Shakespeare and Scandinavia

The International Studies in Shakespeare and His Contemporaries

Jay L. Halio, General Editor

1993

Shakespeare and His Contemporaries: Eastern and Central European Studies, eds. Jerzy Limon and Jay L. Halio

1995

French Essays on Shakespeare and His Contemporaries, eds. J. M. Maguin and Michèle Willems

1998

Redefining Shakespeare: Literary Theory and Theater Practice in the German Democratic Republic, eds. J. Lawrence Guntner and Andrew M. McLean

Japanese Studies in Shakespeare and His Contemporaries, ed. Yoshiko Kawachi

Russian Essays in Shakespeare, eds. Alexandr Parfenov and Joseph Price

Strands Afar Remote: Israeli Essays on Shakespeare and His Contemporaries, ed. Avraham Oz

1999

Italian Studies in Shakespeare and His Contemporaries, eds. Michele Marrapodi and Giorgio Melchiori

2002

Foreign Accents: Brazilian Readings of Shakespeare, ed. Aimara da Cunha Resende

Shakespeare and Scandinavia: A Collection of Nordic Studies, ed. Gunnar Sorelius

Shakespeare and Scandinavia

A Collection of Nordic Studies

Edited by Gunnar Sorelius

Newark: University of Delaware Press
London: Associated University Presses

Associated University Presses
2010 Eastpark Boulevard
Cranbury, NJ 08512

Associated University Presses
16 Barter Street
London WC1A 2AH, England

Associated University Presses
P.O. Box 338, Port Credit
Mississauga, Ontario
Canada L5G 4L8

The paper used in this publication meets the requirements of the American National Standard for Permanence of Paper for Printed Library Materials Z39.48-1984.

Library of Congress Cataloging-in-Publication Data

Shakespeare and Scandinavia : a collection of Nordic studies / edited by Gunnar Sorelius.
p. cm.—(The international studies in Shakespeare and his contemporaries)
Includes bibliographical references and index.
ISBN 0-87413-806-X (alk. paper)
1. Shakespeare, William,—1564–1616—Criticism and interpretation.
2. Shakespeare, William,—1564–1616—Stage history—Scandinavia.
3. Shakespeare, William,—1564–1616—Appreciation—Scandinavia.
I. Sorelius, Gunnar. II. Series.

PR2976 .S336 2002
822.3′3—dc21 2002075004

PRINTED IN THE UNITED STATES OF AMERICA

Contents

Acknowledgments

MY THANKS GO FIRST OF ALL TO PROFESSOR JAY HALIO WHO SUGGESTED that I should undertake the preparation of this collection of Scandinavian Shakespeare studies. I have also received generous help in locating the essays published here and in other ways from a number of colleagues and friends. I can only mention a few by name: Professors Erik Frykman, Roger Sell and Kristian Smidt, Dr. Michael Srigley and Mr. Leif Zern. My thanks go also to those scholars who have written essays specially for this collection. Dr. Vetturlidi Oskarsson very kindly provided me with information about Shakespeare and Iceland. Thanks are due also to the staffs of the Library and Archives of the Royal Dramatic Theater in Stockholm and its Head Librarian Dr. Dag Kronlund, and of the Uppsala University Library. I owe a special debt of gratitude to the heirs and copyright holders of the works of Alf Sjöberg and Gunnar Sjögren, Ms. Katarina Sjögren and Lady Wilson respectively, for allowing me to publish their fathers' essays.

Gunnar Sorelius

Introduction

GUNNAR SORELIUS

AS IN MANY OTHER PARTS OF EUROPE, ENGLISH THEATER FIRST BECAME known through the troupes of English actors that visited the Continent and Scandinavia in Queen Elizabeth's time. Thus an English company of entertainers, players and instrumentalists, were active at the Danish court as early as 1579. As Michael Srigley mentions in his essay included in this collection, a troupe containing well-known Elizabethan actors, who later became Shakespeare's colleagues in London, performed at Elsinore in 1586. A troupe of English "players" also spent the years 1590–92 at the court of Duke Charles at Nyköping, the future King Charles IX of Sweden, whose expansionist policies were to become a threat to Denmark. However, as far as we know, no Shakespearean drama was on the repertoire of these troupes. On the other hand there is the interesting fact that the only existing copy of the first edition of *Titus Andronicus,* the 1594 Quarto now in the Folger Shakespeare Library, was found in the early years of the last century in Lund in southern Sweden. It has been speculated that it was brought to Scandinavia early, perhaps in Shakespeare's own time. There are also records of the existence of one or two copies of the First Folio in the eighteenth century. In Denmark one Jens Rosenkrands owned a Second Folio which was acquired by the Royal Library in 1696.

However, if we disregard the remote possibility that the visiting troupes did perform Shakespeare in either Denmark or Sweden, he first became known in Scandinavia in the second half the eighteenth century. Scandinavia took part in the discovery of Shakespeare that was part of early Romanticism in many areas of Europe. On the other hand there is no sign that he was used in the formation and strengthening of a national culture as in many other countries that looked upon translations of Shakespeare as proof of the maturity and capabilities of their national languages. Somewhat later exceptions to this rule may be the Finnish adaptation of *Macbeth* called *Ruunulinna* that appeared in 1834 as a result of the romantic feelings that emerged in Finland after the country had been separated from Sweden to become part of Russia in 1809. Similarly in Norway Ivar Aasen, the creator of *Nynorsk,* used a translation of part of *Romeo and Juliet* to demonstrate the capabilities of his new national language.

Scandinavia soon took part in the cult of Shakespeare that started in England with the Garrick Jubilee in 1769. To begin with, the influence was mediated through German and French translations, even by means of German translations of French adaptations (the Uppsala University Library bought Le Tourneur's French translation in 1780 but five years later it also bought an English edition in nine volumes published in Birmingham, "From Mr. Pope's Edition." The library of the Östgöta University Nation at Uppsala acquired through a donation Theobald's 1762 edition a few years earlier. The records show that these books were read by some of the early Swedish Romantic poets).

As to performances, *Romeo and Juliet* was performed in Sweden in 1776 by a presumably originally German traveling company using a Swedish translation probably based on Ducis's French adaptation. The same play was performed in Ducis's adapted form in Swedish translation in the next decades in Gothenburg. When *Hamlet* was performed there it was advertised as "by the famous Shakespeare." A French troupe also performed Ducis's *Roméo and Juliette* in French at various royal residences in 1782–83.

Although interest in Shakespeare was great in Denmark-Norway during this period, it was not until 1813 that a Shakespeare play, *Hamlet,* as could be expected, was performed on a Danish stage. On the other hand, translation into Danish started early. In 1777 *Hamlet, Prinz af Dannemark,* by Johannes Boye was published, a translation from the English original. This was followed by a series of translations by different translators both in Denmark and Norway. In Sweden the first translation of a complete play into Swedish was printed in 1813, when Erik Gustaf Geijer, who became one of Sweden's foremost historians, prepared his translation of *Macbeth* after his journey to England in 1809–10. Although Geijer consulted Schiller's *Macbeth,* his knowledge of English meant that his version was closer to the original than the German adaptation. A number of other translations followed, some of which were used in the theater. C. A. Hagberg's *Shakspeares Dramatiska Arbeten* (1847–51), a complete translation of the plays, established Shakespeare as a Swedish classic and has remained the standard edition in Sweden. In Denmark and Norway Edvard Lembcke's translation (1861–73) holds a similar position. In Iceland a number of plays were translated in the second half of the nineteenth century and in the last century. The complete plays translated by Helgi Hálvdanarson were published in 1956–75.

The first literary criticism of Shakespeare also stems from the period of incipient Romanticism. Here the influence from French, but above all German critics was strong in both Denmark-Norway and Sweden, but Addison's essays were also important. Visitors to England reported on performances they had seen in London, although their reaction was often to complain about Shakespeare's lack of taste, his coarseness, and his obscenities. But they were also impressed by the dramatic impact that the plays could exert on the audience. The academic interest is illustrated in two Latin dissertations defended at Uppsala. The earliest is called *De poësi tragica* (1774), which in its treatment of Shakespeare shows the influence of Voltaire and Addison. The other exercise of this kind, *De Poësi dramatica Guilielmi Shakespearii* (1843), shows the enthusiasm for Shakespeare that is characteristic of the Romantic age. Many of the dramatists were also influenced by Shakespeare at an early stage. The Swedish actor King Gustav III, the unfortunate hero of Verdi's *A Masked Ball* (1786), is reported to have seen *King Lear* in Paris, and the opera *Gustavus Vasa,* which he wrote in collaboration with a professional writer, contained Shakespearean influences that were discerned even by his contemporaries. In the next century Shakespeare was even more influential in the great period of Scandinavian drama with, above all, Ibsen and Strindberg. Ibsen gave a lecture in Bergen in 1855 on "Shakespeare and His Influence on Scandinavian Art," which unfortunately is lost. Strindberg wrote a number of essays on Shakespeare, one of which is included here.

The modern study of Shakespeare in Scandinavia began with Henrik Schück's *William Shakspere, hans lif och värksamhet* (1883). Schück calls himself an enemy of "speculative aesthetics" and strives after an empirical and historicist study of Shakespeare as a child of his time. But he also wants to study the dramas not principally as separate entities but as stages in "the history of the development of a human spirit" and to show how Shakespeare "elevated himself to ever greater perfection in his art." Accordingly he divided Shakespeare's development into periods, beginning with his early striving for clarity, a second, happy period when his best comedies were written, and a third period when he was deeply influenced by Giordano Bruno. This was a time characterized by success and prosperity but also by bitterness and disgust with life. The fourth and last period was one of greater harmony in Shakespeare's life and work. Schück was interested not only in Shakespeare's life (and his economic circumstances) but also, in particular, as his critical method demanded, in the relationship between the dramatist's works and his historical time and its ideas.

If Schück was a pioneer in Shakespeare study it was the Dane Georg Brandes that was to win international fame and to influence Shakespeare studies and appreciation in a wider context with his monumental *William Shakespeare: A Critical Study* in three volumes, first published in Danish and German in 1895–96 and in English in 1898. Although he was a child of the same philosophy of history and literary study as his Swedish counterpart, Brandes was able to catch the attention of the learned world and the general public in a way that Schück did not. As Niels Bugge Hansen describes in his essay published here, his lively, indeed flamboyant style, and the way in which he related his own life to that of Shakespeare created a work that still inspires its readers. Thus Ingmar Bergman's *Lear* was clearly influenced by Brandes's depiction of that play as "The Tragedy of a World-Catastrophe."

The essay by August Strindberg printed here belongs to the same period. At least in one detail it also seems to have been influenced by Brandes. Its main interest, however, lies in the fact that it is written by one of the many dramatists that learned from Shakespeare. Strindberg may have looked upon himself as a Swedish Shakespeare, not least because he had written a number of chronicle plays on Swedish history starting with Gustavus Vasa, whose place in Swedish history corresponds to that of Henry VIII in England. As he states in the essay published here, in writing *Master Olof,* which deals with the Swedish Reformation, Shakespeare had been his great master. Shakespeare's way in *Julius Caesar* of depicting his characters, even historical figures, "at home" in their intimate private life, had a decisive influence on Strindberg's early historical dramas. The influence has been traced down to specific episodes and characters. Strindberg's essay was written as part of one of his "Letters to the Intimate Theatre," the experimental stage that he created toward the end of his life and no translation can perhaps do justice to his sprightly and irreverent style. Strindberg demonstrates his somewhat reluctant admiration in his treatment of his source of inspiration, who is also a fellow dramatist.

Closer to our own time, Alf Sjöberg (1903–80), who wrote the next essay in this anthology on *Antony and Cleopatra,* was one of Sweden's foremost directors in the theater but also in the cinema. In the latter capacity he is best known internationally for his film of Strindberg's *Miss Julie,* which won a Grand Prix in Cannes in 1951. Sjöberg's painstaking and penetrating analyses of the plays he directed regularly resulted in long essays that were printed in the theater programs. After his death many of them were published in book form. The essay published here is a good example of the director's belief in the theater's important mission as a means of social and cultural analysis and as a vehicle for social criticism. From his early days Sjöberg was a keen critic of the social injustice and the class system that he felt he had suffered from in his childhood. In this he resembled Strindberg, whom he frequently staged. In 1944 he produced the film *Torment* (*Hets*), a classical indictment of the Swedish school system that he (and Ingmar Bergman, who wrote the script) considered to be both oppressive and unfair. Sjöberg's essay also shows the Marxist ideology that was strong in intellectual circles in Sjöberg's time. Toward the end of his career he also introduced Bertolt Brecht, whom he looked upon as a kindred spirit, on the Swedish stage.

Whereas Alf Sjöberg was a professional through and through with a long career in the theater (he directed 138 plays and a number of films), Gunnar Sjögren was an economist and businessman who at the age of fifty-seven retired to devote the rest of his life to the consuming interest of his youth, a study of Shakespeare and his time and the relationship between the Elizabethan stage and Scandinavia. One of his most fascinating books deals with the Swedish noblewoman Helena Snakenborg, who became a favorite lady-in-waiting at Queen Elizabeth's court, and also Marchioness of Northampton, and after the death of her first husband, wife of Sir Thomas Gorges. The first essay by Sjögren printed here, on *Othello,* is an example of his method of patient, unbiased investigation and weighing of the evidence. The conclusions reached seem unusually sane in a field of study that is usually characterized more by prejudice than sound scholarship. Sjögren's other essay, "The Geography of *Hamlet,*" draws attention to the fact, often forgotten, that not only was the political map of Scandinavia different from what it is now, but also the knowledge in Shakespeare's England of the physical map of the Northern countries was uncertain and erratic. Knowledge of these circumstances can help to clear up difficulties that the readers encounter in understanding important aspects of *Hamlet.*

These form the historical section of the present collection of essays. We turn now to the work of scholars still active. The first two contributions concern the study of the structure of Shakespeare's plays and the ways in which Shakespeare's attention to dramatic planning, and in some cases revision, affect and enhance the meaning of the dramas. The essay of the grand old man of Scandinavian Shakespeare studies, Kristian Smidt, considers in a close analysis of the loose ends and contradictions of a number of plays the ways in which Shakespeare through a process of continuous inspiration, new starts and improvisations, additions and rearrangement of scenes, arrived at his final goal and perfection of his plots. Often the discontinuities and inconsistencies add to the intensity of the dramatic effect and enrich the enjoyment of the dramatic experience.

Keith Brown's essay "On Construction and Significance in Shakespearean Drama" is rooted in his chance discovery that the first and last six scenes of *Hamlet* are not only symmetrical in content, but also frame what in the study of nondramatic Renaissance texts would be considered a classic instance of "mannerist" double centering. This observation led him to a general reconsideration of Shakespeare's dramatic constructional techniques (adding to a substantial body of Norwegian work on this aspect of other Elizabethan texts). Shakespeare, however unique, was clearly even more truly a Renaissance artist than is generally recognized: faithful to the basic aesthetic and compositional principles of his age, but in ways that vary interestingly from stage to stage of his career.

In one of the Finnish contributions, Shakespeare again figures as an author of the most self-conscious kind. In proposing a "Shakespearean philology," Roger D. Sell is interested not only in the way the plays have been interpreted by scholars, directors, editors and others, but also in language and its workings as understood by Shakespeare himself. *Henry V,* in particular, can be read as a study in communicative pragmatics, raising fundamental questions about the relationship between language use and the exercise of power. Henry, by being such an effective speaker, is actually much more like Shakespeare himself than is the poet-king Richard II, whose poetry is solipsistically weak. Yet not even a Henry or a Shakespeare can wield language in such a way as to achieve total and final control. In order to work at all, their words have to be received by other people who will always have their own ideas and viewpoints. Shakespeare, who was perfectly well aware of this, paradoxically uses the Chorus not only in an effort to tighten his grip on the audience, but also as the channel for a metalinguistic commentary on what his own text is thereby doing. To some extent, both Shakespeare and Sell would tend to condone the tendency of late twentieth-century new historicist criticism to de-authorize literature. But Sell is also at pains to say that Shakespeare's use of language nevertheless achieved, and continues to achieve, a very great deal, for which we are likely to give him credit. Communicatively speaking, the text of a named individual in a literary tradition is not at all the same thing as, say, an orally transmitted ballad.

The other Finnish contribution is also concerned with the pragmatics of language, this time the problems caused by prosodic differences between the two languages in translating Shakespeare into Swedish. Clas Zilliacus, who is himself a translator, points to the importance of seeing prosodic choices in relation to the meaning conveyed by the metrical form of Shakespeare's lines as well as by the signification of the words as such. He also discusses the thou/you variation and the ways in which the corresponding Swedish opposition between *du* and *ni,* which does not correspond exactly to the distinction between the two English pronouns as described by E. A. Abbott in his classical *Shakespeare Grammar,* can and should be used in translating Shakespeare.

Niels Bugge Hansen's essay gives an account of important aspects of Georg Brandes's influential Shakespeare criticism. Brandes not only constructed a life for Shakespeare from his works, "recognis[ing] him in his work," the resulting biography also coincided with the critic's own life, oppressed by the same bigotry that Brandes argued Shakespeare encountered in the Puritan England of his time. Brandes's work became the study of "Branspeare." In the reprinting of his *Shakespeare* in his collected works Brandes defended his method against those who pointed to the conventionality of, for example, the sonnet genre. Brandes had relied prominently on the Sonnets for his account of Shakespeare's life and especially for what he described as his pessimism, his misanthropy, his misogyny and his scorn for common people.

Michael Srigley's essay paints a picture of the relationship between the Danish and English courts in the time of James I, and not least the drinking habits of Christian IV, James's brother-in-law, and his court. It is suggested that *Hamlet,* which would of course have been of special interest to Danish guests, was performed in connection with the visit of the Danish king to London in 1606, and that Shakespeare's play was revised and lengthened to suit the occasion and to make Hamlet more like Christian, as the Danish Renaissance prince. It is also observed that the preparations for war that occur in the play were in part inspired by actual rearmament in Denmark in anticipation not of a Norwegian invasion but of an attack from Sweden, whose warlike King Charles IX was threatening Denmark's supremacy in the Baltic.

My own contribution, finally, "The Stockholm 1944 Anti-Nazi *Merchant of Venice:* The Uncertainty of Response" discusses a very successful production by one of the contributors to this anthology, Alf Sjöberg, at the Royal Dramatic Theater in Stockholm at a time when the extent and magnitude of the Nazi persecution of the Jews were beginning to become widely known. It was meant to be an attack on the German persecution of Jews, a manifestation of the director's hatred of suppression and inhumanity that characterized his life, and in particular his hatred of Nazism, a feeling he shared with Ingmar Bergman, as is clear from Bergman's work at this time and earlier. At the same time it is evident from the reactions of the theatergoers and reviewers of the time that the message of the director, and of the production as such, was often ineffective and misunderstood. Audiences brought their own prejudices and predilections to bear on their understanding of the play.

Shakespeare and Scandinavia

Julius Caesar: Shakespeare's Historical Drama

AUGUST STRINDBERG

WHEN YOU WANT TO WRITE A HISTORICAL DRAMA, THIS BECOMES OF COURSE something of a school essay, or an exercise in topic-writing: variations on a theme or a transcription of a piece already composed. Shakespeare's *Caesar* was already in his own time one of his most popular plays, and it can still pay its bill, despite the fact that it is not really entertaining. You know what will happen beforehand, even what is going to happen to the protagonists; there is no love, which can otherwise spice up the simplest and driest dishes; there is no fool to amuse the audience, no exciting intrigue, no hobgoblin—just a ghost, who is, however, poorer than that in *Hamlet.* But the play can nevertheless engage an audience, like everything from Shakespeare's hand, because it is infused with an inner tension, although here this is sometimes slackened.

When in 1869 I read *Julius Caesar* for the purpose of learning the language in my English classes[1] (although I hardly knew the pronunciation of this finicky language), the piece was chosen because the language was easy and the text contained no coarse language. We young people, who were very critical, immediately observed that the drama should have been called *Brutus,* since Caesar evaporates in the third act. And the world's greatest hero, whom we knew from world history as well as from his own *De Bello Gallico,* we thought was badly drawn; a henpecked milksop who believed in premonitions and apparitions so that he wanted to stay home from the senate because the lady of the house had had a bad dream and begged him to take no risks. These main reservations from twenty-year-olds have indeed been made before and after by famous commentators, and when I now at the age of sixty reread my *Caesar,* which because of these explicatory classes I attended in my young days I know best of Shakespeare's plays, the same shortcomings came forcefully to mind.

When now I analyzed Caesar's part again, which I had done before, I found, now as before, a certain weakness in the depiction of his character, which must not be transformed into a virtue because you like Shakespeare. Let us now look at the weave, singling out the warp from the weft, and scrutinize the shafts.

Already in act 1, scene 2, Caesar comes into a public place with his wife Calpurnia. As is well-known, you do not talk about Caesar's wife, and a Roman did not parade his wife in the street. When Caesar, the world-shaker, opens his mouth, this is to ask his wife to place herself in the way of Antony in the race, so that Antony can touch her, because "our elders say, / The barren, touched in this holy chase, / Shake off their sterile curse." Commentators have explained this thus: Caesar at the age of fifty-five is now tired, or decrepit, so that for this reason (?) he is, quite simply, becoming superstitious. Could one not instead accept that things are what they are? Caesar is at the summit of his power: imperator, pontifex maximus, adjudged (literally) divine worship. Still, he has no children by his wife (but by Cleopatra he had Caesarion), and now when he senses his end, he wants to live on in his offspring, or found a dynasty.

Then comes the soothsayer who warns against the Ides of March, but now Caesar refuses to listen and calls him a dreamer. So he is not superstitious, at least not in respect of this. This presentation takes up one page in its printed form, and furthermore comes too early, as we moderns would think.

After a while, in the same scene, Caesar returns and provides some very sharp characterizations of the conspirators, which are meant to intimate that he suspects them. The commentator says that Shakespeare's knowledge of human nature is demonstrated in this way. Then he leaves again and is seen no more in the first act.

The conspiracy is worked out, and in act 2, scene 2 Caesar enters in his nightgown and slippers, frightened by the thunderstorm and Calpurnia's shouting in her sleep. He sends a servant to the priests to ask for sacrifice and prophesying (from the entrails of the sacrificial animals). This is not superstition, but Roman religious practice, like the oracles in Greece. Now Calpurnia appears from her bedchamber. She has never believed in omens before but now they frighten her, and she asks her husband to be careful: "When beggars die, there are no comets seen." And there she is so right.

Now the servant returns and announces that the priests in connection with the offering have found a sacrificial animal with no heart. Caesar replies to this in a boastful way, which is not like this levelheaded, highly educated man, and which therefore seems untrue to us. He says, "Danger knows full well that Caesar is more dangerous than he"? Julius Caesar, who wrote the dispassionate history of the Gallic Wars, did not express himself in this way.

Calpurnia, a loving wife and not unwomanly, implores him not to go to the senate: "call it my fear that keeps you in the house." Caesar humors his charming wife's wish, not to worry her, and there is no sign of the henpecked husband here. Then comes the friend in the house, Decius Brutus, who manages to arouse Caesar's manly pride so that he changes his mind, puts on his toga and goes to the senate. The conspirators enter and Caesar greets them, without any visible sign of mistrust. He throws an accidental question at Brutus, which could be just by chance: "[A]re you stirr'd so early too?" They all then proceed to the Capitol.

Act 3: The Capitol. The soothsayer warns again. Artemidorus delivers his petition. Decius Brutus hands over Trebonius's request. In vain: Caesar goes to the senate. Metellus Brutus sues for mercy for his exiled brother. Caesar turns nasty. Brutus and Cassius press forward and support the petition for mercy. Caesar answers like a Vielgeshrei:[2] He is constant as the North Star, of which "there is no fellow in the firmament." "So in the world: 'tis furnished well with men, and men are flesh and blood, and apprehensive; yet in the number I do know but one that unassailable holds on his rank, unshak'd of motion; and . . . I am he!" And so he is cut down! With the words *Et tu Brute* in the English, which Hagberg translates into Swedish.[3] In other words, with the first scene of the third act the hero of the piece has disappeared, which has always been criticized as a fault in the composition. But now come the critics of the new century who acquit Shakespeare of this defect, something that is generally agreed upon, but not by all. Israel Gollancz has in his 1908 edition, the following piece of information, which may be true: "Mr Fleay (I do not know him! [Strindberg's comment]) thinks that the present form of the play belongs to the year 1607, and that it is an abridgement of a fuller play. . . . The same critic holds that Ben Jonson abridged the play."[4]

The mysterious thing about Shakespeare is that as soon as you write a word about him you are in the middle of a quarrel, with authorities for and against. I cannot decide if we have *Julius Caesar* entirely in Shakespeare's own redaction, and I therefore leave the question open and keep to the present drama as we have read it from our young days.

The main charge that the hero disappears at the beginning of act 3 can of course be spirited away thus: "Call the play *Brutus* or whatever else you like" and the problem is solved. One commentator has tried to hide the truth by saying that Caesar does not disappear from the drama in act 3 because he returns in acts 4 and 5, that is, as a ghost, and his powerful person lives on as a memory, occupying and haunting the acting characters to the end. As we remember, Brutus's last words are: "Caesar, now be still, I kill'd not thee with half so good a will," which is easily said.

But portraying the world's greatest hero as a coward? How can this mesh with Shakespeare's aristocratic attitudes elsewhere? You can answer that the human qualities, including the weaknesses, are what interests us; how do you want to paint the ruler, the statesman, the historic figure, on the stage? Should he drift about with his legions on the battlefield? Should he sit at his table drafting laws, or perhaps be shown composing *De Bello Gallico?* This is not dramatic; thus what remains is the private life. But involving him in a love affair, for example with Cleopatra, would not be nice, and of no importance to Caesar, because he went through his affair with Cleopatra unscathed, whereas Antony went under. What remains is "Caesar *intime*,"[5] at home, as Shakespeare has done, bar the bedchamber scene with the dressing gown. We see Caesar as a good husband, indulgent in little things, as a friend, as statesman and ruler, in the senate. Command does not consist in tearing around on the stage, since for this you need battlefields and armies. Cassius's description of the Caesar figure is just another example of the constant mistake of demagogues that all people are alike. The fact that Caesar cried for help when close to drowning is in the eyes of the democrat a sign of insufficient heroism; that Caesar had a fit in Spain, and that he asked for something to drink, becomes to Cassius a sign of "a feeble temper"—and all of this petty account becomes nothing but the story of Cassius's small-mindedness and envy, for Shakespeare seems to have harbored a naive admiration for Caesar, and he might as well have told the story of Caesar and his luck in the boat.[6]

As to the historical drama in general, the difficulty is to find the golden mean in the historical part and as well as in the depiction of private life. History in its broad outlines is Providence's own construction, and Shakespeare is a providentialist, as the ancient tragedians were, and therefore he does neglect history but lets the highest justice be done even down to the petty details. Examples: Caesar has brought about the fall of Pompey, his co-triumvir; Caesar is cut down at the foot of Pompey's statue. Cassius has stabbed Caesar with his sword, and Cassius falls on the same sword:

Caesar, thou art reveng'd
Even with the sword that kill'd thee.

But Shakespeare has also slavishly followed history as Plutarch wrote it, and has even copied entire passages quoted by Gollancz (1908). As for the main character, or Brutus, he is an ideal and related to Hamlet who was conceived in the same breath. Brutus philosophizes about everything he does, even delivers a soliloquy on suicide, sees a ghost, speculates about his fate and existential problems. Brutus has no flaw, but he commits one gigantic mistake when he interferes in the counsel of Providence and murders Caesar, and this is his downfall, after having first understood what a rabble he has collaborated with, and what the men were like that succeeded the tyrant. Antony doctors Caesar's testament, Cassius is greedy and takes bribes, Lepidus is an ass. The people in act 1, scene 1 that cheer Caesar have just before "clim'd up to walls and battlements" to celebrate Pompey; after the death of Caesar they cheer Brutus, immediately afterward Antony, and then Caesar again when the will has been opened. Brutus has sacrificed his friend's life to the fickle multitude; on the altar of abstract popular freedom he has slaughtered the abstract idea of the tyrant, which is but a bad translation of ruler.[7]

As is well-known, Caesar kept all the outer republican forms but made himself into an absolute ruler. The fact that he arrogated to himself divine worship (the apotheosis) a Greek tragedian would have introduced as a sufficient motif for his overthrow (hubris).

Shakespeare's way of characterizing his hero is not successful, because instead of having the character appear from the action he has Brutus telling us who Caesar is; and in the famous little detail, his concern for the sleepy servants, he poses as a noble person, in my opinion, and is a little too mawkish for a Roman. Brutus declaims, as we moderns would say, and he is over-hasty in his panegyric on the dead Cassius, whom he has just exposed as a greedy knave:

The last of all the Romans, fare thee well!
It is impossible that ever Rome
Should breed thy fellow.

It is the partisan's way of praising himself in his accomplice.

Cruel is the picture of the new men's cruelty, when they have come to power and issue death sentences in Antony's house. Octavius demands that Lepidus condemn his own brother; Lepidus assents without protest. Lepidus demands that Antony's nephew must die—"He shall not live." Antony answers, "Look, with a spot I damn him." Compare this with Caesar's refusal to pardon Metellus Cimber, which became the excuse for killing Caesar! Now the two men commit the same crime, without qualms. Nothing changed. In the delineating of Brutus it has always been considered a weak point that Brutus simply accepts Cassius's call and becomes his tool, standing under the influence of him, the lesser man.

Caesar's friendship with Brutus is not emphasized in any scene; on the other hand, Brutus's boundless love for Caesar is strongly stressed. Of what nature this love was is not known; an uncertain tradition has made him Caesar's natural son, something which used to be alluded to by means of the free translation [into Swedish] "You too, *my* Brutus." (Hagberg translates Et tu Brute as "You too, Brutus.")[8] But who is Brutus! Shakespeare, who does not suffer from too much learning and who is somewhat careless (He calls Decimus Brutus by the name of Decius!), has Brutus descended from Lucius Junius Brutus, who banished Tarquinius Superbus, but who was himself nephew to Rome's last king (after Lucretia's misadventure). I too thought that this was so in my younger days, but learn now that Caesar's Brutus, Marcus Junius, was the son of a tribune "of the same name," and of Servilia, younger sister to Cato the Younger. Here I want to call attention, in passing, to the fact that the elder Brutus feigned madness in order to escape from Tarquinius's persecution, and that Shakespeare possibly conceived the Hamlet motif while dealing with Brutus (in *Julius Caesar,* which preceded *Hamlet).*

In any case, Brutus is a splendid man, upright, human, unselfish, and not even his enemies suspected him of dishonest motives. He says himself about the murder: "As Caesar loved me, I weep for him; as he was fortunate, I rejoice at it; as he was valiant, I honour him; but, as he was ambitious, I slew him." It is about the same as Hamlet's "I have to be cruel to be kind."

But there is one important figure in Shakespeare's *Caesar* that ought to have been portrayed with care, since he plays the same role as Fortinbras in *Hamlet*. This is the man that Shakespeare calls Octavius Caesar but who later becomes the Emperor Augustus. It is true that originally he was called Caius Octavius, and was the adopted son of Caesar, but also the son of Caesar's niece, and that he later called himself Caius Julius Caesar Octavianus, and at the time of the battle of Philippi he should have been called Octavianus. (It is not until the year 27 that he was awarded the honorary title of Augustus by the senate and people.) All right, I know how dangerous it is to try to correct Shakespeare, because one usually meets with opposition in his text, but I shall try! When Caesar is introduced in scene 2, act 1 he expresses his concern that he has no successor, as his marriage with Calpurnia is childless. He is surrounded by a large crowd of people (Cicero is a super!), but the adopted son is not present. It is true that Caesar expresses hopes of having a son by Calpurnia and asks her to stand in the way of Antony in the chase. As he is murdered soon afterward it seems obvious that the adoption must already have been a fact, and there is here an excellent opportunity to prepare for the existence of Octavianus in order that he will not be thrust upon us in act 4. I wondered for a moment if Shakespeare knew who his Octavius Caesar was, but this question can be considered to be too impertinent, and the criticism also, as it is possible that the missing scene has been cut when the play was abbreviated. I should have cut out Cicero, as he is a neglected figure, despite the fact that he speaks Greek. And to listen to Cicero speaking for six hours from a rostrum I do not want, having been tormented all my youth by his awful eloquence.

But the future emperor Augustus is not neglected, although he is not present, not even at the murder. He first appears in scene 1, act 4 and asks to have Lepidus's brother killed. He puts in a good word for Lepidus, who Antony compares to an ass and then to his horse. Then he is not seen until act 5, at Philippi; there he argues already with Antony about the battle-order. "Why do you cross me in the exigent?" The future ruler who is to defeat Antony at Actium answers: "I do not cross you; *but I will do so.*" Soon afterward, divining what his star has in store for him, he answers, "I was not born to die on Brutus's sword." After Brutus's death Octavius Caesar takes all Brutus's servants in his employ, and as a magnanimous victor he delivers an oration to the memory of his fallen enemy: "according to his virtue let us use him . . . within my tent his bones tonight shall lie."

Good, but the audience ought to know that he is Augustus, and that he will one day succeed Antony, because then the drama achieves an infinite perspective, without beginning, without end, something of the eternity of world history, where the actors succeed each other but the theater remains, where the audiences are ever new, but where the good old drama remains the same: where "Imperious Caesar, dead and turn'd to clay, might stop a hole to keep the wind away." Pompey, Caesar, Brutus, Antony, Augustus. That is a series in which each term is, so to speak, the root of the preceding one.

The structure of *Caesar* is characterized by a simple, almost classical treatment; and it pleases tired people to be able to survey the artistry of a work of art without any difficulty. Nothing is lacking in the design because the murder is prepared for in two acts, takes place in the third, and then the tragic consequences are rolled out all the way to the catastrophe, which is followed by renewal and the perspective of the future. Caesar lives on, in the form of his ghost (revenge or justice), in fame, and in his adopted son.

The women, Calpurnia and Portia, are, in Shakespeare's sense and in the sense of all healthy people, true women, that is to say feminine, concerned about their honor, concerned about their husbands, submissive. Calpurnia is soon forgotten but Portia is more of a true Roman of the strong kind. Both of them are therefore well treated by their husbands, like true friends, whom you listen to but do not obey in everything. Theirs is a so-called happy relationship, which in the case of Caesar is not even disturbed by the wife's sterility.

Cassius, the third person, is a domineering figure, who does not brook having anybody above him, but he does not seem to be very popular among the common people. "Dry Cassius" is also a miser and something of a cheat.

Casca is a duplicate Cassius and unnecessary; perhaps he came into being through a mistake, for when you read Hagberg, where the names are written in abbreviated form as *Cass.* and *Casc.,* they are often confused. Shakespeare seems to have noticed this flaw, because he takes the trouble of characterizing Casca in several places, without succeeding in making us interested in him. He is said to be indolent; he gossips; others say that he is a grumbler and dissimulates. And so he is forgotten.

Decius (Decimus) Brutus I cannot get a grip on, and the minor characters are too many to be kept apart; perhaps the author has not even considered this necessary—like our modern directors he wanted to fill the bill. And you do Shakespeare a disservice by praising his little mistakes.

In *The Two Gentlemen of Verona* (as Hagberg notices) Shakespeare has introduced two Eglamores. "Possibly Shakespeare has here forgotten that at the beginning of the play he has given this name to Julia's suitor." These things happen.

Gollancz believes that Shakespeare has slipped in the same way in *Julius Caesar,* when Lucius on one occasion seems to be confused with Lucilius. For this reason I take the liberty of believing that the two Cinnas in *Caesar* also have seen the light of day somewhat haphazardly. These are little things that the director must be allowed to put right without the reviewers accusing him of sacrilege.

There is a little scene that I have noticed as being well-made. This is scene 3, act 3 (actually the fourth) where Brutus has a controversy with Cassius. This scene is instructive as being the archetype of a quarrel.

Cassius has practiced extortion and has sold offices. Brutus confronts him with this outright. At first Cassius denies the obvious (typical!): "*I* an itching palm!" When he cannot prevaricate any longer he appeals to the fact that he is "Older in practice, abler than yourself to make conditions." Brutus cannot agree with this. Cassius: "I am." Brutus: "I say you are not." Then they proceed to terms of abuse. Brutus: "Away, slight man!" Then they start bragging, and the bickering starts. Cassius: "I said, an *elder* soldier, not a better." (Here he lies, because he said—see above—"older in practice".) "Did I say better?" (Here they have both forgotten their own words; because Cassius said "abler than yourself to make conditions" and not a better soldier.) Brutus answers, as is customary after the quarrel has reached its peak: "If you did, I care not." (About time!) Then they start being ashamed, feeling sorry, and proceed to the reconciliation. What did Shakespeare mean by this scene? That Cassius was not unselfish in his fight for freedom, but that Brutus was? Or quite simply that all people, even the greatest, suffer from weaknesses, and that a human being without weaknesses is unreal. Not even Caesar himself could he make into a god, but this does not mean that he has degraded him. Caesar's heroic deeds are looked upon as known, and in the play we are introduced to the human being, who interests us.

As late as 1754, David Hume writes in his *History of England:* "If Shakespeare be considered as a *man* (Hume's emphasis) born in a rude age, and educated in the lowest manner, without any instruction, either from the world or from books, he may be regarded as a prodigy: If represented as a *poet*, capable of furnishing a proper entertainment to a refined or intelligent audience, we must abate somewhat of this eulogy. In his compositions, we regret, that many irregularities, and even sometimes absurdities should so frequently disfigure the animated and passionate scenes intermixed with them; and at the same time, we perhaps admire the more those beauties, on account of their being surrounded with such deformities. A striking peculiarity of sentiment, adapted to a singular character, he frequently hits, as it were by inspiration; but a reasonable propriety of thought he cannot, for any time, uphold. . . . Nervous and picturesque expressions, as well as descriptions, abound in him; but 'tis in vain we look either for continued purity or simplicity of diction. His total ignorance of all theatrical art and conduct," and so on.[9]

I must confess that I have never understood Shakespeare's sonnets, which are said to be about *Männerliebe*. C. R. Nyblom, who has translated them into Swedish, claims in the preface that he has understood them.[10] Oscar Wilde says that these sonnets have had the same impact on him as Plato's works have had on young people in a certain university town. In Shakespeare's works I can only remember that this delicate matter is touched upon in *Hamlet*. The matter is delicate because if you overlook the problem and say that you understand, you become suspect; and if you disapprove you will be wrongfully accused—for something else. In act 2, scene 2, Hamlet says to Guildenstern and Rosencrantz: "[M]an delights not me; no, nor woman either, though by your smiling you seem to say so."—Rosencrantz: "My lord, there was no such stuff in my thoughts."—Hamlet: "Why did you laugh, then, when I said 'man delights not me'?" Does this mean this? I do not know, and I have not seen that any commentator has interpreted it.

I will finish this with a confession and an acknowledgement that I have made long ago. Shakespeare's way in the drama *Julius Caesar* of portraying historic figures, also heroes "at home," intimately, became a decisive pattern for my first long historical drama, *Master Olof,* and also, with certain reservations, for the subsequent ones after 1899. This freedom from "theater," from the calculated effect which I took as a guide, was for a long time held against me, until Josephson[11] at the Swedish Theater [Svenska Teatern] discovered *Master Olof* in 1880. But as late as 1908 Molander[12] held the opinion that my *Erik XIV* was unactable. After reading this play he explained: "Is this play going to be put on? It has only got two scenes!" For Molander was so stuck in the French technique that by "scene" he meant "effect." I do not remember if Molander saw the production of *The Three Musketeers* in the Swedish Theatre. In this piece all the old effects had been put together in one play, and the theater manager expected an enormous success. But the play was but coldly received; the effects looked like tricks that were immediately exposed.

Grandinson[13] went beyond Molander's superficiality and gave me credit where I was right, understanding as he did that the effect or impact of a drama depended on something quite different from suggestive situations or a spectacular decor. Grandinson's refined but simple taste for deeper values made it possible for me, after Fredriksson's[14] retirement, however, to have plays like *Crime and Crime*, *To Damascus I*, *Easter*, *Charles XII*, all directed by Grandinson, performed at the Royal Dramatic Theater. *Damascus* was an innovation and a masterpiece of directorship.

Notes

Only the first part dealing with Shakespeare of this long "Letter to the Intimate Theatre" is included here. The full title is *Julius Caesar: Shakespeare's Historical Drama as well as some Observations on Criticism and the Actor's Art and a Supplement on the Theatre Crisis and Problems*. This pamphlet was published in Stockholm by Björck & Börjesson in 1908. The translation from the Swedish was made by the editor from this text but I have also consulted the text in *August Strindbergs Samlade Verk 64: Teater och Intima Teatern* (Stockholm: Norstedts, 1999), here called "Nationalupplagan." The endnotes (with the exception of note 8, which is Strindberg's) were supplied by the editor.

1. Strindberg attended English classes in the autumn of 1867 and in 1870–71 during his years at the University of Uppsala. The date of 1869 seems to be a slip.

2. Vielgeshrei was a comic figure in the German popular theater of the seventeenth century.

3. C. A. Hagberg's complete translation of Shakespeare's dramas in 12 volumes into Swedish was published 1847–51.

4. William Shakespeare, *Julius Caesar,* ed. Israel Gollancz, (London: Dent, 1908), viii, note.

5. Strindberg is probably influenced here by Georg Brandes's essay " 'Det oendeligt Smaa' og 'Det oendligt Store' i Poesien" (" 'The infinitely small' and 'the infinitely large' in poetry"), published in *Illustrert Tidende,* Sept. 1867. See Nationalupplagan, 64: 501.

6. According to Plutarch (*Lives of the Noble Grecians and Romans,* North's translation, vol. 5), Caesar, who had first disguised himself as a slave, when the small ship he was traveling on met with a storm, revealed himself to the master of the boat, who had wanted to turn back, encouraging him with the words: "Good fellow, be of good cheere, and forwardes hardily, fear not, for thou hast Caesar and his fortune with thee" (Tudor Translations, 1896) 11:40–41. See also Nationalupplagan, 54: 501.

7. Strindberg is referring to the fact that "tyrant" originally signified an autocrat regardless of whether he used his power in an arbitrary or despotic way or not. See Nationalupplagan, 64:501.

8. Gollancz says on p. 130 that according to Plutarch Caesar called out to Casca: "O vile traitor, Casca, what dost thou?" while Suetonius makes him address Brutus in Greek "kaj sy teknon," you too, my son? *Teknon* does not mean that Brutus was Caesar's son, because son is *hyios,* while teknos is a pet name, corresponding to our "dear child." Accordingly, Paulus uses *teknon* to Timotheus, who was not his son (2 Tim. 2:1). In "David's son," son is hyios, and child is pais. The mistake, Decius, instead of Decimus Brutus is said to be derived from a misprint

in Amyot's French translation of Plutarch, which was the basis of North's translation into English, used by Shakespeare.

9. David Hume, *The History of England from the Invasion of Julius Caesar to the Revolution in 1688,* 8 vols. (1763), 6: 131.

10. C. R. Nyblom (1832–1907) was one of Strindberg's teachers at Uppsala.

11. Ludvig Josephson (1832–99) actor, director and dramatist. Josephson's production of *Master Olof* actually took place in 1891. See Nationalupplagan, 54: 335.

12. Harald Molander (1858–1900) director at the Royal Dramatic Theater and other theaters. Molander in fact staged *Erik XIV* in 1899 at Svenska Teatern. Strindberg seems to have misdated an earlier reaction by Molander. See Nationalupplagan, 54: 504.

13. Emil Grandinson (1863–1915) was First Director at the Royal Dramatic Theater, 1900–1911.

14. Gustaf Fredriksson (1832–1921) was an actor at the Royal Dramatic Theater, 1862–1907 and its director, 1905–7.

The Secondary Role: The Vision of Master and Servant in *Antony and Cleopatra*

ALF SJÖBERG

Lepidus. But small to greater matters must give way.
Enobarbus. Not if the small come first.

(2.2.11–12)

FEW DRAMAS HAVE A MORE SOLID REPUTATION FOR SPECTACULARITY THAN *Antony and Cleopatra* and few plays inspire the same expectations of extensive scenery, swarming crowds and magnificent battle scenes. And this is how the play has been staged, not least in Swedish theaters.

Yet there are, in fact, few dramas that resist this kind of treatment more radically than this. Right from the start it is understood that the drama moves in a world of ruinous oppositions. Antony is on the brink of destroying himself in Egypt, and he has hardly set foot on the stage before he wishes the whole of Rome to undergo the same fate. All external greatness and splendor is immediately broken down to a shadow of itself, and this ruinous and destructive picture running counter to something which at the same time is said to exist in splendor and honor, is upheld throughout the drama. It is as if the drama possessed two *levels of articulation,* one that seeks expression through rhetorical magnificence and verve and another that attempts the opposite. It is as if the action was driven by an inherent wish to cut down the dimensions of the enormous subject matter and to reduce it to its smallest possible substance, large enough or small enough to fit into the little wooden O as Shakespeare calls his minute stage. It is as if the realization of the relativity of all measurements has inspired him with an urge to destroy his enormous theme, which describes one of the largest invasions ever undertaken by the Roman Empire, in fragments and details and in violent meetings that he locates in the margin of the scenery in this theater without scenery.

He catches the whole action, broken into a thousand quick reflections as in a prism. He looks upon his vision as an astronomer looks upon the cosmos, where the huge earth has lost its place and become a grain of dust in infinity. There is a diminishing of all dimensions on all fronts, even down to the limit of the barely visible, which makes even invisibility a criterion of the uniquely real and true. (It is not by chance that the play contains the shortest line in all drama. "O" says Cleopatra on one occasion, and this "O" contains a world of irony, disappointment, sadness—a complete world view reduced to the same sign that is the sign of Shakespeare's stage. Can the meeting between image and sound that we all want be expressed more clearly? It is at such a moment that Shakespeare at once exceeds all limits and reduces all measures to the least possible, thus uniting oppositions between play and reality.)

Of course he fills the stage with visions, but these are visions in the characters' imaginations and it is this floating, uncertain fabric that makes up the only scenery in the play. Here battlefields, palaces and galleys whirl by, all of the immense empire from Rome to Alexandria, but in a stream of visions that the characters of the drama light up in the spectator's inner eye, while at the same time giving him the opportunity to observe critically with his outer eyes the simple elements that constitute this imaginary greatness.

Black Vesper's Pageants

The monumentality of a Shakespearean drama is founded on the paradoxical relationship between a poetical, radiant text and the poverty of the base, the nakedness of the stage and its smallness. There is not one scene that does not because of this relationship achieve a new perspective in relation to a preceding scene or a new dimension in relation to a following one. The empire grows up by means of constant displacements, just as in one of Piranesi's gigantic palaces; but as in an *invisible construction*, unreal and grandiose, and just as quickly lost in mist and fume, as in the scene in which Antony believes that he has been deserted and betrayed in his love.

Antony. . . . Thou hast seen these signs,
They are black vesper's pageants.
Eros. Ay, my lord.
Antony. That which is now a horse, even with a thought
The rack dislimns, and makes it indistinct

As water is in water.
Eros. It does, my lord.
Antony. My good knave Eros, now thy captain is
Even such a body: here I am Antony;
Yet cannot hold this visible shape . . .

(4.14.7–14)

The role, the identity, can shift and dissolve as quickly as the poetical vision. What is left is the nakedness of the stage as a thing in itself. The gigantic world-embracing battle can shrink to a circle around one single individual, torn between east and west in his inner life. All measurements are transformed as through a Copernican revolution. All distances in time and space are dissolved, just as the individual himself disappears with his visions and dreams.

Left on the empty stage is the actor, dressed in his gaudy rags and motley, which he now wants to divest himself of as a sign of his longing to find his way back to himself. What are roles and what are feelings in these constant unmaskings? It happens that the performers applaud each other's most fervent tirades, as if everything was a game of words and there was no difference between the genuine and the acted. It is as if the acting was directed by a secret agent, a spoilsport with a clear bent to expose the playacting and the vacuity of the gaudy words. The magnificent visions that want to rise so steeply are met with ever more violent opposition. One is reminded of Tolnay's statement in relation to Michelangelo's fresco *The Last Judgment:* "Before the spectator has yet understood the meaning of the work as a whole he experiences the voluptuousness of a destruction in a higher order."

This higher order can be described briefly as the creative principle as such, not just of Michelangelo's fresco but of all great Renaissance works in all areas of art and culture. The foundation of this is Plato's doctrine of ideas involving the soul's yearning for eternity and a return to the world of ideas; a synthesis between oriental Christian mysticism and the doctrine of Eros in Antiquity. This doctrine received its first poetical form in Dante's *Divine Comedy* and the vision of Beatrice, the image of Divine Love manifested in the shape of the beloved, destined to lift the soul to that heaven which it could never reach of its own strength. Formulated by the Neoplatonic academy of Florence this philosophy rapidly gained ground and was transformed into a way of life embraced by the ruling classes all over civilized Europe. With Castiglione's *Courtier* it found its way into the palaces. But like all doctrines that have been enthusiastically embraced by a ruling class this also contained a strong element of repression. Behind the sublime concern for one's own exclusivity there lies a hidden urge to negate the existence of the exploited classes. "The slave" is repressed from consciousness and transformed into a symbol of the soul's battle against the material world, becomes a code, is deprived of his real, human content. In this way an outcast class is stripped of its political importance. This is how we see the slave in Michelangelo's grave sculptures, encased in a fixed structure that expresses the moral battle that the feudal class, and subsequently the bourgeois class, fights with itself, its dreams of transcendence, disturbed by mysterious forces and voices from the deepest layers of the mind.

This philosophy, which is built so strikingly on an elite's dreams of a superman, was to prove to have a tenacious vitality throughout the centuries. Not just Michelangelo, Leonardo and Shakespeare but also Goethe and Strindberg would in time find inspiration and material in this meeting between heaven and hell, chosenness and damnation.

It is no coincidence that in the violent oscillation between bliss and despair in the love scenes, between tenderness and hate, between tragedy and vulgar comedy, we recognize typically Strindbergian strains in Shakespeare's drama. During the most difficult crises in his life Strindberg found the way to this traditional philosophy of ideas which was to become a liberating force in all of his subsequent writing. His Inferno visions, his Road to Damascus, are derived from the same circle of ideas that form the basis of *Antony and Cleopatra*. And having understood this in relation to Strindberg it is possible for us to approach Shakespeare's drama with a renewed understanding, and to appreciate better not just its organization and dramatic methodology but also its ultimate *structural transformation*. Because just as Strindberg, with his ambivalent nature, never left an idea where he found it, so under similar circumstances a restructuring of the dramatic pattern takes place also in Shakespeare.

Castiglione's book describes the pilgrimage that the soul must undertake step by step through the inferno of this world in order to reach that height of perfection to which it is elevated through the agency of Divine Love. Also the *outer architecture* is informed by this vision, an architecture which by means of its different levels and elevations provides a background to the action and supports it—an architectural facade that contains the same visible elements in Michelangelo's grave sculptures and in Strindberg's house facades in the chamber dramas, as those on Shakespeare's own stage. They all emanate from the same iconography, that is they are governed by the same signifying elements on their different levels, in their relationship to high and low, to ground floor and upper floors. By placing these different versions of the same theme next to each other, despite the difference in time, we can better understand difficult passages in the dramas. We understand, for example, more clearly the meaning of the mysterious "monument" to which Cleopatra flees and the real meaning of the scene in which she draws Antony up to the elevated level of the stage balcony. By comparing the relations of the different versions to the iconographical pattern we can also see the transformations that take place, and identify with greater precision those moments of time when the original code, that is the underlying system of thought, is broken down and transformed.

An aesthetic-philosophical system is in no way different from other human creations: it lives and dies, is perhaps revived but is changed with the ideological march of history. It can from the start be charged with *latent* potentialities that suddenly reverse the situation. What is up can become down and be turned around, and this is exactly what happens with the Neoplatonic doctrine in Shakespeare's play, exactly as in Strindberg's dramas. For Strindberg the aristocratic doctrine ultimately became too narrow and he threw it away; the same disintegration, the same renewal, happens in Shakespeare's play. By juxtaposing these plays and seeing them as correspondences on a common theme, we can extract new values which have previously not been perceived. The dimensions of the Antony figure become clearer if we look upon him in relation to Strindberg's Inferno visions.

In the East Antony has been sucked into a world of shadows where he is at the point of losing himself. He appears to the world and to his own consciousness as a shadow of his former self. Like one of Strindberg's Strangers he experiences his alienation as an increasing feeling of degradation and divorce from reality. In a desperate attempt to break out of the petrified world that is Rome and above all the growing competition with Caesar he has lost all self-control. In Dionysian and sexual orgies he attempts to break out of his physical and mental limitations. He believes (as the Renaissance man he is) in a unity beyond all reason that with one stroke is going to burn away all sexual difference. He is under the illusion that in the sexual ecstasy he will be able to liberate himself, reconcile all the oppositions of existence and achieve that equilibrium, that *coincidentia oppositorum* in which humankind is transformed and loses its sexual nature. Here comes to light the dream of the androgyne, that sexless synthesis of man and woman that haunts so many romantic works of art, and that with us has found its most perfect Nordic vision in Carl Jonas Love Almqvist's *Tintomara.*

In Cleopatra's final scene we can see that she in turn believes that she has reached the same synthesis, the same negation of male-female. It is against all these sexual excesses and speculations that Rome, the headquarters of the manly lifestyle, turns in disgust and contempt.

Caesar

A closed system like the Roman one can only uphold its stability and structure by means of ruthless steering and self-control and a minimum of permissible changes. Caesar stands out as the incarnation of this pitiless control, with the puritanism of a seventeen-year-old. He is one of Shakespeare's last variations on the theme of puritanical man that he, with his aristocratic-aesthetic view of life, had always seen as his natural enemy. In Malvolio in *Twelfth Night* he had in an earlier phase of his work with malicious delight ruthlessly exposed the type. But in Caesar the tone has deepened because the historical circumstances have changed.

He had always looked upon the Puritan as a threat, against the joy of living as well as against his art, which in the fantastic seeks to reveal the nature of existence and the sovereignty of humankind. This art he had pitted against a Puritan fanaticism that had disowned his aristocratic vision, opposing it with bigotry and baseness. But with the new century and the new monarch and far from the court and the king's control, the Puritan movement had grown in the life of the people into a political and religious movement of altogether new dimensions. Increasingly this had been colored by the growing longing for political freedom which characterized the new era and which competed on the fundamental level of reality with the aristocratic doctrine of the liberation of the spirit, which was cherished by the court and which not least had kept its grip on Shakespeare's poetry.

This gives Caesar, who is seen by Shakespeare as the self-appointed leader of this sober and realistic front, a better starting point in relation to Antony, who is now reduced to a secondary role, not because of Caesar's superior intelligence but because of his historical representation, a change in the political climate which Antony does not understand but which Caesar uses coldly and brutally. It is interesting to notice the ruthless scorn with which Caesar observes the ordinary man. Here we can see the rise of the superman, the new Machiavellian dictator, far away from the aesthetic-aristocratic schema. Shakespeare is beginning to get his eyes opened to the new variations of elitism and self-deification of the time. But Antony understands nothing of this new arrangement in the historical development. He sees only an inferior soldier who wants to take his place and relegate him to the backwater of his former fame. He begins to feel old and tired but cannot understand the cause of his depression. It is in this demotion through time that Shakespeare has found the invisible center, the black hole that will disclose the simultaneous maturation and growth of the change.

The Sonnets

It may seem unexpected and paradoxical to find forgetfulness and aging as themes in a poet who has so definitely conquered time in the poetry of his youth. But even in the sonnets, where the Dark Lady makes her entry as his life's great disappointment in love, Shakespeare gives expression to his fear of growing old and passé. He envies his more modern colleagues who in every sense he finds more intelligent than himself, at the same time as he feels deep disgust at the state of society and everything to do with sexuality and love. Even here is fully formulated the dark and embittered view of life that with such renewed intensity will return in his last tragedy. The moral degradation is felt already in every line of these grim poems on how he had believed that he had found a new Beatrice in the Dark Lady. And he has been cruelly deceived not just by her but also by the young nobleman who had accepted him, not just as a poet and actor, but as his equal as an aristocrat and as a friend.

He is twice deceived when he realizes that a friend of the nobleman is the Lady's lover, and also an idolized poet, whose amateurish verses have superseded his own poetry. He is the servant who thought he was master, brutally put back in his place.

And with this experience Shakespeare's view of the entire Neoplatonic pattern is dislodged. Now the secondary role emerges as a theme in his poetry, at the same time as he stubbornly refuses to lose the original vision completely out of sight. All of his subsequent drama will deal with the theme of demotion. From Hamlet to Brutus and Othello he puts forth a privileged hero who—because of an attack on his identity—reacts destructively against the aristocratic model that has formed him. It is then, in the dizzy fall toward the bottom, in the luxurious urge for annihilation, that Antony suddenly discovers that the depth is populated.

He discovers the banished, the constricted, the slaves on society's lowest level. And then the nature of the death wish changes; it becomes an expression of the eternal battle between suffering and oppression. A *change* that will affect the structure of all of the gigantic system of ideas. A *self* that will break out of its limitations, not in sexual liberation, but through identification with the conditions of the banished, a self that will rediscover itself by accepting the conditions of the role of the slave.

Antony gathers his servants around him on the eve of the last, decisive battle:

> Well, my good fellows, wait on me tonight:
> . . . and make as much of me
> As when mine empire was your fellow too,
> And suffer'd my command, . . .
>
> (4.2.20–23)

Like a gleam in a piece of broken glass flashes the picture of another night of sacrifice, when a group of servants take farewell of their master and are entrusted with the future fate of the world: the last supper in the New Testament. It is surprisingly rare that Shakespeare uses biblical motifs compared to his use of motifs from contemporary art. Shakespeare is the "poet of secularization," he transposes the religious motifs to make them serve that creative process of mankind that is the grand theme of his poetry. Seen in this perspective the model of the Neoplatonic world order is suddenly exposed as a falsification. The banished slaves are transformed from empty forms and symbols in an aristocratic-aesthetical code into human beings of flesh and blood.

It is the same transformation as we experience today when in the confrontation with Michelangelo's grave sculptures we are captivated more by the anguish and existential conditions of the slaves than by the composition as a whole and the subtlety of its higher superstructure. This is of course primarily because the sculptor has given these contorted, fighting limbs such a strong concreteness, but above all because we, in our own historical situation, look upon them as an expression of our own fight for freedom. We see their painful wrestling with the stone as an image of the rebellion against oppression and tyranny of the awakening poor nations. And we identify this awakening with our own revived awareness of being bound to their fight.

It is in the same way as in Shakespeare's drama, where Antony is awakened to awareness of being bound to the fate of the slaves:

> Every time
> Serves for the matter that it is then born in't.
>
> (2.2.9–10)

With this identification both the theme of the play and Antony's role are changed. And we read it now, because of our own historical situation, as a reflection of the liberation theme, precisely as this is reflected in the other roles of the play. They are all variations on the theme of the secondary role, the servant theme. Even Eros, the demigod of ancient abstraction, is given human form, steps down together with the whole of the Neoplatonic system from his lofty niche in the world of ideas, to the earth, to be changed there into a living being in the role of a simple servant. And in what seems an important scene he exchanges this role with his master in order to give him a lesson in dignity, in what it means to liberate oneself from degradation and disgrace.

With this descent to the earth all of the grandiose Neoplatonic construction changes form, just as all roles will change identity in relation to the vision of liberty. We get a range of all the different ways of relating to this vision: treason, contempt, ignorance, paralysis, indifference to the possibility of freedom, but also the complete transformation to loyalty, and solidarity, with its concomitant message.

It is in this way that Enobarbus goes through *his* transformation, his pilgrimage through the inferno of treason, in the same way as the irresponsible young girls around Cleopatra are to find in death their way to the freedom of unconditional faithfulness. But first and foremost the greatest transformation happens through Cleopatra herself; it is through her that the theme of liberation gets its most exalted purgation and grandeur.

Cleopatra

With Cleopatra Shakespeare revenges himself for the greatest degradation of his life. He writes himself free from the traumatic memory that he has tried to liberate himself from through his infinite poetical transformations. What luxurious pain in tearing away the mask from the Dark Lady—but at the same time what a victory for his unshakeable belief in the possibilities of transformation.

What a picture he makes of the black gypsy he puts on the stage, a caricature of the Cleopatra myth, past her prime, vulgar and crude, grotesque and wild, but also with a soft humanity behind her split nature, just as with Antony whose illness she sees through because she suffers from the same disease herself, of being neglected, having to play a second-rank role in his love, when she is accustomed to being the foremost and most adored one in these hunting grounds.

Aristotle's idea of man as never being able to become more than a being of the second rank, because he can never rise to the idea of man, seems to have an uncanny manifestation in her role as well as in Antony's; they never become more than shadows and reflections of the pictures they have painted of each other. Because of this they throw themselves at each other's throats like wolves, as if they wanted to tear out with their teeth those confessions of absolute love they have never had a chance to hear from the other's lips, but which they know are there, behind all the lies and all the dissimulation. In their grotesque meetings, in their sadomasochistic attacks they can never find the words, they can only throw themselves in each other's arms in silence, as if in the contact of their bodies there was a language more eloquent than words. What a break with the idealistic credo, when this vulgar cocotte finally takes over the role of Beatrice in lifting her Antony from the lowness of the earthly level up to final purification. Her fire burns away the last remains of his degradation, and in her arms he finally rediscovers his lost identity. He can greet Caesar in the way a Roman greets a victor. He achieves liberation by accepting his fall, in his elevation, and in this way his death becomes a reconciliation of the oppositions inside him, a coincidentia oppositorum.

But the greatest change (which is at the same time the greatest deepening of the original theme) happens through Cleopatra. The despised old whore, who conducts her lover to his liberation, grows to something more than a reflection of the angelic Beatrice. When she has lost Antony, the battle of the sexes finally seems to abate, and her grief transforms her into a human being in whom the male-female opposition has melted down and lost all importance:

> O, wither'd is the garland of the war,
> The soldier's pole is fall'n: young boys and girls
> Are level now with men: the odds is gone,
> And there is nothing left remarkable
> Beneath the visiting moon.
>
> (4.15.64–68)

But what human resources she has and what powers they give her to break out of the marble picture when she is forced to leave her protected retreat of cool androgyny upstairs and once again step down to the downstairs of the slaves.

At first she does this in order to find a metaphor for her grief. High and low have lost every meaning; it is only in a comparison with her lowest servant that she can find words for her loss and for her own self:

> No more but e'en a woman, and commanded
> By such poor passion as the maid that milks,
> And does the meanest chares.
>
> (4.15.73–75)

She follows the same road as Antony: from the heights of cold abstraction she climbs down to the warm earth and exchanges there her role as ruler and master with an identification with the slave. She no longer glorifies the paradise of blessed Dantean visions—instead she wants to throw her royal scepter at the evil gods as a protest against their cruel games. Here there are no gestures of reconciliation toward the divine, no confessions of surrender and humility, neither to heaven nor to earth, the gypsy of the East captures without help from others the Roman citizenship that has been denied her, not just by Caesar but even by her beloved Antony. Against the divine demand for submission, she poses the picture of the beloved elevated to cosmic proportions, and conquers heaven and earth for a dream of his greatness. As Juliet makes of Romeo a being who exceeds all God-given measures for man, Cleopatra puts before us the picture of Antony, to the destruction of all gods. She is mortal humanity confronted with a cosmos devoid of all divine assistance. In her existential forsakenness she musters up strength to endow the theme of freedom with a final greatness.

She meets Caesar, and the prisoner, considered to be a slave, conquers her conqueror. With Caesar the puritan morality of cleanness has reached its final perfection and revealed its hidden fascism. The manipulator steps forward as the dictator of the new republic. He leaves after the meeting with Cleopatra in the false belief that his despotic civic rationality has conquered eastern unreason. But Cleopatra has long seen through the confusion of roles between master and slave. It is he who is Fortune's slave, a poor lackey of the morality of progress, and therefore doomed. In order to demonstrate the paradox she arrays herself a last time in her queenly rank as a sign of a majesty that has finally taken farewell of all visible, earthly power. The Black Vesper's Masquerades are drawing toward their close—also for her. (Perhaps this was the author's calculated effect taking advantage of the waning light in his theater in the afternoon. The plays were performed in daylight. The way home was beginning to darken for the audience also.)

> *Iras.* Finish, good lady, the bright day is done,
> And we are for the dark.
>
> (5.2.192–93)

With dusk the last mask falls from the aging cocotte, and clean and clear as dawn rises the undamaged vision of human integrity—measured not by puritan ideals—as uncontaminated by the mud as the water lily in the water.

The greatest poet of the Renaissance created his work at a time when a dying aristocracy had lost its foothold. A world in the process of restructuring, with new, rising classes on the way to breaking out of political oppression in order to make new demands of their existence, it would only take twenty years before the first European revolution had been carried through, monarchy abolished and the Puritan republic become a fact.

The poet anticipated this impending transformation—but he also defended himself against the contempt of the imagination and the spiritual impoverishment he feared would follow in its wake. Divided in his attitude to the aristocratic philosophy he himself destroyed, he has not yet found the new form that the disrupted situation requires. Instead he builds on the broken fragments of the old already superseded system, his vision. He has it conveyed by already aging characters, who can see that what is new in the new age is already losing its bearings. Their message is tragic because of the falling darkness around the vision of man's capability for integrity. But despite darkness, old age and decay this vision rises up with redoubled strength against the blight of unimaginative ideas, against spiritual capitulation, against slavery and oppression with redoubled strength. Through the thickening darkness is heard Hamlet's meditation on the creative process: "What a *piece of work* is man" (italics mine).

It could be translated as: "What a *result of human endeavor* is man." His striving becomes a paean to man's ability of self-creation, to the ability to form a vision of an unshackled human community, despite the tyranny and evil of the material world. For us who experience our own struggle in our own time, the liberation theme in *Antony and Cleopatra* stands out with a new and unexpected intensity as a counteraction against the annihilation of man, against his degradation, against his loss of identification. The confrontation, between east and west, between the new world and the old, is concentrated and takes shape in human and apprehensible form.[1]

Notes

1. This essay was translated by the editor from the text in Sverker R. Ek, Ulla Åsberg, Elsa Sjöberg and Katarina Sjöberg, eds., *Alf Sjöberg: Teater som besvärjelse, artiklar från fem decennier* (Stockholm: Norstedt & Söners förlag, 1982), 124–39.

Was Othello Black?

GUNNAR SJÖGREN

> *Cornwall:* Why dost thou call him knave? What is his fault?
> *Kent:* His countenance likes me not.

PERHAPS IT SHOULD BE: *IS* OTHELLO BLACK—BECAUSE IT IS OF COURSE NOT a question of a historical person with a completed life, but of a fictional figure who still *is*. The question may be justified if the aim is primarily to throw light on the question of whether Shakespeare himself conceived of Othello as black—in other words whether he *was* black in the eyes of the audience that *Othello* was written for. To begin with it can be argued that this is nothing to argue about: Shakespeare called his tragedy *Othello, The Moor of Venice* and Moor is (roughly) the same as Arab. And therefore the problem should be solved: Othello is not black. But nevertheless this is very much a moot point, and the question is particularly interesting because the role has often been played by a black actor opposite a white Desdemona.

To start with, what do the authorities say? Georg Brandes wrote in his big Shakespeare study in 1912:

> . . . [I]t is quite unreasonable to suppose . . . that [Shakespeare] thought of [Othello] as a negro. It was, of course, inconceivable that a negro should attain the rank of general and admiral in the service of the Venetian Republic; and Iago's mention of Mauritania as the country to which Othello intends to retire, shows plainly enough that the 'Moor' ought to be represented as an Arab. It is no argument against this that men who hate and envy him apply to him epithets that would befit a negro. Thus Roderigo in the first scene of the play calls him "thick-lips," and Iago, speaking to Brabantio, calls him "an old black ram," and Brabantio talks of his "sooty bosom." That Othello calls himself *black* only means that he is dark. . . . As a Moor, Othello has a complexion sufficiently swarthy to form a striking contrast to the white and even blonde Desdemona, and there is also a sufficiently marked race-contrast between him, as a Semite, and the Aryan girl.[1]

Henrik Schück in 1916 does not expressly commit himself on the question of Othello's race, but he calls him "African," which seems to indicate that he thinks of him as black.[2] Per Meurling in his study of Shakespeare published in 1952, on the other hand, is quite sure: "Of course the Moor is not black and he should not be acted as black. He is quite simply an Arab. The Duke says to Brabantio: 'your son-in-law is far more fair than black.' Othello is brown like a sheikh."[3]

Coleridge, too, looked upon him as an Arab, whereas Bradley in *Shakespearean Tragedy* (1904) on the one hand does not want to argue that Shakespeare differentiated between Negroes and Moors, but he feels almost certain that he envisaged Othello as black rather than light brown.[4] Granville-Barker in his famous Preface (1930) does not discuss Othello's race but says unhesitatingly that he is black.[5] And in recent years the general opinion has swayed more and more in that direction.

The yearbook *Shakespeare Survey* (1957) contains an essay by Albert Gerard who writes: ". . . it is obviously impossible to retain the Romantic view that Othello is not a real Negro."[6] In the introduction to the edition of *Othello* in the series *The New Shakespeare* (1957), the prominent Shakespearean John Dover Wilson writes: "Bradley was undoubtedly correct in his belief that Shakespeare intended us to think of him as a Negro. That is what 'Moor' meant to Englishmen in the Middle Ages and at the time of Elizabeth and James. Roderigo's contemptuous reference to 'the thick-lips' may be prejudiced evidence, but it should at least have warned nineteenth-century producers and their successors that to present the Moor of Venice as a bronzed and semitic-featured Arabian prince might seriously disfeature the play."[7] In the spring of 1958 a new edition of *Othello* was published in the respected series *The Arden Shakespeare,* revised by M. R. Ridley. Ridley shares John Dover Wilson's view that Shakespeare thought of Othello as black, not overly negroid but pitch black.

If it was true that "Moor" to Shakespeare and his contemporaries quite simply meant "Negro," this would be a fact of decisive importance. But is this so? The following quotations will answer the question:

Boorde (1547): "Barbary—the inhabitants be called the mores; ther be whyte mores and black moors."

John Pory (1600): "This part of the world is inhabited especially by the Africans or Moores, properly so called; which last are of two kinds, namely white or tawney Moores and Negroes or blacke Moores."

> Lithgow (1632): "A towne inhabited by christians, arabs, and Moores, not blacke Mores, as the Africans be, but . . . a kinde of Egyptians."

Even if the definitions do not agree altogether it is still obvious that during all of this space of time a distinction is made between white and black Moors, and therefore Dover Wilson's assertion does not hold good.

It now remains to investigate whether Shakespeare himself distinguished between different kinds of Moors. In addition to *Othello* (1603) there are Moors in another two of his dramas, Aaron the Moor in *Titus Andronicus* (probably written about 1590) and the Prince of Morocco in *The Merchant of Venice* (from around 1595).

That Aaron is intended to be black there is no need to doubt, despite the fact that he is the lover of the Queen of the Goths. In two places he is called "coal-black" and he talks himself about "my fleece of woolly hair." He is also pictured as a child of nature, a pagan and a jolly barbarian. In addition we have a very compelling indication that he acted as a Negro; there exists a pen drawing showing a scene from the play, which is considered to be very early, perhaps from 1595, and in it he is quite black and has pronouncedly negroid features. This drawing is by all appearances the earliest illustration we have of a Shakespearean drama and shows the main characters dressed in classical Roman clothes, while the soldiers are dressed the way Elizabethan soldiers were. Dover Wilson, who was not afraid of daring conclusions, suggests that Aaron's black profile belongs to the famous actor James Burbage, and that behind Titus's beard Shakespeare's own features are concealed.[8] In any case there is no doubt that the skillful artist who drew the sketch has seen a black man—and not a Moor in our sense—on the stage. The prominent Shakespeare scholar E. K. Chambers writes about this drawing: "Incidentally it may inform students of *Othello,* as well as of *Titus,* that to the Elizabethan mind a Moor was not tawny but dead black."[9]

As we have seen from the quotations from more or less contemporary authors this is not quite true, and when we turn to the Prince of Morocco, who is one of Portia's suitors in *The Merchant of Venice,* we find that Shakespeare himself differentiated between different kinds of Moors. In the stage directions to the 1623 Folio we read: "Enter Morochus a tawney Moore in all white." Thus he is exactly that kind of tanned or light brown Moor that Pory describes. Even if we cannot be sure that the stage direction is by Shakespeare's own hand, it nevertheless shows that the Prince of Morocco in any case was not *acted* as a black man.

About him Portia says—but this is before she has seen him: "If he have the condition of a saint, and the complexion of a devil, I had rather he should shrive me than wive me." (Desdemona argued the other way round.) He himself says about his color: "Mislike me not for my complexion, / The shadowed livery of the burnish'd sun." This is a paraphrase of the Song of Solomon: "Look not upon me, because I am black, because the sun hath looked upon me." The Prince of Morocco is very like Othello in many ways, the same self-confident dignity, the same way of expressing himself, the same somewhat affected pose, and like Othello he is of noble birth. He is proud of his complexion: "I would not change this hue, / Except to steal your thoughts my noble queen." And the quiet way in which he accepts his defeat shows that he is a gentleman, a "good loser."

It is easy to feel pity for him; he is often played down to the level of ridicule, but he is too good a man for such treatment. In fact he deserved to win Portia, because his choice of the golden casket, instead of those of silver and lead, is logically correct: "never so rich a gem," he says about Portia, "was set in worse than gold." She is rich, she is young and beautiful, and her interior corresponds to her exterior. It is difficult to think of a worse illustration to the saying that all is not gold that glitters. Hagberg in his translation has made matters even worse by giving the poor Prince an awful last line which does not convey the dignity of the original.[10]

Since the Prince of Morocco is expressly said to be a tawny Moor and not black, there is hardly any reason to think that Othello was not of the same race; it is also a fact that he comes from the same part of the world as the Prince does. It is true that he is called black, but not coal-black—but this means just dark-skinned. There are far too many examples of this kind of language use in Shakespeare and other writers for there to be any reason to doubt this. That the duke says of Othello that he is "more fair than black," on the other hand, has hardly any weight of evidence; this does not refer to his appearance but to his inner qualities, as the lines in their entirety read: "If virtue no delighted beauty lack, / Your son-in-law is far more fair than black." There is a parallel passage in *Twelfth Night:* "None can be call'd deform'd but the unkind. / Virtue is beauty." In English the expression "he is a white man" is still used to refer to a decent human being regardless of skin color. Thus Shakespeare's text gives us no absolute certainty, but the similarity with the Prince of Morocco is an especially strong support for the opinion that Othello also is no more than "brown like a sheikh" as Meurling writes.

When Brandes pointed out that it was unthinkable that a black man could be entrusted with the post as supreme commander in Venice, this is a little beside the point—the question is if Shakespeare considered it to be unthinkable, and this is not quite so certain. To answer this question it will be necessary to investigate what was known about black people in England in Shakespeare's time. This was presumably not much, not much more than that they were savages who were transported on English ships as slaves from Africa to the West Indies. According to K. L. Little's *Negroes in Britain,*[11] a certain John Lok in 1555 first brought a number of black slaves to Britain. According to the same source they got on well, although "the colde and moyst aire doth somewhat offend them,"[12] which is not surprising. The English participation in the slave trade was rather modest to start with, and very few slaves seem to have been brought to England until toward the 1660s, when this traffic became more extensive and it became common, and fashionable, to have black servants. One can form an impression of their situation, at this time, from an advertisement printed in 1659 in the *Mercurius Publicus:*

> A Negro-boy, about nine years of age, in a grey searge suit, his hair cut close to his head, was lost on Tuesday last, August 9th at night, in St. Nicholas Lane, London. If anyone can give notice of him to Mr. Thomas Barker at the Sugar Loaf in that Lane, they shall be rewarded for their pains.[13]

Ten years later Pepys writes in his famous Diary: "For a cookmaid we have, ever since Bridget went, used a black a moor of Mr. Bateliers's, Doll, who dresses our meat mighty well, and we mightily pleased with her."[14]

~

But this was long after Shakespeare's time, and there is reason to believe that to *his* contemporaries Negroes were most probably exotic curiosities, who were closer to the "Cannibals, that each other eat; / the Anthropophogi, and men whose heads / Do grow beneath their shoulders," that Othello speaks of, than to Othello himself.

But what about the Moors; what did Shakespeare's countrymen know about them? Did they live in blissful ignorance of the astonishing fact that Britain had at one time been ruled by a Moor, even by a Moor with Negro blood in his veins? This was the Roman soldier emperor Lucius Septimus Severus who was born in Leptis Magna in Tripolitania and became emperor in the year 193. From 208–211 he was in Britain busy quenching rebellions, and he died—in York. He was succeeded by his sons Bassianus and Geta—the former killed the latter and became emperor, best known under the name of Caracalla. There is in the Musei Capitolini in Rome a bust of Severus which clearly betrays his exotic origin; his is not the usual profile of a Roman emperor. But the bust of Caracalla in Naples shows even clearer negroid features; his head is round like a ball—and he looks surprisingly like Orson Welles in his film of *Othello* some years ago.

In Shakespeare's time the main source of knowledge about England's history was Holinshed's *Chronicles,* from which the playwrights derived much material for their plays. It may therefore be of interest to see what he has to say about Severus:

> . . . such was the state of this Isle about the yeare of our Lord 195. In which season, because that king Lucius was dead, and had left no issue to succeed him, the Britains (as before ye haue heard) were at variance amongst themselues, and so continued to the comming of Seuerus, whome the British chronographers affirme to reigne as king in this Isle, & that by right of succession in bloud, as descended of Androgeus the Britaine, which went to Rome with Julius Cesar, as before ye haue heard.

And about Caracalla (Bassianus):

> [Severus left] behind him two sonnes, the one named Geta, and the other Bassianus. This Bassianus being borne of a British woman, succeeded his father in the gouernement of Britaine, in the year of the incarnation of our Lord 211. The Romans would haue had Geta created king of Britaine, bearing more fauour to him because he had a Romane Ladie to his mother.[15]

Holinshed is not correct on this point—both Bassianus and Geta were children of Julia Domna, who was, by the way, a very remarkable woman born of obscure parents in Syria. Holinshed tries to do the best he can with the unpleasant fact that his country was dominated by Rome, and tries to legitimize the Roman rulers as best he can. Probably he acted in good faith.

Thus there is nothing to be learned from this. Shakespeare's contemporaries did not know that a Moor had at one time intervened in their history. On the other hand we know that the English knew very well the role that the Moors had played in the Mediterranean countries, and that they stood in high esteem as soldiers—they had for centuries held Europe in terror. England had also since a long time back traded, at least sporadically, with Morocco. With his considerable knowledge about Italian matters, Shakespeare would also have known that the Venetians on principle employed a foreigner as commander of their military forces in order to avoid the risk of power abuse that a native commander-in-chief might present. We are of course dealing with mercenary troupes, and other officers in *Othello* were foreigners as well—Cassio, Florentine, and Iago, to judge by the name, Spanish.

If circumstantial evidence thus indicates that Othello is an Arab, there is *one* strong reason to assume that in Shakespeare's time he was nevertheless presented with his face black; that is the tradition in the theater. We know that after the Restoration in 1660 Othello was acted with blackened face, and it is impossible, according to Bradley, that Othello's color should have been forgotten so soon after Shakespeare's own time. He also holds it to be unlikely that the color had been changed deliberately from brown to black,[16] which is more questionable. Such a change could have been a result of the fact that black people, as has been mentioned, had become increasingly more common in England.

However, it is interior rather than exterior criteria that critics rely on when they want to make Othello black. They believe that he has certain traits of character that are typical of black people, and here we enter upon very treacherous ground. Albert Gerard, who has already been mentioned, points out that crime reports in newspapers teach us that those who murder their wives out of jealousy are mentally defective, and that although it is true that Othello has a high position in society, and is of a noble disposition, he must nevertheless be intellectually underdeveloped to do what he does. He is stupid and gullible, and he speaks of himself in the third person in an infantile way. He is like a child that feels self-pity.

All this, according to Gerard, indicates that Othello is a Negro, a person with a primitive emotional life and an undeveloped intelligence. He is, as Iago says, a barbarian. This contribution to the discussion by Gerard is perhaps not one of the more weighty ones, but it is symptomatic of the turn to a more realistically psychological evaluation that was started by T. S. Eliot in his essay "Shakespeare and the Stoicism of Seneca." It is a reaction to the Romantic school, represented by, for example, Brandes, and to the theater historian school, whose foremost representative is Stoll, according to whom we should not try to find any coherent psychological explanation for the behavior of the characters: they quite simply behave in the way the dramatic situation requires.

Dover Wilson stresses particularly Othello's trustfulness and naivete, character traits that he considers to be typical of a black person:

> The Moor a free and open nature too,
> That thinks men honest that but seems to be so:
> And will as tenderly be led by the nose . . .
> As asses are.

Iago's disdainful bragging does in fact sum up the relationship between blacks and whites for the past three and half centuries, is Dover Wilson's bitter comment.[17]

He bases this view primarily on the experience of having seen Paul Robeson perform Othello: ". . . and I felt I was seeing the tragedy for the first time, . . . the fact that he was a true Negro seemed to floodlight the whole drama. Everything was slightly different from what I had previously imagined; new points, fresh nuances, were constantly emerging; and all had, I felt, been clearly intended by the author. The performance convinced me in short that a Negro Othello is essential to the full understanding of the play. . . . The marriage between an African with a 'sooty bosom' and an Italian girl with 'whiter skin than snow' sets the problem in its extremest form."[18]

Paul Robeson himself says in an interview: "This play is about the problem of minority groups—a blackamoor who tried to find equality among the whites. It's right up my alley." His director, Miss Webster, explained: "There is no mistaking it, . . . Othello is a black man. That being so, all the elements of the action fall automatically into place, as they do not when he's merely played in blackface."[19]

But in actual fact, the race problem is not very prominent in the drama, if you look at it objectively. Othello is eminently respected: Desdemona's father—as Othello says himself—liked him and often invited him to his house. He has a high position and holds a position of trust, and Montano, the Governor of Cyprus, spontaneously offers his highest appreciation when he is told that Othello is coming to the Island to take command. Furthermore, Othello is not himself as conscious of his race, as for example Shylock is; he is not afflicted with an inferiority complex—his worry is as much that he is so old and not a lady's man, as that he is black.

The racial difference between Othello and Desdemona is one component in the tragic conflict, but this does not mean that Othello should be played as a Negro. Many people would find the racial difference sufficiently strong if he were an Arab. It is characteristic that Brandes, who was Jewish, thought that Othello as a Semite was sufficiently contrasted with the Arian girl. Hitler's Germany was to prove him dreadfully right.

The assertion that Othello is so gullible, or plain stupid, and that this can only be explained as a racial feature, rests on two false assumptions: that Negroes are more stupid than other people, and that Shakespeare and his audience had an opinion of what was characteristic of Negroes in this respect. But it is not necessary to refer to any racial characteristics to explain Othello's behavior. It is true that the tragedy is often performed in such a way that Othello is made to look too stupid for words, but this is not necessary.

The view that people are what they look like, that a villain looks like a villain, that anyone that looks honest also is honest, is still very widespread and is the basis of the impostor's business. In the sixteenth century this view was even more common than now, and especially in the theater it was easy to differentiate between the good and the bad. Richard III is as deformed in body as in soul, while Hamlet is not just "a noble soul," but also "That unmatch'd form and feature of blown youth." In the latter play we can find another example that is very illuminating.

To many people the long scene in act 3, scene 4 in which Hamlet shows his mother the portraits of her two husbands becomes a stumbling block. It appears as if he is applying purely aesthetic criteria to his mother's behavior. He first points to his father's portrait: "See what a grace was seated on this brow . . ." and so on, and then he points to that of Claudius:

> . . . Look you now, what follows;
> Here is your husband; like a mildew'd ear,
> Blasting his wholesome brother. Have you eyes?
> Could you on this fair mountain leave to feed,
> And batten on this moor? . . .

Madariaga writes: "Is there in all this sermon a single word to show that Hamlet would have objected to the Queen's 'act' had Claudius looked like King Hamlet and King Hamlet like Claudius?"[20] But this is an absurd construct; on the contrary the quotation shows that ethical and aesthetic considerations concur. Hamlet is convinced that appearances do not deceive, that the shell shows what the content is, and he thinks the queen is blind who cannot see this.

The quotation is of particular interest for our argument, since it also throws light on the use of the word "Moor." In the text of the First Quarto (1603) of *Hamlet* that is called Q1, which is considered to be a mutilated rendering of an early stage version, Hamlet describes his father in this picturesque way:

> Looke you now, here is your husband,
> With a face like *Vulcan.*
> A looke fit for a murder and a rape,
> A dull, dead hanging looke, and a hell-bred eie,
> To affright children and amaze the world.

In the complete version that was printed the following year in the Second Quarto edition, called Q2, the passage runs the way I quoted before. The text here contains a pun, or at least a play on words, which is significant. "Moor" means heath, but the spelling with a capital M gives the double meaning "dark-skinned person." This is clear from the earlier version where he is likened to Vulcan: both designations are intended to point out that he is swarthy, and it is understood that this means that he is villainous.

But in *Othello* Shakespeare reverses the key signatures. "Honest" Iago, who looks so confidence-inspiring, is a monster, Desdemona, who has appearances against her, is innocence personified, the wanton Emilia has a heart of gold, and Othello is "black" outside—how black we can leave open for the moment—but "white" inside. This is one leading principle in this ingeniously constructed tragedy, and a device that may have shocked the audience that Shakespeare was writing for.

Does Desdemona really have appearances against her? Indeed, Venice was considered to be a sinful city; the redheaded Venetian courtesans were world-famous. "The name of a Cortezan of Venice is famoused over all Christendome," writes a contemporary. Just as for Victorians much later in time the very word "Parisienne" was to carry associations of indecency, so Shakespeare no doubt had to count with the fact that his audience harbored preconceived opinions about the moral standing of the Venetian Desdemona. And he keeps them in this delusion: she has deceived her father and she is having an affair with a colored man—that can make anyone's blood boil. And she has, which is clear from Othello's own account, proposed herself—something outrageous. Her father also gives Othello a word of advice: "She has deceiv'd her father, may do thee."

Desdemona is no milksop; on the arrival to Cyprus she does not object to the rather blatant flirting on the part of the courtly Cassio and the grosser Iago—we cannot really make up our minds about her. Note the way Othello describes her:

> . . . 'tis not to make me jealous,
> To say my wife is fair, feeds well, loves company,
> Is free of speech, sings, plays, and dances well.

She cannot in other words be very different from the young ladies in waiting that Queen Elizabeth never managed to prevent from having affairs with her own favorites. And Othello's description is given added force when one remembers where Shakespeare took it from. It appears in the introduction to the collection of short stories, the *Hecatommithi,* by the Italian Cinthio, from which Shakespeare derived the action of *Othello.* There occurs a warning against the traps that are laid by beautiful courtesans, whose charming social graces conceal their evil intent. Singing, games, dancing and pleasant conversation are among the studied accomplishments that serve to deceive credulous men. In other words they behaved exactly like Desdemona.

And what can Othello—and the audience—think when she tries to twist Othello round her little finger in order to influence him in an official matter, running through the whole gamut of the art of seduction from coquetry to tears. And for whom? For Cassio who has everything that Othello lacks, who is young and handsome, who has an upper-class education and comes from the same social class as Desdemona does. Is it strange that he becomes jealous?

Interfering in their husbands' work is probably the last thing that newlywed officers' wives should do. "Our general's wife is now the general," Iago says, and she herself says to Cassio when he has fallen into disfavor:

> . . . my lord shall never rest,
> I'll watch him tame and talk him out of patience;
> His bed shall seem a school, his board a shrift, . . .

"This is called curtain-lectures," Strindberg writes,[21] who quotes these words enthusiastically and also Desdemona's words to Othello:

> . . . Michael Cassio
> That came a-wooing with you, and so many a time
> When I have spoke of you dispraisingly,
> Hat ta'en your part . . .

"The fact that Cassio serves as a lightning-conductor or *Hausfreund* is an important incidental circumstance," Strindberg writes.

But even Desdemona's obstinacy in spite of Othello's evident disapproval shows how utterly inexperienced she is, through and through. It does away with what remains of the scepticism that we, the audience, ought to feel up to this point. And then, when Othello showers her with accusations, our sympathies go unreservedly to this frightened, and as we now understand, completely innocent young girl, who does not even understand his insinuations, but is loyal unto death to her incomprehensible husband. But if she is depicted as a little snow-white lamb from the beginning, the drama loses an element of suspension for anyone who is perhaps ignorant of the story, and the Othello figure loses in stature.

Othello is a leader who commands respect. He has stature. He is credulous but he is not stupid. He is pure-hearted but not silly; naive, but not childish. "He speaks as great men do," Henri Fluchère writes, "hardly raising his voice, always calm, radiant, dignified, until the moment when uneasiness undermines this nobility."[22] But he is also something of a poseur; he acts a part. He is well aware of his position in relation to his entourage; as soon as he appears and opens his mouth, everybody listens; when he orders something, everybody obeys. Between him and the others there is an invisible line that nobody oversteps.

Many high-ranking officers fall for the temptation to over-dramatize themselves. From our own time we can think of Montgomery, MacArthur and de Gaulle. It is almost an occupational hazard. There is a story about the French generalissimo Joffre in the First World War that whenever news of the not infrequent military setbacks reached him, he used to walk about in the headquarters patting his own head and murmuring to himself: "poor Joffre, poor Joffre." He talked about himself in the third person, exactly as Othello does. De Gaulle did the same at the well-known press conference on 19 May 1958: "de Gaulle thinks this, the Gaulle does that."

Othello's indisputable naivete is not that of a child of nature but is the result of the isolation from natural social intercourse with other people that a leader is subject to. It is this distancing that makes him prone to listen—as regards questions that are out of his experience—to anyone who has his confidence.

It is the not too far-fetched notion that Desdemona may equally well be wanton that Iago makes use of, when from her father's words, which have just been quoted, he gets the idea to make

Othello jealous, and thus make him discharge Cassio. To secure Cassio's office for himself is the limited aim of his plot, which then unintentionally grows to such a devastating storm that it sweeps away all the participants, except one—and here lies one of the ironies that the play is so rich in—this one person, Cassio, becomes governor of Cyprus and pronounces judgment on Iago.

In Hagberg's translation Cassio and Iago are called lieutenant and ensign respectively—we would have been able to form a better picture of the conflict if they had been called chief of staff and aide-de-camp. Even in the first lines of the play we get to know that Iago has been passed over at the appointment of a "chief of staff," and this in spite of the fact that he has had powerful intercessors. As a professional soldier Iago has come up the hard way and has considered himself to be the obvious candidate for the position. And then—what is more, on purely military grounds—he is passed over by an armchair strategist, who has never felt the smell of gunpowder, an upper-crust fop, a lady-killer. Iago's vanity is wounded, it hurts, and he wants to hurt others, and he starts by waking up Desdemona's father.

The bitterness of a rejected officer at seeing a younger man overtake him can, in a person with a bad character, find expression in the most perfidious ways. And Iago definitively has a very bad character. Many have wanted to see in him the incarnation of the very nature of evil, and to interpret the play on the symbolical level as a description of the predominance of evil over good. But Iago is also very human, as has been pointed out by others. He is proud that he is free from all illusions, and he believes that he is completely clear-sighted. To him Cassio is a blockhead, Othello an ass, Emilia an idiot, and he despises Desdemona for having been taken in by Othello's boastful stories about his heroic deeds. But he is completely blind to their inner qualities.

Iago is a master of deception, and his disguise is the most difficult to see through: it is the straightforwardness of the simple soldier and his rough outspokenness. It is a role that has become second nature—perhaps he was such once—and it does not occur to Othello to distrust his upright aide-de-camp. Iago is perhaps not sufficiently skilled to be worthy of promotion, but he is, as Othello thinks, "honest." What a starting point for an impostor.

In order to avoid deceiving his audience Shakespeare makes him reveal his dark plans—this gives him a free hand to employ all his ingenuity against Othello. If Iago were not completely convincing Othello would look silly, and that he is least of all. He is no easy prey, he is dangerous as a bull, and Iago has to work fast, adroitly and fearlessly like a bullfighter. I did mention that he is a Spaniard? The smallest slip and he is dead. It is a cruel but fascinating spectacle. But his plans do not proceed as he had thought—soon he finds himself in extreme danger, he becomes desperate, strikes down Roderigo, but Cassio is only wounded, and he does not manage to silence Emilia before she has already spoken. It is the same crescendo as we know from countless detective stories—confronted with the danger of being exposed the murderer lashes out blindly and takes ever greater risks. But when Iago is exposed it is too late—Othello has strangled Desdemona.

Othello is about jealousy but Othello is not jealous by nature. And you have to do him justice; his jealousy is not grounded on wounded vanity, or even a feeling of inferiority—although for a moment this also catches hold of him in his moment of doubt—but is caused by the fact that he has built his view of life on trust in his fellow beings. Just as he is himself loyal he takes it for granted that other people are equally loyal: a commander has to be able to trust his officers, a man has to be able to trust his wife—for him this is an axiom. When he becomes convinced that his wife has betrayed his confidence his world picture falls to pieces, his personality is dissolved, he ends up in chaos. And face-to-face with the truth of her innocence he is ceased not so much with remorse for his rash act as with relief that the horror was not true, and that the divine order, as he had understood it, had never been disturbed. He feels as if he has woken up from a nightmare, and he recovers his majestic and sonorous diction from before the catastrophe.

This egocentricity, as has been pointed out especially by T. S. Eliot, is very human, and Shakespeare demonstrates here as usual how keen an eye he has for human weaknesses, and how unconventional he is in his portrayal of his characters. When he depicts the standard characters of the Elizabethan stage, the villain, the victim and the hero, he gives them the ability to awake a response in generation after generation because he makes them living human beings.

It seems we had distanced ourselves a long way from the question of whether Othello is a Negro or an Arab—he is a human being; this is the important thing. But this does not mean that the racial question is unimportant; far from it. He has to be sufficiently different racially to motivate the indignation that this ill-assorted marriage causes. And it is important that the audience understands fully the apprehensions involved, perhaps not with their minds but with their feelings. And even if we, as enlightened viewers, can ignore our dislike, because Othello is such a splendid human being, an element of the alien, the somewhat frighteningly exotic behind the normal, the usual, must be there to burst forth in the final scenes. Then, if not before, we understand that Othello is not one of us, that there is in him something we cannot understand, whether this is in his race, his nature, his background, or in all these things together.

It is obvious that if Othello is played by a black man the racial tensions become particularly striking, something which can add to the dramatic effect of the play as a whole. This has often happened. In 1857 the black American Ira Aldridge played the title role in Sweden in a famous guest appearance. Not long ago Othello was acted in Brussels by a native Congolese, and Paul Robeson has, as we have experienced, created an unforgettable Othello.

On the other hand, white actors have not always been so lucky when they have made him into a black man. In 1745 the great Garrick failed completely in this role. He was small in stature, and when he entered the stage with blackened face and a big turban on his head the audience could not escape thinking of the little Negro boy with a teapot in one of Hogarth's popular prints. Somebody shouted: "Where is the teapot?" and the whole audience burst out laughing. Despite his great popularity he did not manage to win the favor of the audience in this role, and he gave up after a few performances. The failure was perhaps due in part to the fact that his facial expressions were hampered by the blackened face, and this is an important reason why Othello should not be made to look darker than necessary when he is played by a white actor.

Mounet-Sully in 1899 in the Comédie Française also failed dismally. With blackened face and with black arms and legs he presented an unfortunate likeness to those sculptures of black men carrying candelabras, and the audience never got over its mirth.

At Max Reinhardt's guest appearance at the Royal Dramatic Theater in Stockholm during the First World War, Paul Wegener, Carl Laurin writes, made the moor into "an Ashanti chief or a Njam-Njammer. . . ." "For six or seven tableaux this jealous Othello roared to the extent that even sincere friends of the Central Powers were left exhausted." And he points out quite correctly that "you do not have to be black to be jealous."[23]

From Nils Molin's *Shakespeare och Sverige (Shakespeare and Sweden)* I derive the following item about the reaction to the 1827 production of *Othello* in Nicander's translation: The magazine *Granskaren* writes that the drama and its characters are intolerable. To begin with Othello is black "which is not likely to affect us pleasantly" and Desdemona, who ought to be a well brought up girl, "runs away from her father to surrender herself to a Moor who is anything but young." Othello is "a bad character worthy of society's contempt, a dirty villain, a cannibal despicable to God and man, a wild animal . . ."[24]

The conclusion would be that Othello should be made exactly as dark as is needed to achieve the desired result, and it depends on the audience whether he should be lighter or darker. "A nuance in the color" can be important. (In countries where racial awareness is particularly strong, as for example in the American South, it is hardly possible to perform *Othello* at all. When Verdi's opera *Othello* was to be performed in Atlanta in connection with a guest appearance of the Metropolitan in 1958, it had to be exchanged for something else. What was suggested as a substitute was—*Madame Butterfly*!)

Strangely, it is in fact possible that the original model for Othello was neither black nor Arab, but a white man. Shakespeare derived the Moor from Cinthio's sententious story, and follows the main features of his account. To Cinthio the story serves to illustrate what happens if two married people are too different, and Desdemona's fate is a warning to Italian girls not to marry men who differ too much from themselves in race (*la Natura*), religion (*il Cielo*) and manner of living (*il modo della vita*). However, there was in Italy a very powerful family by the name of Moro, and in the fifteenth century one Christofal Moro was Venice's governor in Cyprus at a time when an attack from the Turks was expected, a situation very like that found in *Othello*. His wife died in Cyprus under very mysterious circumstances. "Moro" can mean both mulberry and Moor. Did Cinthio get the idea for his story by thinking of this Moro and changing "Christofal Moro of Venice" into "the Moor of Venice?"[25]

One can speculate whether Shakespeare knew this. The fatal handkerchief that Othello gives to his wife is in Cinthio's novella embroidered with arabesques. Shakespeare changes this to strawberries. Was this a "translation" of the three mulberries that Moro carried in his coat of arms, it has been asked. Or could it be that the strawberry pattern was fashionable in London in 1603?

I have amused myself by looking into this question on a visit to the Victoria and Albert Museum in London. And yes, this pattern was popular at this time. It can be seen on a bodice decorated with big red berries, and on a sampler dated 1600 I discovered a complete strawberry plant with flowers, leaves and berries. It was such a sampler that Helena tells us that she and Hermia shared as children in *A Midsummer Night's Dream:*

> We, Hermia, like two artificial gods,
> Have with our needles created both one flower,
> Both on one sampler, sitting on one cushion,
> Both warbling of one song, both in one key, . . .

But I also found a sampler with a mulberry branch, so there was no need for a "translation" from mulberry to strawberry. Mulberries were well-known in England—by an old tradition Shakespeare is said to have planted a mulberry tree outside his new house in Stratford. The explanation is probably much simpler: the strawberries were motivated by theatrical reasons so that the audience would more easily recognize the handkerchief. There is no need to assume that Shakespeare knew about the possible background to Cinthio's novella.

After this was written a new document has come to light which is an important contribution to the debate about Othello's race and color. This is a portrait of a Moor, which has recently been acquired by the Shakespeare Institute at Stratford. The portrait represents Abdul Guahid (Abd-el-Ouahed), emissary from Barbary (Morocco) to Elizabeth's court, and was painted in 1600. We can see a fair-skinned, black-bearded, tall man without any traces of negroid features.

Bernard Harris, who has written an essay about the portrait in the *Shakespeare Review* (1958, no. 11), rightly emphasizes the importance of this ocular proof of how a high-ranking Moor was seen in England at the time of the writing of *Othello*. He also explains the immediate circumstances of the embassy that Abd-el-Ouahed led. To all appearances its secret aim was no less than investigating the possibilities of forming an alliance between Morocco and England against Spain. The intention was to attack this country and to capture Spain as well as her rich overseas territories! It was a magnificent plan that had been hatched by the ruler of Morocco, Muley Hamed, encouraged by what he had heard about the successful English raid against Cadiz in 1597. But officially the embassy was a simple courtesy visit linked to business negotiations and discussions concerning certain financial disagreements that had occasioned an exchange of notes.

The embassy, which consisted of sixteen people, arrived in August 1600 and was quartered in a private house in the Strand that was ordinarily used on such occasions. A contemporary gives this account of the audience with Queen Elizabeth, who was residing at Nonsuch:

> The Ambassadors of *Barbary* had Audience vpon Wednesday last: here was a roial Preparacion, in the Manner of his receuing; rich Hangings and Furnitures sent from *Hampton* Court; the Gard very strong, in their rich Coatees; the Pentioners with their Axes; the Lords of the Order with their Collars; a full Court of Lords and Ladies. He passed thorough a Gard of Albards to the Cownsell Chamber, where he rested; he was brought to the Presence, soe to the Priuy Chamber, and soe the Gallery; where her Majestie satt at the further End in very great State, and gaue them Audience.[26]

There was good deal of theorizing about the real reason for this mission and the guesses went in all directions. The Queen was probably not very interested in the extravagant proposal, and left the matter in suspense, as was her wont. It turned out to be difficult, however, to find a passage home for the Moroccans, who were to stay for almost six months in England. Officially they were treated with great courtesy, but the attention they received in London, which was at this time a rather isolated backwater in the world in comparison with, for example, the cosmopolitan Venice, was not especially flattering.

The mistrust of these infidels was great and many rumors circulated: the real purpose was said to be commercial; they used all kinds of stratagems to find out about home market prices of such merchandise as was exported to them and of the prices charged for imported merchandise. They also collected samples of English commodities to take home, which was evidently considered less than honest. In addition, "such was their inveterate hate unto our Christian religion and estate as they could not endure to give any manner of alms, charitie, or relief, either in money or broken meat, unto any English poore, but reserved their fragments and sold them unto such poore as would give most for them." Their customs also were met with disapproving surprise: "They killed all their own meat within their house, as sheep lambs poultry and such like, and they turned their face eastward when they killed anything." It was also rumored, presumably incorrectly, that they murdered their interpreter, a Moor born in Spain, "because he commended the estate and bounty of England."[27] It is not difficult to recognize the attitude that exists even today to embassies from alien cultures.

Nothing came of Morocco's high-flying plans. Further negotiations were to be conducted via the English resident in Morocco, but Queen Elizabeth carried on simultaneous negotiations with Spain, and the whole thing petered out. Two years later both Elizabeth and Muley Hamed were dead.

But it is evident that after this famous visit of a mission from Barbary with a Moor of the kind that Shakespeare called "tawnie" at its head, he could not put a pitch-black man on the stage and describe him as a Moorish general. On the contrary it is perhaps not too rash to assume that precisely the visit of this delegation was a contributing reason that Shakespeare, with his often documented feeling for the topical, chose to make a similar Moor the principal character in his next tragedy. At the time of Abd-el-Ouahed's visit he had *Hamlet* on his mind and there is almost complete agreement that *Othello* was his next attempt.

In Cinthio's novella the Moor is a Muslim, but Shakespeare makes him Christian. I consider this a very important change and believe that it was intended to make the Moor more acceptable to English audiences, for it was against the religious views of the Moorish guests that people had reacted. For the man in the street the decisive dividing line was not between whites and colored people but between Christians and pagans. One can think of how strong the religiously motivated hatred was against the Jews, for example, as this is illustrated in *The Merchant of Venice*. Nobody wants to touch Shylock with a barge pole, but nobody objects to the fact that Lorenzo marries his daughter Jessica, since he has her baptized at the same time and makes her a Christian and therefore "one of us." It is not the race but the religion that matters.

A romance followed by marriage between a Christian Moor with an appearance similar to that of el-Ouahed and a white, rather emancipated girl from a good family seems to be suitably acceptable and yet sufficiently adventurous to have created in the first-night audience that curious suspense as to the outcome, without judgment for or against, that at the end of the first act should have been awakened in any audience. The spectators would not be disappointed. As usual Shakespeare gave them more than good value for their money.

Notes

This essay was translated from the Swedish by the editor using the text in *Var Othello neger? och andra Shakespeareproblem* (Stockholm: Natur & Kultur, 1957). The endnotes have been added by the editor.

1. George Brandes, *William Shakespeare: A Critical Study,* 2 vols., trans. William Archer, Mary Thomson and Diana White (London: William Heinemann, 1898) 2: 116.

2. Henrik Schück, *Shakspeare och hans tid,* 2 vols. (Stockholm: Hugo Gebers,

1916) 2: 293. This is Schück's second Shakespeare study. The first is called *William Shakspere: hans lif och värksamhet* (Stockholm: Jos. Seligmann, 1883).

3. Per Meurling, *Shakespeare* (Stockholm: Wahlström & Widstrand, 1952), 200.

4. A. C. Bradley, *Shakespearean Tragedy* (London: Penguin, 1991), 187.

5. Harley Granville-Barker, *Prefaces to Shakespeare,* [1927–47] 5 vols. (London: Batsford, 1963), 4: 306.

6. *Shakespeare Survey* 10 (1957): 99.

7. *Othello,* ed. Alice Walker and John Dover Wilson (Cambridge: Cambridge University Press, 1957), ix.

8. *Titus Andronicus,* ed. John Dover Wilson (Cambridge: Cambridge University Press, 1948), 99.

9. *Shakespearean Gleanings,* (London: Oxford University Press, 1944), 200.

10. Carl August Hagberg's *Shakespeares dramatiska arbeten, 12 volumes, 1847-51.* This is still the standard Swedish translation. Morocco's last two lines in the Swedish are: "Farväl, o Portia! Alltför stor är sorgen / För långa avsked; fort man far med korgen."

11. K. L. Little, *Negroes in Britain: A Study of Racial Relations in English Society* (London: Kegan Paul, 1947).

12. Ibid., 166.

13. Ibid.

14. Ibid.

15. Raphael Holinshed, *The First and Second Volumes of Chronicles,* n.p. (1587) ("The fourth Booke of the historie of England,"), 54.

16. A. C. Bradley, *Shakespearean Tragedy* [1904] (London: Penguin Books, 1991), 197–98.

17. *Othello,* ed. Alice Walker and John Dover Wilson (Cambridge: Cambridge University Press, 1957), xii.

18. Ibid., ix–x.

19. Quoted by Robert Withington, "Shakespeare and Race Prejudice," *Elizabethan and Other Studies in Honor of George F. Reynolds* (Boulder: University of Colorado Studies, 1945), 172–73.

20. Salvador de Madariaga, *On Hamlet* (London: Hollis & Carter, 1948), 79.

21. August Strindberg, *Shakespeares Macbeth, Othello, Stormen, Kung Lear, Henrik VIII, En Midsommarnattsdröm* (Stockholm: Björck & Börjeson, 1909), 25 (*det kallas sparlakansläxor).*

22. Henri Fluchère, *Shakespeare,* trans. Guy Hamilton (London: Longman, Green and Co., 1953), 226.

23. Carl G. Laurin, *Ros och ris,* andra samlingen 1914–18 (Stockholm: Norstedt, 1918), 260–61.

24. Nils Molin, *Shakespeare och Sverige intill 1800-talets mitt* (Göteborg: Elanders Boktryckeri, 1931), 155.

25. On this see Brandes, 2: 116–17.

26. Quoted by Harris, 92.

27. Ibid., 95.

The Geography of *Hamlet*

Gunnar Sjögren

So geographers, in Afric-maps
With savage pictures fill their gaps;
And over uninhabited downs
Place elephants for want of towns.

—Jonathan Swift, *On Poetry*

No doubt Shakespeare intended to give his play about the Danish prince a touch of local color when he made Polonius use the word Danskers instead of Danes in his advice to his servant Reynaldo: "Inquire me first what Danskers are in Paris." We do not know if this word elicited any catcalls from those sailors among the groundlings who plied the Baltic and knew better. But with English scholars Shakespeare was indeed successful—in modern editions of Hamlet Danskers invariably are equated with Danes.[1]

The eminent scholar Dover Wilson explained in his glossary to the Cambridge edition: "DANSKER, a Dane. The correct Danish term, not found elsewhere in English though Danske (i.e., Danish) occurs rarely." The mistake is a natural one: in modern Danish Dansker does in fact mean a Dane. But in Shakespeare's time it was not so. Dansker then signified something coming from Danzig.[2]

The city of Danzig was and is today called Gdansk in Polish. The name derives from the fact that the place was once a Danish settlement and a part of the kingdom of Canute. Foreigners trading with this important city usually spelled the name Dansk, Dantsk or Danske. Purchas's "brief Memoriall" of the travels of George Barkley, Merchant of London, is a case in point. Barkley goes to "Elsinore . . . where the Danish custom is taken, to Coppenhagen, thence to Bornholm, thence to Danske, a towne subject to the Pole." In the margin: "Danzik." And he tells how the amber found there is gathered by "the Danske Officers."[3]

England had a considerable trade with Danzig, and a whole range of commodities were labeled "Danske": *a danske chiste, danske pint potts, danske flaxe, danske yron,* and so on. And, what is more important, the inhabitants were called Danskers by people in the know, for instance "One Megg, a Dansker."[4]

It is perfectly clear that Danzigers, not Danes, is meant. In the chapter entitled "Of the traffic of Germany" Fynes Moryson relates how the English merchants moved their staple from Danzig: "the English Merchants trading for Poland . . . first had their Staple at Danzk in Prussen. . . . But when the Dantzkers under pretence of the Suevian warre, exacted of them a doller for each woollen cloath . . . they settled their Staple [in Melwin]."[5]

Another instance is found in Purchas. He prints a letter from Master Henry Lane to the worshipful Master William Sanderson. Under a pointer in the margin: "The first trade to the Narve, 1560" he writes: "And at this time was the first trafficke to Narve. . . . The trade to Rie [Riga], and Revel, of old time hath beene long since frequented by our English Nation, but this trade to the Narve was hitherto concealed from us by the Danskers and Lubeckers."[6]

It is evident that Master Lane does not mean the Danes. They were quite content to collect duties from all ships that passed through the Sound. The passage quoted implies that the English merchants, following their usual policy at this time, had once more succeeded in circumventing the merchants of Lubeck and Danzig, and had established direct relations with yet another port, Narva, situated to the east of Riga and Reval. The Polish king protested in vain on behalf of "our subjects of Danske."[7]

All skippers and merchants, of course, knew perfectly well that Dansk was just another name for Danzig.[8] So also did other people whose business it was to be well informed. Francis Bacon, in his *Notes on the State of Christendom* mentions Stephan Batory's siege of Danske, thereby showing that he knew that this town was identical with Danzig. Many more instances could be quoted.

Nevertheless there were people who confused Dansk with Denmark, probably because in Danish Dansk means Dane. Moreover, the same word was often used to denote both the country and its inhabitants, for example, Sweden for Swedes, China for Chinese. So, among English literary men at least, Dansk (or Danske) became just another name for Denmark, like Helvetia for Switzerland, Muskovy for Russia, Gaule for France, and Almaine for Germany.

William Warner, for instance, relates in *Albion's England* how the Danes invaded England, until "of England, Danske, and Norway, then Canut was perfect Lord." And when John Webster in *The White Devil* makes Giovanni say "so he makes a noice when he's a' horseback like a Danske drummer" it is evident that he is alluding to the big kettledrums displayed in the suite of the Danish King Christian V when he visited London, to the amazement of the citizens.

But while the name Dansk was used as a synonym for Denmark and Danish in literary contexts, the English also seem to have had a hazy idea of some sort of connection between Dansk and Danzig—and hence also between Denmark and Danzig. At least some people believed that Danzig was situated south of the Danish islands.

This is quite clearly demonstrated by the case of Michael Drayton in his charming work *Poly-Olbion*.[9] When he praises the traffics and discoveries of the English in Song 19 he follows Hakluyt's *Principal Navigations* very closely, often almost word for word.[10] But when he comes to Wolstan's voyage from Hedeby to Danzig, on the mouth of the Vistula, he makes a significant deviation from his source, evidently to suit the facts to his own preconceived geographical notions. He skips Wolstan's seven days and nights' voyage eastward into the Baltic, and makes the river of Wixel (Vistula)—which he calls "the greatest river of Danske"—flow into the Sound of Denmark. Evidently he believed that the city of Danzig was situated south of the Danish Islands, and that it belonged to the country which he sometimes calls Denmark and sometimes Dansk.[11]

That great traveler Fynes Moryson is another case in point. Although he made the voyage himself in an English ship he gives the distance from Elsinore to "Dantzk" as only about a quarter of what it really is.[12] From "Falsterboden" in Scania to a point off "Rosehead" (Rixhöft) he reckons the distance at fifty-eight English miles, which would have taken him to the coast of Germany—if he had sailed due south instead of almost due east.

Robert Greene's geographical ideas are exuberantly fantastic, but they seem to mirror the same notion of Danzig's westerly position:

> . . . troop with all the western Kings,
> That lie alongst the Dansick seas by East,
> North by the clime of frostie *Germany*,
> The *Almain* Monarke, and the *Saxon* duke . . .[13]

"By East" signifies "to the east of"—but there are no western kings to the east of Danzig.

If the theater manager Henslowe also believed that Danzig somehow belonged to Denmark, this may be the solution of the old problem of the identity of *The danyshe Tragedie*, in earnest of which he paid Henry Chettle one pound. Chambers and Fleay tentatively identified this play with the *Howghman,* which is almost certainly the play known to us as *The Tragedy of Hoffman.* This identification has been rejected on the grounds that there is no adequate reason for it, as *Hoffman* is not "strictly speaking, a Danish tragedy at all."[14] The setting is in or in the vicinity of "Dantzike" on the Baltic coast. A shipwreck occurs on the way from "Lubecke" and the passengers are cast ashore under "Reschopscurre" (Reserhoft, that is, Rixhöft). Indeed, there is no mention of Denmark, but Henslowe may well have thought that Danzig belonged to Denmark and for this reason called the play a Danish tragedy.

There is a further conclusion to be drawn which has a direct bearing on the geography of *Hamlet.* Danzig was the principal port in the English trade with Poland. If at the same time Danzig was vaguely felt somehow to belong to Denmark, then Poland moves westward with Danzig. There are in fact indications that Poland and Denmark were thought of as neighbors. Danes and Poles are sometimes thrown together: "How silly the *Polander* and the *Dane* / To bring us Crystall from the frozen Maine?" writes Michael Drayton in *England's Heroical Epistles.*[15] There is another instance in the anonymous *The Raigne of King Edward the Third:* "The sterne Polonian and the warlike Dane."[16]

If Shakespeare believed that *Danskers* were *Danes*, he may also have given credit to the supposition that Poland bordered on Denmark.[17] This would fully explain the otherwise rather unlikely idea that old King Hamlet had fought "the sledded Polacks on the ice."

And what about the position of Norway? Fynes Moryson—who had been in Elsinore in 1593 and visited the castle—wrote: "In this village a strong Castle called Croneburg lyeth upon the mouth of the Straight, to which on the other side of this Narrow sea, *in the Kingdome of Norway*, another Castle is opposite, called Elsburgh"[18] (italics mine). As a matter of fact Norway was fairly remote from Elsinore. It was Danish territory Moryson saw, and it stretched northward along the coast for one hundred and fifty miles. Now, who could have misinformed Moryson? Evidently not a Dane—both sides of the Sound had been Danish since time immemorial. But a foreigner, even a resident in Elsinore, could have imagined that the Sound constituted the dividing line between the two countries—to him it would not matter anyway as Norway was a tributary country governed by Danish officials, to all intents and purposes a part of Denmark.

Moryson's misconception may well have been shared by Shakespeare. I suggest that when he shaped the opening of the play he had this geographical situation at the back of his mind. A *hostile*

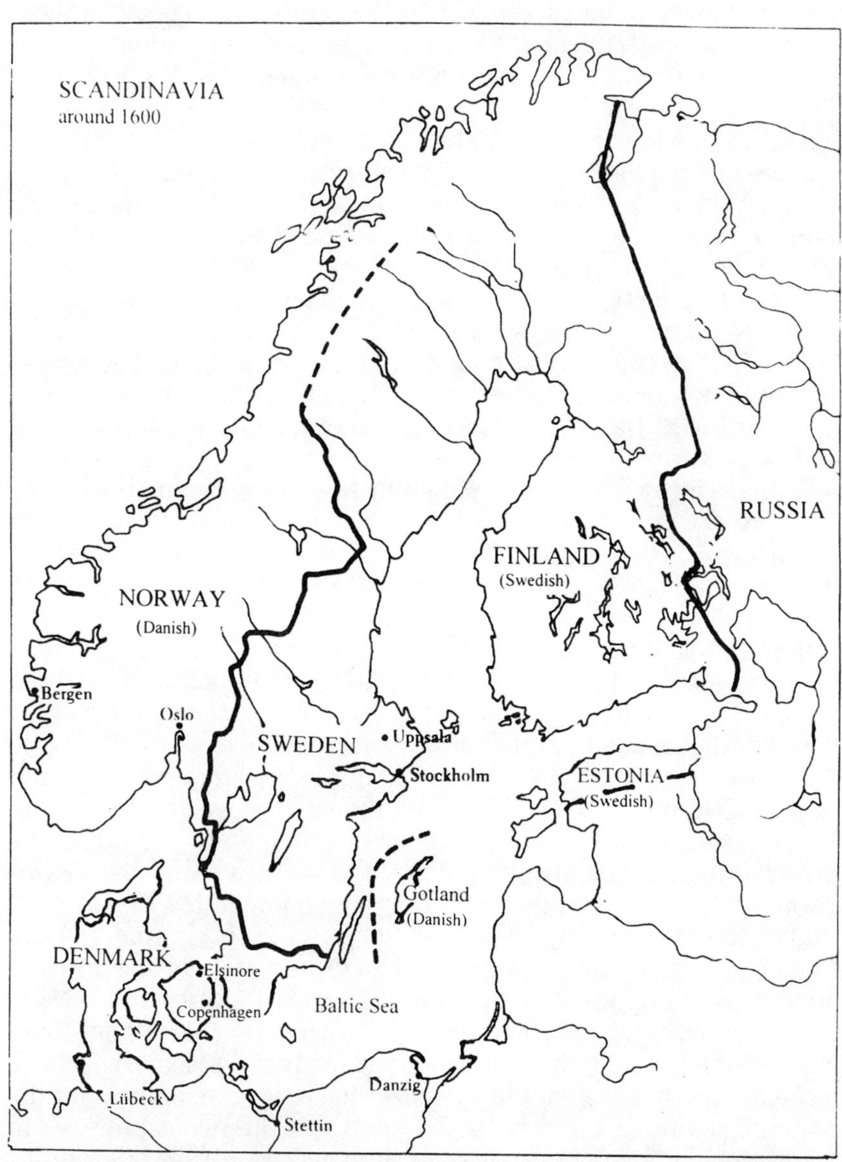

Map of Scandinavia around 1600, by the Editor, based on maps and other information in Ulf Sundberg, *Svenska freder och stillestånd 1249–1814* (Hargshamn: Arete, 1997).

Norway on the other side of the narrow strait would be no laughing matter. Shakespeare created an atmosphere of imminent danger. A strict and most observant watch had been ordered. At any moment a commando of Fortinbras's lawless resolutes might try to take the castle by surprise. This makes the guardsmen nervous and generates a heightened dramatic tension throughout the first scene.

On the supposition that Poland and Norway were situated on the borders of Denmark, the Fortinbras story becomes much more realistic. Also, it provides an answer to the question of how Hamlet—on his way to the ship which was to carry him to England—could encounter Fortinbras and his army. Editors have been in a quandary about this. The First Quarto has only "Enter Fortenbrasse, Drumme and Souldiers," the Second Quarto has "Enter Fortinbrasse with his Armie ouer the stage" and the 1623 Folio "Enter Fortinbrasse with an Armie." In 1709 Rowe made it "A Camp." Theobald elucidates: "A Camp on the Frontiers of Denmark." In 1768 Capell alters this to "A Plain in Denmark." Dover Wilson has "A plain near to a port in Denmark." It seems to be implied that the encounter takes place somewhere in Jutland, Fortinbras having landed his army in the north to march southward, and Hamlet being on his way to a port on the west coast—where no ports worth the name existed.

To the Elizabethans there were virtually only two ports in Denmark: Copenhagen and Elsinore. Thus Hamlet is naturally supposed to sail from Elsinore, just as Laertes had done when he went to France, Polonius being able to watch the ship set sail from out his window. That Hamlet also sailed from Elsinore is evident from the King's order to him:

> Therefore prepare thyself,
> The bark is ready, and the wind at help,
> Th' associates tend, and everything is bent
> For England.

This is still more abundantly obvious from the wording in the First Quarto:

> It is our mind you forthwith goe for England
> The wind sits faire, you shall aboorde to-night.

And if Norway extended as far south as opposite Elsinore, this is where Fortinbras would cross with his army. That he is not far from the King's castle is implied by Fortinbras's own words:

> Go, captain, from me greet the Danish King,
> . . . .
> If that his majesty would aught with us,
> We shall express our duty in his eye,
> And let him know so.

So it must be on his way from the castle to the harbor that Hamlet encounters Fortinbras's army.

It is logical to suppose that the Norwegian prince had marched with his small army from Oslo to Helsingborg opposite Elsinore—along the same road that James and his Queen had followed after their wedding in Oslo to the repetition of the ceremony at Kronborg in Elsinore in the winter 1589–90. One may infer that Fortinbras would also march through Denmark to the Polish border.

Now we understand how it comes that Fortinbras turns up in Elsinore in the last scene. He simply returns from Poland the same way he came. Nothing could be more natural.

The notion of the geographical contiguity of Norway, Denmark and Poland greatly enhances the plausibility of the Fortinbras subplot, and from a geographical point of view it is shown to be perfectly consistent with prevalent ideas of the time. The Norwegian prince and his army were not thrown in haphazardly for dramatic effect. The Fortinbras subplot emerges as a carefully planned and integral part of the play.

Notes

1. So in The Riverside Shakespeare: "*Danskers*, Danes." The Complete Works edited by Hardin Craig and revised in 1971 has a somewhat curious note: "*Danke* [*sic*] was a common variant for Denmark, hence Dane."

2. Otto Kalkar, *Ordbog til det aeldre Danske Sprog*, (Copenhagen: Thiele, 1881–1918) is quite definite on this point.

3. Samuel Purchas, *Purchas his Pilgrimes*, Hakluyt Society Works. 20 vols. (Glasgow: James MacLehose, 1905–07), 13:451.

4. "One Megg, a Dansker," *Merchant Adventurers*, Publications of the Surtees Soc. 101 (Durham, 1899), 44. This instance was quoted by Gösta Langenfelt who early established the real meaning of Dansk and Dansker in his dissertation *Toponymics* (Uppsala, 1920).

5. Fynes Moryson, *Itinerary*, 4 vols. (Glasgow: James MacLehose, 1907–08), 4:21–22.

6. *Purchas*, 12:53.

7. Richard Hakluyt, *The Principal Navigations, Voyages, Traffiques & Discoveries of the English Nation,* 12 vols. (Glasgow: James MacLehose, 1903–05), 2:487.

8. The compiler of the Index to Hakluyt's *Principal Navigations* does not seem to have been aware of this.

9. J. William Hebel, ed., *The Works of Michael Drayton*, 6 vols. (Oxford: Blackwell, 1961), 4.

10. As has been pointed out by Robert R. Cawley in "Drayton and the Voyagers," *PMLA* 38 (1923): 530–56.

11. This notion of Danzig's proximity to Denmark was probably not restricted to Englishmen. Mr. Martin Holmes has kindly drawn my attention to plate 345 in Cesare Vecellio's work on dresses: *Degli abiti antichi e moderni* (1590). This plate shows a servant's dress "from Danzig, Pomerania or Denmark."

12. *Itinerary,* 1:127.

13. Robert Greene, *Friar Bacon and Friar Bungay*, act 2, scene 2.

14. Harold Jenkins, *The Life and Work of Henry Chettle* (London: Sidgwick & Jackson, 1934), 240.

15. *Works*, 2:248.

16. Tucker Brooke, ed., *The Shakespeare Apocrypha* (Oxford: Clarendon, 1908), 82.

17. Curiously enough the title page of John Stow's *Annales* shows a picture of "A Dane" who is dressed in a long coat with straps across the breast and armed with a scimitar, a Turkish curved sword, in fact the dress described by Moryson as worn by the Polish courtiers he encountered in Danzig. This apparent confusion of Danes and Poles may perhaps account for the incongruous name Polonius in *Hamlet*.

18. *Itinerary*, 1:124.

Improvisation and Revision in Shakespeare's Plays

Kristian Smidt

In the beginning of *The Tempest*, just after we have witnessed the dramatic shipwreck, there is a long expository scene in which schoolmaster Prospero, under cover of an explanation to Miranda, whom his speech continually threatens to send to sleep, tells us why and how he and his daughter came to their desert island, whom they found there and what they have been up to there since. Prospero asserts to Miranda: "I have done nothing but in care of thee," who, he says

art ignorant of what thou art, nought knowing
of whence I am, nor that I am not better
than Prospero, master of a full poor cell,
and thy no greater father.
Miranda: More to know
did never meddle with my thoughts.
Prospero: 'Tis time
I should inform thee farther.

Which he begins to do. But after only nine lines which it takes twenty-five seconds to speak, he tells her again:

Sit down,
for thou must now know farther.

And Miranda this time replies:

You have often
begun to tell me what I am, but stopped
and left me to a bootless inquisition,
concluding, "Stay, not yet."

Obviously Miranda's contradictory statements—"More to know did never meddle with my thoughts" and "You have often . . . left me to a bootless inquisition"—cannot have both been meant for inclusion in the finished play, and one may wonder why editors do not omit one of them; in fact the editors of the First Folio should evidently have done so. Notice, too, that Miranda's first statement is introduced by Prospero's "'Tis time I should inform thee farther," and her second, contradictory, statement by a repetition of virtually the same remark: "for thou must now know farther." As if Shakespeare struck out, or intended to strike out one passage in his draft and rewrote it with more or less the same opening words. I see this kind of repetition as a clear sign of authorial revision, probably during work in progress,[1] and we may bear this mini-example in mind when we come to look at cases of more extensive revision.

A little later in the same scene, when Miranda has finally fallen asleep, Ariel is called in for some more exposition, and after a temperamental exchange Prospero promises him that "after two days I will discharge thee." But such is the precipitation of the plot that Ariel is discharged in the end after only about four hours, and Shakespeare seems to have forgotten Prospero's initial time limit. Without attaching too much importance to this little discrepancy, we may perhaps see it as an instance of the way in which Shakespeare could feel his way along as he wrote, making new decisions and leaving inconsistencies behind, in other words as an example of improvisation.

How carefully and in how much detail did he plan his works before he began to write?

The earliest collected edition of Shakespeare's dramatic works contains eleven plays classified as tragedies. In the case of six of them they were provided by the editors with a complete division into acts, and three of them with a further division into scenes. And this was no mere embellishment. In all instances the act divisions correspond pretty closely to distinct movements or blocks of action in the plays, and a similar anatomy may readily be found in the tragedies which are not formally divided. There is a neat five-act structure in every one of them, conforming to the pattern which T. W. Baldwin has demonstrated in Shakespeare's drama in general.[2]

Shakespeare entertained certain preconceptions about dramatic structure, and the five-act model was obviously one he accepted and turned to good account. But the act-and-scene division was only the external sign of an internal completeness and cogency of theme, plot, and character portrayal which we can all experience when we read or see his plays. Most of them were based more or less directly on narrative material with a fully developed story and a well-defined cast of characters, and Shakespeare firmly tightened and soldered what he found in his sources.

The regular structuring of the plays can hardly have been achieved without prior planning. General plot outlines, the high points of the action and its progress toward a fit conclusion must have been mapped out in advance of actual composition, and the characters must have been conceived as possessing the essential features which they were intended to exhibit. But occasionally even main roles and basic issues were perhaps not fully clarified before writing began, so that there remained a certain need for improvisation from point to point. And in other cases changes of mind may have occurred as the plays took shape, or new inspiration may have come either seeping or flashing to modify the characters or give a new twist to the story. This is natural enough: Shakespeare was after all human. But it is incredible how unwilling critics have been for the past one and a half centuries, and to some extent still are, to recognize this element of indecision in the great poet. I would maintain that we can get really close to his plays only by taking a straight look at their bends and breaks, in addition to watching the consistent unfolding of the action to a logical conclusion. And the bends and breaks include their unexpected strokes of genius as well as their imperfections.

In practically every one of the history plays, from *King John* to *Henry V*, we are led in the opening scenes to expect developments which in the event do not take place. The first part of *Henry IV* will illustrate this oddity. King Henry's title to the crown is weak and there is a rebellion in the North. The rebels support the claim of Edmund Mortimer, the Earl of March, and in the first scene of the play and the long council scene at Windsor where the King confronts the Northumberland lords, the name of Mortimer is sounded loudly no fewer than sixteen times. Harry Percy, or "Hotspur," swears he "will lift the down-trod Mortimer as high in the air as this unthankful King." Mortimer appears in person in the Bangor scene, in Wales, where he, Glendower and Hotspur produce a big map and divide England and Wales between them. Mortimer is to have all of southern England including the capital. It is Mortimer who tells us of the rebels' appointment to meet the King's army at Shrewsbury and of his own intention to join them. And it is Mortimer who has the last words in the Bangor scene: when Glendower calls him "to horse immediately," he answers cheerfully, "With all my heart," and we must suppose him ready to gallop off. But he never gets to Shrewsbury, and there is no explanation. He is not even missed by his companions in the decisive battle, though they are worried by the default of others. He does not appear in the remainder of the play and is only barely mentioned in the final acts. Mortimer apparently, after the promise of his importance, became a superfluous character when improvisation took over and *Henry IV* took a turn from its original direction. It is Prince Hal who becomes the center of interest and Hotspur who becomes his chief antagonist. Shakespeare seems to have been carried away, too, by his exuberant creation of Falstaff, so much so that he had to improvise a second part of the play to contain the fat knight, and failed to solve completely the resulting problems of adjustment.[3]

Another character he seems to have been carried away by is Shylock. The play in which Shylock appears is entitled *The Merchant of Venice*, and the opening scene introduces us to the merchant Antonio and his mysterious sadness. We naturally become curious, as his friends do, about the reasons for his depression, and we are only partly satisfied when we realize it has to do with Bassanio. As if to emphasize the importance of this sadness motif, we have a similar situation when Portia is introduced in the second scene and we learn not only that she is "aweary of this great world" but that she has tender memories of the same Bassanio. Without asserting that this is what Shakespeare had in mind, I would suggest that we might have had an interesting play about the rivalry of Antonio and Portia for the love of Bassanio. But then Shylock gripped the playwright's imagination to such an extent that the Jew became the dominant and easily the most fascinating character of the play—at least up to the point when the denouement had to be achieved and Shylock was left out of it. By that time Antonio had become peripheral and was left out in the cold with only his ships to console him.

Although *Hamlet*, as we have it, is a maturer play than *The Merchant of Venice*, one is not perhaps equally surprised to find signs of indecision in the tragedy of the Prince of Denmark, being itself a play about indecision. To some extent this effect may have come about fortuitously by the coexistence of two plots or themes which both vied for the author's full attention, that of revenge, which primarily relates to the King, and that of redemption, which primarily relates to the Queen. Or, to put it differently, by the conflict of plot versus character. The plot which Shakespeare borrowed in its broad outlines from Saxo by way of Belleforest and possibly an *Ur-Hamlet* is essentially a revenge plot. The character of the Prince which Shakespeare worked out for himself on the basis of hints from Belleforest is that of a sexually aroused Platonic idealist with strong affections, long shielded from the wickedness of the world. The revenge plot dictates attention to the King. At its center is the duty imposed upon a fully capable son to avenge his murdered father by dispatching the murderer. The character of the Prince, on the other hand, draws his and our attention to his mother. Hamlet is not chiefly interested in revenge and finds all sorts of excuses for delaying it. Significantly, it is when he thinks he finds Claudius in Gertrude's bedroom that he springs to action, and his revenge is fulfilled vicariously and emotionally by the killing of Polonius. After the bedroom scene the poor Ghost exits from the play for good, and though the revenge plot is technically wound up when Claudius is both stabbed and poisoned at the end of the play, Hamlet's incentive for revenge in that final scene is not the murder of his father but the poisoning of his mother. Notice the dialogue. Laertes cries out with his dying breath: "Thy mother's poisoned. I can no more. The King—the King's to blame." Hamlet stabs the King and then forces the remaining poison down his throat as he shouts:

> Here, thou incestuous, murd'rous, damned Dane,
> Drink off this potion. Is thy union here?
> Follow my mother.

Another scene, in the middle of the tragedy, is equally revealing. I refer to the staging of the *Gonzago* play, by means of which Hamlet hopes, as he says, to "catch the conscience of the King" by provoking him to betray his guilt. Hamlet determines to observe Claudius closely during the performance and enjoins Horatio to do likewise:

> For I mine eyes will rivet to his face,
> And after we will both our judgments join
> In censure of his seeming.

Part of this scheme, of course, they carry out. The King starts up "upon the talk of the poisoning." At this moment Hamlet and Horatio undoubtedly watch him, and this is in agreement with the main revenge plot. But until the poisoning speech Hamlet has riveted his eyes not to the King's face but to the Queen's. As the audience on the stage settles down to watch he remarks to Ophelia, "Look you how cheerfully my mother looks and my father died within's two hours." When the Player Queen declaims

> In second husband let me be accurst;
> None wed the second but who killed the first.

Hamlet mutters, obviously watching Gertrude, "That's wormwood." He has no similar comments for Claudius. Then, during a short interval while the Player King sleeps, Hamlet tests Gertrude's (but not Claudius's) reaction: "Madam, how like you this play?"

It seems clear that Shakespeare improvised the details of the *Gonzago* scene and that he allowed his empathy with the Hamlet character to push the revenge plot out of focus. Hamlet is more intent on stirring his mother's conscience than on probing his uncle's. But the revenge plot has to proceed. And it cannot be denied that the superimposition of the revenge plot on the emotional preoccupations of the protagonist has made for a much more complex and fascinating tragedy than we might have had if everything had been composed neatly from a mental blueprint.

In *Othello* there are several instances of definite information being supplied at one stage and contradicted at another, either because Shakespeare forgot what he had written first or because he changed his mind and neglected to make adjustments. Thus the manner of Othello's wooing of Desdemona is represented in two mutually inconsistent ways. In act 1 we have Othello's own story of how he was invited to her father's house and she was entranced by the account of his adventures and misfortunes to the point of hinting that he should propose to her. When they marry in secret not even Othello's friend Cassio is informed. But in act 3 the story is very different. Far from encouraging Othello's courtship, Desdemona apparently had certain misgivings about her suitor to overcome: she now reminds Othello of Michael Cassio

> That came a-wooing with you, and so many a time
> When I have spoke of you dispraisingly,
> Hath ta'en your part, . . .

Cassio, in this version of the story, was not only Othello's confidant and knew of his love "from first to last," as Othello himself tells us, but he was evidently a much-needed go-between. The accounts are so much at variance that there can be no way of reconciling them.

The most remarkable and remarked-upon contradiction, however, has to do with the time scheme. Othello and Desdemona embark for Cyprus in separate ships before their marriage has been consummated. Cassio sails in a third ship and arrives first. Yet on the day after their arrival—at least there is every indication that it is the very next day—Iago succeeds in suggesting that Desdemona has been unfaithful to her marriage bed with Cassio. On the evening of that very same fateful day Othello in his distraction imagines

That she with Cassio hath the act of shame
A thousand times committed.

Only Emilia has the sense to ask, "What place, what time, what form, what likelihood?" On that first day in the island, too, various characters talk as if they have been there for a long time.

Shakespeare evidently began writing with a general intention of condensing the duration of the action in comparison with the source he drew upon for his story,[4] which speaks of months and years, but he had incompatible conceptions as to how the central intrigue should be managed. Perhaps even the marriage of Othello and Desdemona on the same night as Othello sets sail for Cyprus was invented without forethought of how it might affect Iago's opportunities for deception. Shakespeare must have realized as he wrote that he would need a relatively long backward perspective to make Iago's inventions plausible, and had possibly completed the first two acts when this became clear. But instead of starting afresh he went on and committed himself to a double calendar, extending the marriage backward into an imaginary period for which there is in reality no room.

It is impossible to suppose that he was unaware of the double calendar he adopted. And the "double time" effect has been highly praised as a wonderfully ingenious device which Shakespeare frequently and deliberately exploited,[5] nowhere more successfully than in *Othello*. Perhaps we should ask the irreverent question whether the double time scheme was a desperate remedy rather than the illusionist marvel we are asked to admire? But when all is said and done his success is all we need bother about. One may possibly admit that the scrupulous confinement of the main action to one day somehow goes unnoticed, leaving us with an impression of headlong speed, of "violent pace," which is really the important thing. In any case the ambiguous impression that events in Cyprus happen both quickly and slowly affects not so much our sense of the theoretical possibility of Desdemona's adultery as our experience of Othello's escalating madness.

If we move on to *King Lear*, we shall find that a number of promises relating to the minor, or secondary, characters are not kept, apparently because certain developments that Shakespeare at first had in mind proved in the event to be unwanted. We are prepared from the very first for dissension between the Dukes of Albany and Cornwall. The opening dialogue concerns the Dukes, not the King's daughters, and assumes that they are to be the beneficiaries of Lear's abdication. "I thought," says Kent, "the King had more affected the Duke of Albany than Cornwall." Very soon there are rumors of impending war between them. But nothing comes of this conflict, and just before he is killed by his servant, Cornwall speaks as if he is oblivious of any quarrel between himself and Albany. It may be in lieu of this quarrel that we are offered the subplot of Goneril and Regan in rivalry for Edmund. But still it is natural to wonder why the anticipated clash is aborted.

Two of the puzzles of *King Lear* are the petering out of the role of Kent and the disappearance of the Fool after the storm on the heath. Kent and the Fool are both closely associated with the King but are seemingly turned off by the author after great expectations have been built around them in the first half of the play. Kent is the kind of irrepressible character, with plenty of humor, who is unafraid of Fortune and who, as we think, has to come out on top. His mere presence is reassuring. But having been Lear's staunch defender, he is nowhere when the King runs wild in the fields at Dover. And where is he in the final battle? His age and weakness seem to be invented as excuses for his inaction, and by the end of the play he is ready to die. But though he gives his years as forty-eight when he seeks service with the King, forty-eight after all was no hoary age even in the Jacobean era, and Kent in the first half of the play certainly gives the impression of having the vitality of youth. It seems likely that Shakespeare at first planned a more active part for Kent in the fourth and fifth acts than he eventually found he could afford if he was to have enough room, for instance, for Edgar and Gloucester—not to speak of Cordelia, whose return also makes the Fool superfluous.

In *Macbeth* there is a problem of consistency in the curious indecision with regard to the respective shares of Macbeth and his wife in criminal initiative and responsibility. Before Macbeth comes home from battle, he feels that the prophecies of the witches begin to come true and is already shaken inwardly by the idea of regicide which they suggest to his imagination. When Malcolm is proclaimed as Duncan's successor, Macbeth seems determined to remove all obstacles to his own possession of the crown. His faith in the prophecies is confirmed in his letter to Lady Macbeth, who fears that his scrupulous nature may prevent him from achieving his ambition. When a messenger brings news of Duncan's imminent arrival, she resolves to murder the King herself:

> Come, thick Night,
> And pall thee in the dunnest smoke of Hell,
> That my keen knife see not the wound it makes.

This determination is reasserted when Macbeth enters upon the heels of the messenger and she assumes sole responsibility for the "great business" to be dispatched:

> He that's coming
> Must be provided for; and you shall put
> This night's great business into my dispatch;
> . . . .
> Leave all the rest to me.

Then the roles are again reversed. In scene 7 we find Macbeth struggling with his conscience and unwilling to perform the crime which once more has fallen to him. Lady Macbeth upbraids him for his cowardice and reminds him of the deep oaths he has sworn: "When you durst do it, then you were a man." To encourage her husband Lady Macbeth suggests a joint action. In the event she drugs Duncan's grooms and lays their daggers ready, while Macbeth performs the actual murder. But there is a reminder of her determination to act on her own when she confides to us in soliloquy, "Had he not resembled / My father as he slept, I had done 't." Apparently Shakespeare ultimately wanted to make Macbeth and his wife equal sharers in guilt. And if at one time he contemplated a more dominant part for Lady Macbeth, his final solution was surely of incomparably greater artistry.

In the examples of improvisation we have looked at so far—the improvisation of a genius, remember—it is impossible to tell whether Shakespeare may have had two or more successive versions down on paper before he was satisfied, or whether the texts we have represent his first and only solutions. In the examples that follow we find clear signs of revision, either because there are extant Quarto and Folio editions of the same plays with indicative differences, or because the author left telltale clues when he deleted, or meant to delete, passages he did not want; or when he interpolated new lines and speeches into a finished sequence; or when he rearranged the order of scenes.

In *Henry V* there is a disappointment of expectations, as in the other history plays; disappointment, that is, in technical terms, not in terms of enjoyment. The high point of the council of war in the first act is when King Henry, expecting ambassadors from the King of France, receives instead messengers from the Dauphin, who present him insultingly with a "tun," or tub, of tennis balls. This insult provides him with a totally different motive for war than that of his legal title to France, which we have heard more than enough about. It is now a question of revenge, and we can hardly be blamed if we expect in the sequel to see Harry and the Dauphin banging or slanging at each other. But they are never brought face-to-face, and even the antagonism between them is forgotten as the play proceeds. The Dauphin plays an inconspicuous part at the battle of Agincourt, and after the battle he vanishes without a trace as far as the play is concerned. So much for Harry's "chiding this Dauphin at his father's door," as he promises to do in act 1. I suggest here that Shakespeare at first followed an earlier, anonymous play, *The Famous Victories of Henry the fifth* quite closely. In this the Dauphin and the tennis balls are very much in the background. Then, in revising his manuscript, he may have felt that the play lacked color and that the forefronting of the quarrel between the English King and the French Prince would make it more temperamental. He actually introduced the Dauphin into the Agincourt scenes, without historical warrant, to be put to shame in the ignominious defeat of the French. But beyond that he did not trouble to accommodate the Dauphin.

The famous night scene in *Henry V*, where the King at Agincourt goes round the camp in disguise and talks to some of his soldiers, may well have been interpolated into the text after completion of the play and bears strong witness to Shakespeare's unremitting creativity. The most substantial clue is the King's repetition of the order to the English lords to assemble at his tent in readiness for the battle. He first tells the Dukes of Bedford and Gloucester:

> Brothers both,
> commend me to the princes in our camp;
> do my good-morrow to them; and anon
> desire them all to my pavilion.

He also tells Erpingham, who offers to attend him, "Go with my brothers to the lords of England: / I and my bosom must debate a while." He then, in what I take to be the interpolated passage, wanders off into the night to debate, not with his bosom, but with Pistol and three privates. He subsequently soliloquizes at some length on the responsibilities of kingship, and when Erpingham comes to look for him because the nobles are, understandably, "jealous of [his] absence" he again instructs the faithful captain:

> Good old knight,
> collect them altogether at my tent:
> I'll be before thee.

And only now does he debate with his bosom and his God, as he falls to his prayer, "O God of battles! steel my soldiers' hearts." It was when he revised and added the night scene that Shakespeare found it necessary to tie up what preceded and followed the additional passage by having Harry repeat the initial order for assembly at his tent.

In *Hamlet* there are signs of a major rearrangement of scenes. Not only two but three printed texts of this tragedy survive from the author's lifetime and shortly after. And though the First Quarto (1603) is a very "bad" quarto, it is generally agreed that it derives from the play as performed and spoken in the theater. It has a weak but independent authority and throws an interesting light on some of the readings and arrangements that we find in the Second Quarto and the Folio.

Let us look at the placing of the most famous of all Shakespeare's soliloquies, the "To be or not to be" speech, and the so-called "nunnery scene" which is linked to it. You will remember that in act 2, scene 1 Ophelia enters in a fright to report to her father that Hamlet has behaved very oddly in her closet. Polonius interprets this as "the very ecstasy of love" and tells Ophelia to accompany him to the King. Yet in the versions we are familiar with he goes alone to the King. He tells his story, and proposes a love test:

Pol. You know sometimes he walkes foure houres together
Heere in the Lobby.
Quee. So he does indeede.
Pol. At such a time Ile loose my daughter to him.

Hamlet then appears "reading on a Booke," as the Folio stage direction informs us, and Polonius "boards" him in what we may call the "fishmonger" episode, finds his suspicions confirmed, and again decides to "suddenly contrive the means of meeting / between him and my daughter" ("suddenly" meaning "immediately"). This sudden meeting, however, does not take place till after the long sequence of episodes which begins with Hamlet's encounter with Rosencrantz and Guildenstern, continues with the Players, and ends with Hamlet's third major soliloquy, "O what a rogue and peasant slave am I!" Even then Rosencrantz and Guildenstern have to report back to the King and Queen before we learn that the King has "closely sent for Hamlet hither, / that he, as 'twere by accident, may there / affront Ophelia." However, when Hamlet wanders in he gives no sign of having been sent for. Nor is there this time any mention of his reading a book, although the first line which he now speaks, "To be, or not to be, that is the question," surely has reference to something he has just been reading. It should be noticed, too, that as far as Hamlet's speaking part is concerned the "To be" soliloquy follows on the heels of the "rogue and peasant slave" soliloquy, which ends with the idea of arranging a trap in which Hamlet has good hopes of catching the conscience of the King. It may seem surprising that the Prince should now relapse into such deep despondency as is indicated by the "To be or not to be" speech—which I definitely think must be interpreted as a reflection on suicide.

In the First Quarto there is a much more logical sequence. Ophelia *does* accompany Polonius to the King for her father to report on Hamlet's "frensie", Polonius proposes his love test, to "loose his daughter to him." Hamlet obligingly enters "poring upon a booke" and the plot is put into execution immediately. Hamlet speaks his soliloquy, "To be or not to be," in which the idea of suicide and the everlasting penalty it may entail links up naturally with his earlier ruminations on self-slaughter. Then occurs the shending of Ophelia, which proves to the King that Hamlet's trouble is "some deeper thing" than love, whereupon Polonius offers to "try him every way" himself, and we get the "fishmonger" scene. After this we have Rosencrantz and Guildenstern and the Players, and Hamlet's idea to test the King by means of a play—all in a natural sequence.

Critics have thought that whoever took down the wording of the First Quarto was (or were) stupid enough to get the order of the scenes confused.[6] But there are too many signs of textual disturbance in the so-called good texts, as well as psychological arguments, that tell against this theory. There can be no doubt, I would maintain, that the First Quarto arrangement was composed first and was subsequently revised to produce the order of scenes which we know. As for Shakespeare's motives for this revision, it has to be admitted that logic is not everything and that he may precisely have wished to show his hero relapsing into depression and evasion even after he has planned his *Gonzago* stratagem. By this means the picture of the Prince gains an extension which, if this is what the author wanted, may have been worth the sacrifice of a more predictable succession of events.

There are indications that the whole graveyard scene may be an interpolation made after the last act of *Hamlet* had been written. And the evidence is plentiful. The most important indication is this: In act 4, scene 6, Horatio receives a message that Hamlet is back in Denmark and has urgent news for him: "repair thou to me with as much speed as thou wouldest fly death. I have words to speak in thine ear will make thee dumb." The news is important, we learn later, because it affords documentary proof of the King's treachery. But before it is communicated to Horatio there is the long and mainly slow-paced graveyard scene. There is no communication of news in the graveyard, and Hamlet seems in no hurry to impart it as he muses on death and dissolution. But the news is given in detail and with some vehemence in the dialogue between Hamlet and Horatio which follows, as if in uninterrupted fulfillment of Hamlet's promise. It is very unlikely that the leisurely conversation in the graveyard originally intervened. It is not in Saxo or Belleforest, or, for that matter, in the early German version of the play, *Der Bestrafte Brudermord*.

Many things in the graveyard scene are also at variance with what we know from the scenes that precede and follow it. In telling of Ophelia's death in act 4, scene 7, the Queen leaves no doubt that she was drowned by accident when "an envious sliver broke" as she was clambering to hang her "crownet weeds" on the boughs of a willow. The coroner, too, we learn, "hath sat on her and finds it Christian burial." But there is equally no doubt that she is buried as a suicide. As the funeral procession approaches, Hamlet points out Laertes to Horatio as if the latter is a complete stranger to the Danish court. Laertes should actually have kept "close within [his] chamber" by the King's advice until such time as the duel between him and Hamlet could be arranged. Instead he not only appears at the funeral but partly spoils the effect of the duel by fighting with Hamlet at the graveside. And, for further absurdity, Laertes's presence at court is announced by Osric in the following scene as if Hamlet, after fighting with Laertes, was unaware that he was back from France.

All of which is not saying that the graveyard scene is not brilliant or that one would not rather have the scene *and* the problems than a smoother denouement without it. Hamlet's cynical remarks on death and decay may be seen as an important addition to the thematic content of the play. The setting itself, with graves and skulls visible to the audience, would provide a powerful symbolic spectacle. One of Shakespeare's own additions to the borrowed plot, we may assume, was the story of Ophelia, which is here completed, with the inclusion of the one credible revelation that we have from Hamlet's own mouth of his love for her.

When Shakespeare revised, whether in *Hamlet* or elsewhere, he did not necessarily discard an earlier version in favor of a later. He may well have wished to keep alternative variants, and in the case of *King Lear* it has been forcibly argued in recent years that he did so.[7] The editors of the new Oxford Shakespeare have gone to the length of printing the Quarto and Folio versions of *Lear* as distinct plays, broadly the same but separated by systematic differences produced in revision by Shakespeare himself. If the theory is correct, *King Lear* offers a good opportunity to see Shakespeare having second thoughts and endeavoring to improve his own tragedy.

It does certainly look as if passages lacking in the Folio represent deliberate cuts for the most part, and that those lacking in the Quarto may be mostly additions to the Folio text. In other words, the Quarto would be the original version and the Folio the revised edition. And if we look at the roles of the Duke of Albany and Gloucester's son Edgar, the alterations indicate changing conceptions, which have been much discussed.[8] In a general way the Folio in the beginning gives a somewhat fuller impression of Albany as a peacemaker than does the Quarto. But in the Folio recension of the fourth and fifth acts Albany loses some of his moral elevation and patriotic motivation on account of omissions. And in the end he loses his central standing to Edgar. He does not change radically, but he has more questionable qualities of leadership than in the Quarto version and is no longer, in the Folio, the most natural successor to Lear. The last words of the play are spoken in the Quarto by Albany, but in the Folio by Edgar.

Edgar, then, is brought forward in the revised Folio ending. If we consider his role up to the point of his fight with Oswald this must seem unexpected. Edgar is a bit of an idiot to listen to his brother's lies to start with, and never becomes very credible as a person. His main usefulness is in the scenes with Lear in the storm, where he joins the Fool in a duo of fool and madman, embodying, even allegorizing, a central theme of confusion and reflecting the mind and behavior of the King. Then, as he abandons his assumed madness to conduct his father, he turns philosopher and speaks some of the most balanced wisdom of the play. Still, there is little preparation for Albany's praise of his "royal nobleness": we can only assume that he is being belatedly groomed by the author for the role of ruler which he enters upon at the end of the Folio version.

One difference between the Quarto and Folio versions of *Lear* which has been highlighted more than it deserves to be has to do with the war between France and Britain and the decisive battle in which Cordelia's French army is defeated by the forces of Edmund and Albany.[9] Gary Taylor has maintained that the Folio tends to universalize the war theme by removing a number of references to the foreign nationality of the liberation army. He even goes so far as to say that the audience is encouraged to forget that Cordelia's army is French. But this is not correct. There are still many references to French spies and French landings in the Folio even after cuts in the text, and it should be borne in mind that any reference to Cordelia after the first scene of the play will remind us that she is married to the King of France and that she is herself now the French Queen. Significantly, when Lear awakes to sanity and recognizes his daughter he asks, "Am I in France?" There can have been no serious attempt, in revising for the Folio version, to make us unaware of the French provenance of Cordelia's army. What the omissions do effect is to somewhat reduce the sense of a foreign attempt to conquer Britain, which would have been objectionable to the patriotic sentiments of Shakespeare's audiences. Since Cordelia, and not the French King, is in command, and since she has more or less borrowed her French troops for the interim, her invasion on behalf of the King of Britain has the appearance of legitimacy.

One more difference between the Quarto and Folio versions of *Lear* may be mentioned. I have noticed that a large number of expressions of pity which we find in the Quarto are absent from the Folio, as if there was an attempt to make the world an even harsher place for man than in the original conception. At various points in the play the Folio omits some of Gloucester's words of pity for Kent, some of Kent's and Edgar's pity for Lear, of the servants' pity for Gloucester, Albany's pity for Lear, the anonymous Gentleman's pity for Cordelia, and Cordelia's pity for her father. It would be strange indeed if this sum of reductions bearing on the same emotional theme were purely coincidental.

An argument for two self-contained texts similar to that relating to *Lear* has been put forward by E. A. J. Honigmann in the case of *Othello*.[10] Honigmann has maintained that here, too, the Folio represents a revised version and that a number of passages contained in the Folio and absent from the Quarto did not belong to the original script, as most editors have thought, but were later additions. These Folio additions were part of what he calls a "strategic revision" aimed at strengthening, clarifying, and tying together roles and speeches which were in need of improvement. I am unconvinced by most of the evidence he offers for a Folio revised by addition, and suggest that there is better evidence in this case for a revised Quarto, that is, one revised by omission from the original script.

Let me explain why. When Shakespeare approached the writing of *Othello* he set himself the hitherto unattempted task of depicting the conception and monstrous gestation of a passion, showing how from an itch of doubt it swells into an overwhelming fury. No need this time, as in *Hamlet*, to delay an action which is ripe for execution from the very beginning. Rather, the challenge to the author was the need to delay the ripening, to contain the mental torture of his protagonist till endurance was ready to crack. Working in the turmoil of feelings which he conjured up, Shakespeare must have known something like the problem not merely of premature birth but of premature ejaculation. There must be a certain holding back of the creative impulse in order to allow for the climactic effect. And I think this very special problem of securing a mounting tension till the final eruption of violence may help to account for some of the differences we find between the two substantive texts. In three places in the central part of *Othello* there are Quarto omissions in Othello's speeches which may have to do with the problem of avoiding premature climaxes while still giving scope to passionate outbursts. Othello rises so many times to a pitch of exclamatory intensity that there is a risk of diminishing returns. This actually constitutes a real difficulty in the theater, where the actors, it appears, have often complained of the strain of repeated ravings.[11] The full Folio text therefore is particularly difficult. And the cuts in the Quarto seem to have been primarily motivated by the need for emotional economy. The Quarto entirely omits one passionate speech and most of two others, and it can hardly be by chance that these passages, all belonging to Othello's part, were chosen for major related abridgments. Here, if anywhere, there was "strategic revision."

Many of the differences between Quarto and Folio versions in such plays as *Hamlet, Lear* and *Othello* indicate that revision occurred some time after the plays had reached completion and perhaps performance. In such cases we tend to get one unrevised and one revised version, and Shakespeare may have wanted to keep them both. But if we look at the earliest stage of revision, that which went along with initial composition or followed shortly after as far as we can judge, we will often find mixed states of textual transmission containing both wanted and unwanted matter in one text. More frequently than it is comfortable to contemplate if we wish to think our texts trustworthy, editors and printers disregarded the author's more or less obvious intention to strike out lines and passages or even whole scenes, either because they did not notice the signs for deletion, or because they were so greedy to print everything the author produced that they deliberately ignored them. Miranda's contradiction in *The Tempest* is a case in point. Unfortunately the Folio editors did not have the restraint to leave out the unwanted bit of dialogue. Another well-known example is the double announcement of Portia's death in *Julius Cæsar*. Brutus, now with his army in camp near Sardis, has had news of his wife's death and speaks of it to Cassius. A few minutes later he is informed again of her death as if he has not heard before. Arguments have been urged for the retention of both passages and they have been found to work effectively both together on the stage and on film,[12] but there are verbal as well as factual irregularities which to my mind prove that Shakespeare undoubtedly wished to substitute one of the passages about Portia's death for the other. For one thing, its first mention is both preceded and followed by Brutus's order to his boy Lucius to give him a bowl of wine. This is the kind of redundant repetition we have already seen in *The Tempest* and *Henry V* and which often in Shakespeare signals second thoughts or afterthought: deletion or addition. I am actually a little complacent about the discovery of a large number of repetitions in the plays which may be explained as Shakespeare's way of sewing up rifts in the texture of the dialogue caused by either cuts or insertions.[13]

In cases of revision Shakespeare was not always to blame for the irregularities that appear in the printed texts. His first editors bear a great deal of the responsiblity for not observing his signs. And there is not a great deal modern editors can or should do beyond correcting obvious errors and emending meaningless cruxes. But theater directors should know when a reading is suspect, and particularly when there is reason to think that a deletion has been intended. And students of Shakespeare, both scholars and critics, should be able to read with sufficient discrimination to recognize the signs of revision and form their judgments accordingly.

The discontinuities and inconsistencies that resulted from Shakespeare's changes of intention and his introduction of new perspectives and developments as he composed his plays were generally of his own making. They sometimes resulted in problems of explication. But one thing we may learn from a study of Shakespeare's occasional violations of the expectations he creates, is not to look for subtle psychological explanations of the characters' unpredictable behavior or supplement the plot with ingenious guesses when a far simpler explanation will do. Much too often critics will devise farfetched theories to explain as intentional an effect which was probably the unintended result of a new departure or a modification of the author's original plan.

I have tried to show that in most cases the gain was worth the cost. *Hamlet* is enhanced by the ambiguity involved in a double focus. *Romeo and Juliet*, it may be added, is enhanced by the uncertainty as to whether the characters are responsible for their own tragedy or merely the victims of fate. Both *Hamlet* and *Romeo and*

Juliet, as well as *Julius Cæsar* and *Othello* profit in dramatic intensity by the effect of speed and urgency produced by condensing a great deal of action into an impossibly short space of time.[14]

NOTES

1. See my "Repetition, Revision and Editorial Greed in Shakespeare's Play Texts," *Cahiers Elisabéthains* 34 (October 1988): 5–37.
2. T. W. Baldwin, *William Shakspere's Five-Act Structure* (Urbana: University of Illinois Press, 1963).
3. See my "Down-trod Mortimer and Plump Jack" in *Unconformities in Shakespeare's History Plays* (Basingstoke: Macmillan, 1982), 103–20.
4. Giraldi Cinthio, *Gli Hecatommithi* (1565).
5. This was first remarked upon by John Wilson ("Christopher North") in *Blackwood's Magazine*, Nov. 1849, Apr. and May 1850. See, e.g., Ned B. Allen, "The Two Parts of *Othello*," *Shakespeare Survey* 21 (1968): 13–29; M. R. Ridley, introduction to the Arden edition of *Othello* (1971 repr.), lxvii–lxx; Norman Sanders, introduction to the New Cambridge edition of *Othello* (1984), 14–17.
6. See, e.g., Harold Jenkins, introduction to the New Arden *Hamlet*, 31–32.
7. See my *Unconformities in Shakespeare's Tragedies* (Basingstoke: Macmillan, 1989), 239, n.15.
8. See Michael J.Warren, "Quarto and Folio *King Lear* and the Interpretation of Albany and Edgar" in D. Bevington and J. L. Halio, eds., *Shakespeare, Pattern of Excelling Nature* (London: Associated University Presses, 1978), 95–107; Steven Urkowitz, *Shakespeare's Revision of* King Lear (New Jersey: Princeton University Press, 1980).
9. See Gary Taylor, "The War in 'King Lear,'" *Shakespeare Survey* 33 (1980): 27–34.
10. E. A. J. Honigmann, "Shakespeare's Revised Plays: *King Lear* and *Othello*." *Library*, sixth series 4.2 (1982): 142–73.
11. This was maintained by Gary Jay Williams in a paper read at the World Shakespeare Congress in Berlin (1986).
12. See Thomas Clayton, "Should Brutus Never Taste of Portia's Death but Once? Text and Performance in *Julius Cæsar*." *Studies in English Literature* 23 (1983): 237–55; Arthur Humphreys, introduction to the Oxford *Julius Cæsar* (1984), 80–81.
13. See my *Unconformities in Shakespeare's Later Comedies* (Basingstoke: Macmillan, 1993), appendix, 174–85.
14. For a detailed analysis of all of Shakespeare's plays along the lines represented in this article, the reader may be referred to my four-volume series of *Unconformities* books published by Macmillan (1982–93).

On Construction and Significance in Shakespearean Drama

KEITH BROWN

IT IS THE PURPOSE OF THIS ESSAY TO ARGUE THAT SHAKESPEARE IS A RENaissance artist—in a sense to which too little attention has, as yet, been paid. But the point will perhaps best be made if we first consider certain changes which have taken place in our general picture of the literary art of the English Renaissance over the past forty years or so.

Looking back, it is by now clear that in some respects our picture of the history of English Renaissance literature radically began to alter in the 1950s, after Kent Hieatt's celebrated demonstration of the elaborate correlation between the shape of Spenser's *Epithalamion* and the position of the heavens on the poet's wedding day.[1] Not that Hieatt's discovery was generally felt to be good news: the latent romanticism of mid-twentieth century literary aesthetics made it rather shocking that a major poet, in a major poem, should ever have "descended" to such detailed involvement with mere numerical calculation. Even more distasteful for many was the realization that equally strange numerical possibilities might also need probing in other major texts of the period. But the cat was now out of the bag, and clearly someone had to pursue it. After Hieatt, it was simply no longer safe to assume that among Shakespeare's contemporaries an interest in number symbolism was the concern only of the quaint or the untalented. Subsequently a variety of scholars, braving their colleagues' understandable unease, therefore felt their way forward into the tricky terrain of numerical and numerological explication of Renaissance texts.[2] And the necessary background to such inquiries was made much better known through studies such as Christopher Butler's *Renaissance Number Symbolism*. Today it seems fair to say that—within limits—awareness of the possibilities of number symbolism is cautiously allowed to be at least a valid secondary intellectual tool in the kit of any analyst of nondramatic Renaissance literary texts. An unexpectedly plausible case has been made for the presence of a numerological element even in *Julius Caesar*.[3]

By taking the king, moreover, Hieatt had clearly also taken the rest of the pieces on the board. If a writer of Spenser's standing would go to the extreme of building difficult numerical significances into even one major poem, was it not prima facie likelier still that he would often build simpler non-numerological—but still consciously significant—"architectural" patternings and structures into his compositions, too? And might not his contemporaries, the mainstream writers, not just the fringe eccentrics, be expected to be doing the same? Such possibilities were not merely the logical-seeming implication of one textual discovery by Kent Hieatt; the increasingly detailed picture that was developing of the general climate of ideas in Tudor and early Stuart England already pointed the same way.

It was, after all, an age in which it was natural to reason by analogy, and in which analogy between the artist and his creator was fully grasped. Familiarity with Pythagorean ideas, and with the doctrine that God had created the world "by number, measure and weight," enabled the Renaissance to see the world as "God's poem," and made it natural to view the Divine harmony of the Universe as the highest manifestation of music, the supreme paradigm of art. The poet, giving to airy nothing a local habitation and a name, and boasting half seriously that *his* creations could also stand against Time, was perfectly conscious of following—if at an infinite remove—the pattern of that greater Maker who had coalesced the world out of empty Chaos, and set the first man to name his creatures. In such a climate, it would be natural for any serious poet to tend to develop a peculiar degree of self-consciousness about structural questions; and for such self-consciousness to reflect more overtly "spatial" ways of thinking about literary form than is perhaps normal today. (That this actually happened can be seen, for example, in Drayton's matter-of-fact justification of a particular type of eight-line stanza, comparing its rhyme scheme to the proportions of a Tuscan column![4] For of course the kind of cosmological considerations just adduced meant that it was also natural to regard architecture, with its concern for strength, stability and right proportion, as another prime paradigm of art.)

Perhaps then, in the discussion of Renaissance literature, our familiar critical talk about "structure"—which has nothing whatsoever to do with French structuralism/design/proportion/architectonic and the like—actually needed to be taken with the same unexpected literalness that the notion of the "numbers" of poetry had also turned out to require. Once again, this is a hunch that has proved fruitful. Slowly, over the decades, an increasing alertness to the potential of structure and configuration in Renaissance texts for forming a separate, consciously significant element within the total meaning of any given work, has come permanently to mark the way we see the literature of the period. Our awareness of the association of centrality with the idea of sovereignty is one obvious case in point.

Naturally these developments have met resistance. (As a contributor to *ENGLISH* has ruefully noted in another context, there is an older generation of academic critics who seem haunted by needless fear that their heirs secretly wish to dismantle human consciousness to about the level of a mechanical computer.) Until recently, scornfully impatient references to "line-counting and all the rest of it" resounded at many an academic literary conference. Yet in reality all we were seeing was the next phase of a progressive sophistication in critical thinking that has been going on since the nineteenth century, and of which these hostile older scholars' own work has also formed a part.

This evolution is perhaps to be seen most simply in discussions of the long poem. Nineteenth-century criticism tended to regard long poems as something squeezed by the pressure of inspiration out of the poet's mind like a ribbon of celestial toothpaste; and with a presumed lack of internal structure that made them quite as difficult to get hold of or pick up. All that could really be done with such lengths of verse, was to analyze the ingredients, and give one's personal reactions to flavor or moral taste. But then came the successive development of new intellectual tools which, by helping critics to structure their own responses more tidily, also began to clarify—irrespective of length—the latent articulation of the texts they faced. For some fifty years, advances in science—in our understanding of human psychology and of the nature of language—really underlay this critical progress: "close reading," explorations of the workings of myth and symbol, and "Empsonian ambiguity" were all among its fruits. These were not small gains. But a psycholinguistic critical tradition of this kind, of course, necessarily focuses on those orderings of a literary text that can only be fully developed intuitively or subconsciously. Hence, the familiar exaggerations of the Intentional Fallacy doctrine: blithely insisting, with a hey derry-da, on the irrelevance of questions of "authorial intention" to proper critical response. The realization of the impossibility of maintaining that stance in the face of Renaissance work whose consciously symbolic structure is wholly entwined with other aspects of its meaning, thus jarred on many, precisely because it did put "authorial intention" so firmly back in the picture again.

Yet the basic duty of the New Critic was to try to integrate the full *totality* of any text into his analysis or reading of it. And as William Empson tirelessly pointed out in the 1950s, that frequently requires taking at least tacit account of some aspect of the original author's apparent intentions. Any investigation of the often formalistic mentality with which literary composition was approached in the Renaissance, essentially *completes* the New Critic's program for him. It was an inevitable intellectual development, not an aesthetic absurdity or betrayal.

As already noticed above, however, such "structural" investigation has so far been focused more upon the nondramatic poetry of the English Renaissance than on the parallel wealth of play texts. One good reason for this, of course, is the known slowness of the Elizabethans and Jacobeans themselves in accepting contemporary theater scripts as "literature": the situation was very like what we see today regarding TV scripts. Clearly, in such a climate there was very little reason for the average playwright to work any very elaborate formal scheme into his dramas, and so far investigation seems to confirm the suspicion that they generally did not do so. With Shakespeare, though, one might expect the case to be rather different: after all, he relatively early became the leading dramatist of his day, and his concern for his literary rather than his stage reputation seems suggested by the replacement of the so-called Bad Quarto of *Hamlet* by a good new text arguably too long for the stage. Furthermore, it is generally agreed by modern scholars that the only playwright among his contemporaries from whom Shakespeare seems to have learned very much was Christopher Marlowe; and Marlowe was one dramatist who did make use of a formal symbolic "architecture" in his work.[5]

Why then, in the teeth of an ever-increasing body of evidence, have Shakespeare scholars been so averse to taking account of this aspect of *his* art? Is it because it conflicts with a lingering wish still to believe in the sentimental image of Shakespeare as an untutored genius who never blotted a line? He did blot lines; and an alumnus of Stratford Grammar School was far from untutored. Is it the lingering pressure of the romantic Victorian notion that True Genius must, by definition, achieve its effects spontaneously, without premeditation? By now, we know far more than the Victorians ever did about the sheer volume of solid work that lies behind most strokes of genius. Yet "as far as I am concerned," the then Director of the Shakespeare Institute (Dr. Philip Brockbank) told an approving Stratford conference, "the more Shakespeare calculated, the less Shakespeare he."

How odd it would be if this were true: it would mean that Shakespeare, so alert in countless ways to the life of his own times, was yet completely out of touch with some of its basic aesthetic presuppositions. Let us look, then, at some apparent examples of Shakespearean calculation—asking, at the same time, whether it might not be of practical help to students if their attention was occasionally drawn to this aspect of Shakespeare's dramas. With that extra question in mind, it may be useful to take first the structure of two favorite syllabus texts: *The Tempest* and *Julius Caesar*.

Though of course very dissimilar in other respects, *The Tempest* and *Julius Caesar* are both works with which students tend to experience the same sort of difficulty. Although in each case the main story line may be grasped readily enough, many new students can do little more because for them each play exists only as a patchwork of scenes and episodes, whose very sequence is impossible to remember. *The Tempest* is seen as a distracting interweaving of four story lines (those of Prospero, the lovers, the court characters, and Caliban and the low characters) together with the comings and goings of Ariel, the episode of the Harpies, and the Masque of Ceres. The atmosphere of magic, dissolving confidence in the normal reference points by which we orient ourselves when mentally reconstructing a narrative, increases the uncertainty. The result is to create in retrospect a sort of delightful kaleidoscopic effect, of bright slivers of drama, loosely assembled. Yet when properly staged the play is not like that at all: what we then *experience* is a fully developed work of art, moving with a coherence and harmony whose satisfactions are close to those of music. In *Julius Caesar*, the difficulty comes with the second half of the play. The new student will have no trouble in perceiving a strong story line up to the first countermoves against Caesar's killers, but is apt to feel that a mere clutter of material then fills out the rest.

In both cases however, simple diagrams or tabulations can greatly aid the student's struggle to get a better grip on the text. Many teachers, of course, are deeply suspicious of any use of diagrams in literary teaching, fearing that they can only foster a vulgarized, Procrustes-bed notion of the work in question. But these are merely theoretical worries: as Mark Rose has long since asked, in reality what damage has been done, if the teacher points out to a class that has lost its way in *The Tempest* that the inner seven of the play's nine scenes are symmetrical, from the final segment of 1.2, to the first segment of 4.1, the penultimate scene?[6]

Scene 2	Scene 3	Scene 4	Scene 5	Scene 6	Scene 7	Scene 8
Prosp., Ferd., Miranda	Alonso, Sebas., Anton.	Caliban, Steph., Trinc.	Ferd., and Miranda	Caliban, Steph., Trinc.	Alonso, Sebas., Anton	Prosp., Ferd. Miranda

In the case of *Julius Caesar*, most students are told at some point that in some ways the play can be regarded as two successive tragedies: first, that of the "the noblest man that ever lived in the tide of times" (Julius); then that of "the noblest Roman of them all" (Brutus). But surely they can make much better use of that thought when they also realize that these two halves of the play in fact form a repeated *abcdefg:abcdefg* scheme, hinged around the central Forum scene:[7]

This tabulation is also useful in clarifying the century-old dispute (repeated in the case of *Hamlet*) as to which is the play's central turning point: the Capitol or the Forum scene? Most new students tend to be bemused by this dispute, since they haven't heard of R. G. Moulton's pre-Bradleyan analysis of Shakespearean dramatic construction,[8] and don't see why it should be assumed that the action of either play necessarily has a central turning point at all. And of course in many ways scepticism about this ancient critical squabble is well justified, since identification of the play's center must vary with the way one reads it. If read as two successive tragedies—and the table above shows how the underlying structure of the play validates and reinforces this perception—then obviously the action "turns" in the Capitol, with Brutus stepping into the newly vacant role of doomed leader almost before the blood is dry on his hands. But focus instead on the play as one work, dealing with the establishment of the Caesars as the keystone of the Roman world, sanctioned by the Cosmos much as a true king in Shakespeare's day was regarded as God's vice-regent, and it is equally

First half of the play		Second half of the play
Fickle and disordered Roman street crowd ("Is this a holiday?") celebrates destruction of Pompey's cause.	A ← →	Fickle and now dangerous street crowd kills Cinna, allegedly as friend of Brutus.
Caesar and Antony	B ← →	Octavius Caesar and Antony
Brutus and Cassius	C ← →	Brutus and Cassius
Brutus, Lucius, and Portia	D ← →	Brutus Lucius, (and Portia)
Caesar	E ← →	Caesar's spirit
Death of Caesar at the Capitol	F ← →	Death of Cassius and Brutus
Anthony's private tribute to Caesar at close of Capitol scene	G ← →	Anthony's tribute to Brutus

FORUM SCENE

obvious that the Forum scene is then the play's true center. Neither way of seeing the play invalidates the other—and it seems significant (for *Julius Caesar* is a trustworthy text) that both the Capitol and the Forum scenes can, in fact, also claim to be literally physically central: the one lying across the halfway point of the text, and the other being the numerically central scene.[9] This is unlikely to be accidental, since exactly the same thing occurs in *Hamlet*: Here too, the two scenes that modern criticism has intuitively identified as rival turning points—the Mousetrap and the Closet scene—come at just the same alternative, literally physically central, halfway points in the Q2 text.

Again as in *Hamlet*, both of these rival central points in *Julius Caesar* are also associated, in true Elizabethan fashion, with the idea of sovereignty: in the Capitol Brutus briefly inherits his victim's power, and at the Forum the Caesars regain it. This is strongly suggestive of the mannerist moral structuring that has been identified in many nondramatic Elizabethan texts (where a first midpoint is associated with a falsely sovereign figure or concept: then discredited by the presentation of a truer sovereignty at a second central point, calculated on some other basis). However, in such works the discriminating reader is usually given an extra clue as to the identity of the truly sovereign center by the buildup of a symmetrical "embellishment of the center" around it. If Shakespeare had really been computing the design of *Julius Caesar* in a similar manner, would he not have done the same?

In fact he has done so. In the first place, it may be noticed that Shakespeare has altered his sources in order to arrange that Octavius, the new embodiment of Caesardom, actually enters Rome while the dead yet still powerful Julius, his wounds and will made eloquent by Antony, is in the very act of sweeping Brutus and Cassius out of the city. The King is dead—Long Live the King! Could anything better demonstrate a continuity not only uninterrupted, but indeed *created*, by the assassin's act? This bracketing of Antony's great performance by the announcements, first that Octavius is approaching, and then that he has already entered the city, is deftly executed. But defter still is the use that has been made of the Cinna the Poet episode. Earlier, this scene seemed puzzling to some critics, as a digression that advances nothing in the action. Nowadays it is read as a necessary demonstration of the effects of Antony's speech that also offers a bitterly ironic commentary on what the conspirators' alleged desire to restore the health of the Republic has led to. But its double *structural* function should surely also be noted. By its echo of 1.1, as we have seen, it intitiates the rerun of the sequence traced in the play's first half. But it also serves to frame the Forum scene between two murders, of which the second blackly travesties the first: Cinna the Poet dies merely because of his name, despite thrice insisting that he is *not* Cinna the Conspirator—just as Julius had allegedly been killed because "he would be crowned," despite having thrice refused a kingly crown. (The parallel is underlined by the cynical joke about just tearing Cinna's name out of his breast and setting him loose: a mordant comment on Brutus's wish that he could kill the spirit of Caesar without shedding his blood.)

In short, the essential design of *Julius Caesar* consists of a twice-enacted narrative pattern neatly dovetailed into a symmetrically elaborated center, emblematizing, as it were, some of the main ideas of the play. Surely few would hold that a student's general grasp of this drama would not be helped by some understanding of that underlying scheme.

To what extent a grasp of that aspect of this particular play also helps one to a more general understanding of Shakespearean drama as a whole, however, is another question. In the first place, it is necessary to make a broad distinction between three levels of construction/planning in Shakespearean drama (while the greatest of the comedies seem to lie outside the bounds of this discussion entirely, and follow quite other principles).

On the basic level, Shakespeare is simply being normally human in matters of design. As anyone in a crowded train or restaurant soon discovers, people tell stories all the time from their own experience; and the general liking for filtering the picture of life one is offering through simple patterning and framing devices is unmistakable. Narrators persistently arrange things in threes, or juxtapose experiences in simple diptychs—"it seemed a fine morning until I met Mr. B. Then I met Mr. C. and it was a fine morning again"—a simple moral reflection then closes the tale. They tend to like simple X-shaped plots (*that old cat of a supervisor triumphs at the outset over the nice girl, who then in turn triumphs over her persecutor*) or they may arrange a longer narrative, in a rather *Lear*-like way, as a mounting succession of shocks or surprises. That a man so intelligent as Shakespeare tends throughout to observe this sort of fundamental tidiness—take for example the X-shaped plot of *Richard II*—is hardly remarkable; and it is probably pointless to ask in any given case whether such simple symmetrizing was deliberate or instinctive. At the intuitive level, this sort of basic planning instinct would for example have been reinforced, for a bright child growing up in Elizabethan Warwickshire, by constant exposure to a wealth of oral literature.[10] Shakespeare's many allusions show how deeply folk culture imprinted itself in him; and the trick of strongly patterning (often symmetrizing) material, as a mnemonic aid to performance, was engrained in the oral tradition.[11] At the more deliberate level, one has only to point to the habits of thought inculcated by Elizabethan schooling, with its training in the balanced, symmetrical and antithetical figures of rhetoric.

But it must be emphasized again that, at this level of literary planning, the cultural context in which Shakespeare worked did no more than reinforce constructional habits present in the literature of every age. Their varying *visibility*, in different literary periods, is only the result of varying fashions in literary criticism or scholarship. Thus, it is easy to find reputable works by modern novelists—Virginia Woolf, Lawrence Durrell, and A. S. Byatt are three highly diverse examples—in which a crucially central episode or turning point in the narrative is so placed as to lie astride the physical midpoint of the text.[12] (Two of the above authors explicitly confirmed to the present writer that they had consciously counted pages or chapter sections to achieve this elegance: a fact which may perhaps help conservative Shakespeareans over the distaste they feel at the thought of Shakespeare similarly computing the proportions of his own work.) Yet what scholar or reviewer ever draws attention to this aspect of any modern work of fiction, unless it is obtrusively experimental in form?

A second level of planning has been reached, however, as soon as any pattern, position, or proportion in this kind of scheme takes on a specifically symbolic significance. Thus the underlying planning in *The Tempest*, illustrated above, *can* be just a piece of tidy Shakespearean craftsmanship; but within the context of what has been shown about the Elizabethans' general habits of thought, and about the nondramatic literature of the period, it seems better seen as a characteristically intelligent Shakespearean game with the notion of the sovereign center. The diagram offered earlier shows a triple frame around a central tableau of love: *amor vincit omnia*; and Miranda even thinks she has disobeyed her father to declare her love. Yet this will be a royal union, and if love really were sovereign in that context, it would wreck the order of court and state alike. So the scene is watched over by Miranda's royal father, and it is made clear that all is happening by his will—effectuated through a magic that is itself dependent, of course, upon a favorable conjunction of the heavens.

It may be noted that the scene is not only centric in relation to the rest of the play, but is internally centered also. The text is a good one, and the center of 3.1 is occupied by a matching pair of speeches from the lovers, of identical length (did Shakespeare really never "calculate"?) of which the first ends at line 48—in a 96-line scene—with the whole bracketed by a repeated acknowledgment from Miranda that her father's word is no longer law for her. Ferdinand has, of course, been wanting to make Miranda Queen of Naples ever since he saw her; but it is only at the start of this pair of speeches that he learns her name, and what follows is a little ritual to make clear that this—by the sexist standards of the age—is to be the perfect love match. Ferdinand makes clear that he is not without the male's requisite previous experience, in judging Miranda to be the "only girl in the world" for him; and Miranda then repeats directly to Ferdinand her earlier feminine assurances to her father that she does not need experience of other boys to know that this is the "only boy in the world" for her. (This licenses the crescendo of joy in mutually avowed love which then rises through the second half of the scene.) Meanwhile the symmetry of the matching pair of central speeches is extended, more diffusely, into what precedes and follows them. Beforehand, Miranda tries to serve Ferdinand by carrying his logs for him. After her speech, he avows his determination to serve her. The way of thinking that is exemplified in the internal construction of this scene is clearly continuous with the way of thinking equally manifest in the whole play's overall design.

Symmetrical or center-conscious planning, on either level one or level two (as just defined) thus seems widespread in the canon of Shakespeare's work, and to have been often much more specifically related to the actual physical proportioning of segments of the text than traditional criticism has grasped. Admittedly there are plays (*All's Well That Ends Well* is one) from which the signs of such planning seem to be absent without one sensing the presence (as in the greatest comedies) of some other elusive shaping principle. And of course there are also plays (such as *Love's Labour's Lost*) which would appear to have been so altered as to be outside the scope of this present inquiry. But more often, the question to be asked is whether the manifest element of symmetry in the planning of the work is likely to have been instinctive or deliberately calculated, or whether or not it carries a symbolic loading. Anyone who pays attention to the cleared-stage scene divisions of *A Midsummer Night's Dream*, for example, will find in the layout of the Q1 text an obviously symmetrical plan that seems quite unsymbolic but elaborate enough to have required deliberate calculation. The symmetrical plan of *Coriolanus,*[13] on the other hand seems meant to follow and express in its own way the ideas embodied in the action of the drama. In *Antony and Cleopatra* Shakespeare has made the crucial battle of Actium the numerically central scene of the text, but the general structure of the play has still not yet been sufficiently explored for us to be sure quite how much follows from that particular piece of calculation on the dramatist's part.[14] Analyses of *Macbeth* suggest that even where a play has been substantially cut down in length, an attempt could be made to hack a rough approximation to an original sovereign-centered symmetry back into the text.[15]

In all these cases, it seems clear that what we are concerned with is something that mattered to Shakespeare more than to his colleagues in the theater. It would appear that he delivered scripts to his colleagues stamped with his own unique genius, yes, but scripts that were usually also solidly crafted in harmony with the normal aesthetic assumptions of the age, sometimes further embellished—when his mind had really been ignited by his subject—by those symbolic elegancies of structure that seem to have been part of the literary, not theatrical, taste of his times. The actors, like actors anywhere, then cheerfully chopped and bent his work into something that they felt would work better on stage. This can be seen particularly clearly in the *Dream*, where a subsequently imposed act division, manifestly connected with a preparation of the text for a later production, plows ruthlessly through the symmetrical layout of the cleared-stage scene units of the earlier text.

The surely very modest and unrevolutionary notion of Shakespeare ordering his plays in terms of what we have been calling "level one" and "level two" of constructional planning, has implications for the detective work of Shakespearean textual scholarship. In the arguments such detective work stimulates, it is frequently pointed out that Shakespeare did not necessarily compose his plays by beginning at line one, and then working steadily through to the end of the play. But though the point is generally accepted in the abstract, it is not a thought with which scholars normally seem able to do very much in practice. Yet surely the natural link is between the idea of nonsequential composition, and that of the symmetrical and centric planning, which, in various forms, critics have been accepting in Shakespearean drama at least since the work of R. G. Moulton in the last century. Common sense would suggest (and testimony from other writers confirms) that what is most likely to be left to be composed later, in works written on such a basis, is the "filler" between the main anchor points of the scheme in question. Of course nothing conclusive can be proved on such a basis, but it is perhaps at least a consideration that should be cautiously borne in mind at times, when considering editorial problems in any Shakespeare play with a markedly regular structure. As evidence that Shakespeare did compose nonsequentially, there is of course the text of *The Two Noble Kinsmen* which he appears to have abandoned, for completion by another hand. It is noticeable that the parts of the extant play which seem most unequivocally Shakespearean come at the beginning, around the middle and toward the end.

Earlier in this essay, however, there was reference to three levels of construction or planning that may be distinguished in Shakespearean drama. What is the third? Here, we are not concerned, as before, with modes of design simultaneously or alternately present throughout Shakespeare's career as a playwright, but with traits apparent in some of his work for just a few years around 1600. At this time Shakespeare does appear to have been trying out the possibility of incorporating into his plays precisely those constructional dramas and ironies, with their finesses between truly and falsely sovereign center points, consciously significant proportions, and occasional recourse to number symbolism, that have been observed in some of the nondramatic compositions of the period. Why not?

The construction of one play of this period—*Julius Caesar*—has already been gone into in some detail here. As with *Hamlet*, it really does seem too much to believe that there can be no connection at all between the rival "central turning points" that critics have discerned and disputed over (both of which occupy textual halfway points), and the equivalent configurations in nondramatic texts. Nonetheless, the human brain is so extraordinary an instrument that it must be admitted that it *is* just possible, even in *Hamlet*, (where the content of the cleared-stage scene units of the first two acts pairs with those of the last two acts, in an *abcd:dcba* scheme) that Shakespeare could have achieved this tidily elaborate kind of layout purely "by ear," in perhaps only unconscious imitation of something he had come to admire in the course of his reading. But the same argument is much less plausible in the case of another double-centered play, *Henry V*, where the symbolism implicit in the form seems much more elaborate.

When Shakespeare, for whatever reason, took on the task of dramatizing the story of this hero-king and his battle, it must have been obvious from the outset that the meagerness of the material would cause difficulties. Compared with Shakespeare's other plays, the thinness of the basic plot is almost comic: the King goes to France, wins his battle, and goes home again. What, apart from distracting the audience with a good deal of noise and bustle, could be done with that? One thing that could be done, especially in a period when he seems to have been experimenting—with at any rate part of his mind—with the idea of viewing his play texts as "mannerist" literary artifacts, was to draw upon the familiar Renaissance notion of the great general as a great artist, godlike in the capacity to take the confusion of war and battle and order it according to his will. Listen to Henry V, says the Archbishop in the first scene, "and you shall hear a fearful battle rendered by you in music." He is talking about the King himself, but he is also telling us precisely what the play of the same name is about to do.

Or so it would appear, if one counts the play's twenty-nine scenes.[16] (The dislike of so many Shakespeareans for counting lines, is very understandable, and it is not suggested here that Shakespeare did so except in special circumstances. Even then, he may of course only have been making accurate eye measurements of his manuscript pages, or simply have been guided by an innate sense of timing: after all, Beethoven was able to achieve the Golden Section proportion in some of his compositions purely by ear. But an aversion to Shakespearean line counting need not require an equal aversion to the much more modest—indeed rather commonsensical—notion that when composing his plays he would have been likely to count scenes.) And what scene counting demonstrates in *Henry V* is a play laid out—fortuitously, many will say, but nonetheless with striking neatness—as a tetractys:

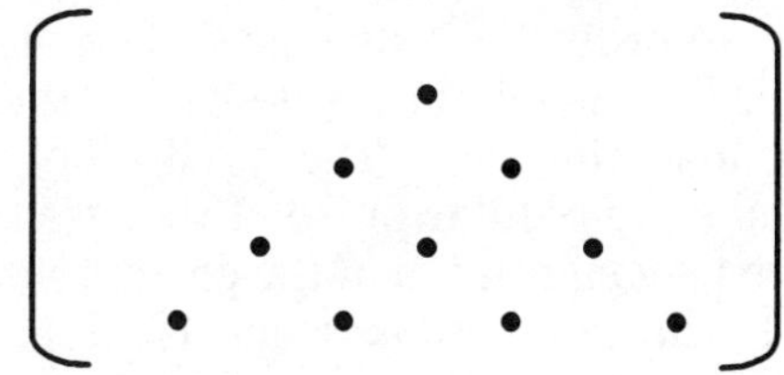

If this is an accident, and that possibility must of course be allowed, then it was a notably happy one, for the proportions of the tetractys correspond to the perfect musical consonances: (unison), fourth, fifth, (octave). Is it to consider too curiously, to suggest that from one point of view *unison* is what the play is all about? It begins with Henry stabilizing the recently regained unity of the English by weeding out a handful of traitors and leading the rest against the French. And it ends on a higher note of unison, with a merging of the kingdoms and royal families of England and France. But perhaps of more interest, especially in view of Shakespeare's repeated references in his works to the psychotherapeutic uses of music, is the fact that the fourth and fifth were considered to represent the ideal relative proportions of the *rational*, *irascible*, and *concupiscible* faculties in the truly harmonious soul. It is precisely these aspects of Henry's own character that the play foregrounds.—"May I with right and conscience make this claim?" "I was not angry since I came to France, until this instant." "I love France so well that I will not part with a village of it; I will have it all mine."

But of course everything said in the last paragraph depends on making good the assertion that *Henry V* is analyzable in terms of the divisions of the tetractys. Certainly, the play's halfway point has been made a characteristically "sovereign" center; for it is in the (numerically central) fifteenth scene of the play that King Henry at last receives the formal defiance of the French king. As in *Julius Caesar*, the play further enhances this midpoint by really extending the episode into a centerpiece consisting of three scenes: first we see the dispatch of the French herald, then Henry's rebuff of the defiance, then the French waiting to arm for the fight that must follow after Henry's response to the herald. Then at the one-third and two-thirds points in the text (tenth and twentieth scene) we find those two astounding jets of heroic verbal energy by which Henry seems to secure victory at Harfleur and Agincourt almost single-handedly: "One more unto the breach" and the Crispin Crispian speech. Dividing the play into quarters are the landmarks in the progress of the unfortunate French court. After the prologue, six scenes elapse before they determine to "fill the proportions [sic] of defence"—that is, to order their defenses; then another six scenes elapse before their King's defiance is delivered; then after a further six scenes, hope lost, they cry "the devil take order now." But through all this runs the regular pulse of Henry's successes, effecting its own five-part segmentation of the drama: scene 6, conspiracy crushed; scene 12, Harfleur taken; scene 18, Henry wins his argument with his men; scene 24, victory at Agincourt is conceded.

Of course there is another five-part scheme in the play. Although it has increasingly become the view of modern editors that the speeches of the Chorus in *Henry V* are essentially to be viewed as scenes like any other, they still mark out a five-act scheme. When viewed in this way, the play has a different halfway point: the numerically central scene, not of the whole play, but of act 3, the central act. This is the charming interlude of the Princess Katherine's English lesson. It is difficult to believe, in the context of what has already been noted here about other Shakespeare plays, and about Elizabethan centric-consciousness generally, that this positioning of Katherine is quite free of symbolism. In short, once more we have, as with *Julius Caesar* and *Hamlet*, a play with an ironic interplay of implications between two alternative "sovereign" center points, the one "truer" than the other.

Here again the traditional critical debate about the play is the pointer to its constructional strategy. True, we do not in this case see a long-standing wrangle about rival central turning points: we could not, for the play's simple line of action does not "turn" at all, but marches straight on to its conclusion, with Katherine herself no more than an essentially passive—if willing—sacrifice to the victor. But what we do have, is a long-standing critical dispute as to whether the play is really belauding Henry and his achievements, or covertly passing a quite severe judgment upon them?

Empson long ago taught us to ask, "why not both?" when faced with such critical disputes; and surely that is the right question in this case. And in such an essentially static drama, where form is in any case likely to take on at least some sort of emblematic aspect, it would be natural enough for the two ways of seeing the moral issues raised by the play to be related to the two ways of seeing the play's organization. (That Shakespeare did build two alternative structural schemes into the play is evident from the fact that the Chorus/act divisions cut through the symmetrical layout of the main action, yet are not [unlike in the *Dream*] a later addition to the text.)

It should be noted, then, that Katherine is the real victor in the play. Henry has not really conquered France, for his empire will disappear within a generation. But Katherine has conquered England, and Wales too, for after Henry's death she will become the mother of the Tudor dynasty, as any educated member of an Elizabethan audience would presumably have been well aware. Apart from her parents (and, embarrassingly, the traitor Earl of Cambridge, whose latent royalty is however wholly concealed in the play) she is the only ancestor of Elizabeth I among all these confidently brawling medieval princes. The irony is clear. The whole play, alike in terms of idea content and of textual layout, seems organized around the Mars-like triumphs of King Henry. Yet it is gay, innocent little Katherine, quietly enthroned at the alternative secondary-seeming midpoint of the play—in a scene so ostensibly unimportant that it can even be in a foreign language—from whose loins the real future will grow, once this vainglorious, brutal medieval brawling is over. If one accepts the Elizabethan association of the midpoint with the idea of sovereignty at all, the implicit judgment here seems clear.

By the time Shakespeare had completed *Hamlet*, however, his curiosity about the applicability of elaborately symbolic modes of mannerist literary construction to writing for the stage seems to have burned itself out. In *Othello*, and *King Lear*, although there are clear signs that a reflective curiosity about constructional issues still persists, it is much more Elizabethan theories of dramatic, rather than literary, composition that appear to be engaging his speculative intelligence.[17] But that is another story—or rather, another chapter of the same story, which remains that of a Renaissance artist whose dazzling various compositions may be for all time, but whose practical compositional habits were much more of a piece with the general practice of his own age than we, in our bardolatry, sometimes care to acknowledge.

Notes

1. Kent A. Hieatt, *Short Time's Endless Monument* (New York: Columbia University Press, 1960). I do not wish by this note to deny credit to Prof. Alastair Fowler, whose own work in this area paralleled and in part preceded that of Hieatt. But my own experience—I was then working in a major North American university—was that, in practice, it was Hieatt's work which made the first impact.

2. A useful showcase of work of this kind is *Silent Poetry*, A. Fowler ed. (London: Routledge, 1970).

3. Thomas McAlindon, "The Numbering of Men and Days: Symbolic Design in *Julius Caesar*," *Studies in Philology* 81(1984): 372–94. Like many studies of its kind, this essay pushes too hard and too far; but its exploration of the quiet play that seems to be made in the drama around the number eight (the number of regeneration) and the name Octavius, must give any fairminded reader pause, and is not inconsistent with other aspects of the construction of the tragedy noted here.

4. J. W. Hebel, ed., *The Works of Michael Drayton*, 5 vols. (Oxford: Blackwell, 1941), 2: 3–5.

5. R. T. Eriksen, *The Forme of Faustus Fortunes* (New Jersey: Humanities Press, 1987).

6. Mark Rose, *Shakespearean Design* (Cambridge: Harvard University Press, 1972). The diagram reproduced here is on p. 173.

7. The analysis of *Julius Caesar* offered here is a conflation and expansion of points made by the present writer in *Essays in Criticism* 27 (1977): 6–7, and by Prof. Kristian Smidt in his *Unconformities in Shakespeare's Tragedies* (Basingstoke: Macmillan, 1989).

8. R. G. Moulton, *Shakespeare as a Dramatic Artist* (Oxford: Clarendon Press, 1885). The enlarged third edition (1893), will be found useful.

9. That is, assuming the Elizabethan practice is followed of counting all the little episodes of the battle as a single scene.

10. As late as the 1920s, in an area only forty kilometers from Stratford-on-Avon, it took one collector only nineteen months to record more than six hundred ballads and folksongs, some over four hundred years old. These were only the remainder of a rich tapestry of seasonal feasts and festivals, folk plays, folk tales, and so on, that survived largely intact well into the last century. Most Elizabethan Londoners had contact with this world.

11. David Buchan, *The Ballad and the Folk* (London: Routledge, 1972).

12. *Mrs. Dalloway* (Woolf), *Tunc* (Durrell), and *The Game* (Byatt) all illustrate the point.

13. Carolyn Grant Wakeman, *Action and Interpretation: The Impact of* Coriolanus *in the Theater*, Ph.D. thesis, Washington University, 1981, see ch.1.

14. Roy Battenhouse, *Shakespearean Tragedy: Its Christian Premises* (Bloomington: Indiana University Press, 1969).

15. William Godshalk, *Patterning in Shakespearean Drama* (The Hague: Mouton, 1973). See especially 118–19.

16. If one counts the speeches of the Chorus as scenes, as does the new Oxford edition—with the implicit blessing of other editors (see, for example, the comment on this subject in the Pelican edition)—then there are twenty-nine scenes in the play, although of course the conventional numbering shows a lower total.

17. Attention is drawn to an article by Keith Brown in *Cahiers Elisabethains* 20(Oct. 1982): 71–82, "Chimeras dire?: An Analysis of the 'Conflated' *Lear* Text." The author would today stand by the main points made in this article, but would wish to revise extensively many points of detail and secondary argumentation.

Henry V and the Strength and Weakness of Words: Shakespearean Philology, Historicist Criticism, Communicative Pragmatics

Roger D. Sell

Ever since modern languages became the object of serious research, they have been studied by scholars who pursue philology in the *Oxford English Dictionary* (*OED*)'s sense 1:

> Love of learning and literature; the study of literature, in a wide sense, including grammar, literary criticism and interpretation, the relation of literature and written records to history, etc.; literary or classical scholarship; polite learning.

Even today, and especially in continental Europe, there are scholars who still cover this brief. Closer to our time's more normal understanding of philology, however, is the *OED*'s sense 3:

> The study of the structure and development of language; the science of language; linguistics. (Really one branch of sense 1.)

And even this meaning is a bit dated. The last example offered by the *OED* (*Compact Edition*, 1971) is from 1852, after which time scholars in the traditions of Saussurian and Bloomfieldian structuralism drove something of a wedge between philology and linguistics. Linguistics tended to be perceived as the synchronically oriented approach to structure, while the diachronies of development continued to be assigned to philology.

At the time, the twentieth-century tripartition into literary study, linguistics, and language history was accompanied by some unpleasant professional and institutional tensions.[1] But in the long term, it meant a specialization that brought clear benefits, and not least by providing new kinds of detailed knowledge on which to base a general understanding that can be richer and more accurate. Nor is it as if scholarly paradigms were now merely marking time. Most obviously, perhaps, the specialized senses of linguistics and philology may actually be entering into rapprochement. After all, the structuralists' focus on *langue* at the expense of *parole* has long been qualified by pragmaticists, who have not only emphasized the importance of contextualization, but are noticing that an adequate account of contextualization must be fundamentally historical, and that pragmatics, no less than phonology, syntax and semantics, has its own history.[2] This is the background to Benjamins' recent launch of *The Journal of Historical Pragmatics*.

The odds are also improving for a reaffirmed and fruitful alignment between language study and the study of literature. Earlier "language-literature" interdisciplinarities—Jakobsonian poetics, for instance, or stylistics, or speech act theory of literature—simply did not see the writing and reading of literary texts as forms of genuine interactivity between situated—albeit disparately situated—human subjects.[3] On the contrary, a lot of such work only compounded the structuralist linguists' behavioristic disregard for meaning and intention with the depersonalizing and de-historicizing aesthetics of New Critical literary formalism. But if present-day language study is much more centrally concerned with contextualized interpersonalities, the same goes for present-day literary study as well. Literary formalism, no less than the universalizations of Leavisian evaluative criticism, Freudian psychoanalytic criticism or Jungian myth criticism, has been seriously challenged by the historicist approaches of Marxist and post-Marxist criticism, new historicism, cultural materialism, feminist criticism, postcolonial criticism, and cultural studies. Increasingly, literary critics and language scholars could well find themselves comparing notes on the pragmatics of real communication, with literary writing and reading sometimes viewed as instances.[4] By the same token, the term "philology" could gradually be regaining something of that oldest and broadest sense of all (*OED* sense 1). Certainly for my own present purposes, I would hope the term can denote a very wide interest in language, in its history, and in its actual uses in various types of communication, literary and otherwise.

One of my aims here is to stress the importance to such a philology of a historicist concern with communicative pragmatics. Another point is that historicism needs to be carefully thought through. More particularly, historicist literary criticism, though it has already brought the study of literature closer to the socio-pragmatic study of language, is sometimes open to question in its account of the relationship between human beings and society, and therefore in its account of communication as well. After proposing what I hope is a more adequate view of things, I move on to my main task, which is to illustrate its implications for a Shakespearean philology, with *Henry V* as my prime example.

By "Shakespearean philology," part of what I mean is the comprehensive kind of philology as applied to Shakespeare. I am focusing on Shakespeare because he has already proved extremely interesting to language scholars and literary scholars alike, so that his chances of bringing them together are the best possible. Approaches could move either from Shakespeare toward a fuller understanding of language, its history and its communicative uses in general, or from a general knowledge of language, its history and its communicative uses toward a fuller understanding of Shakespeare. But ideally speaking, philological scholarship of the kind I have in mind would constantly move in both directions at once.

What "Shakespearean philology" can also suggest, perhaps, is that this bidirectionally philological study of a literary author will at the same time be a study of literary authorship itself as a philological praxis, and in the same broad sense. For one thing, authors have a professional understanding of language, which will inevitably be reflected in their own usage, and quite possibly in metalinguistic commentary as well. For another, it is very much as language users that both authors themselves and their intradiegetic characters become real for us. Literature's actual instantiations of language in use go a very long way to constituting the human worlds which it offers to its audience's contemplation. Not only that, but an author's philologizing is often a matter of both portraying and activating something we might call the philology of everyday life. On the one hand, the characters in the story are shown as applying essentially philological types of enquiry to each other's words, in order to work out what to think, feel and do. On the other hand, the story's audience is drawn into the very same process.

One of the earliest and best treatments of the philology intrinsic to Shakespeare's plays was Gladys D. Willcock's *Shakespeare as Critic of Language* (1934).[5] Above all, Willcock demonstrated that Shakespeare was quite exceptionally self-conscious about language and language use; that he made it the theme of a sustained sociocritical commentary in *Love's Labour's Lost*; and that in other plays he foregrounded matters of pragmatics and style at precisely the dramatic high points. Examples of this tendency include: Richard II's comment on the dying words of John of Gaunt, "Can sick men play so nicely with their names?"; Hamlet's reply to the outraged

Laertes, "I'll rant as well as thou"; and Dolabella's interruptions of Cleopatra's poetical climaxes.

True, Willcock's scholarship itself, though basically far ahead of its time, showed traces of the mid-twentieth century's specializing polarization of language and literature. As an enthusiastic and very sensitive reader, she clearly grasped that the linguistic interests in Shakespeare's earlier plays are much more on the surface, whereas in the later ones they are integrated with a fuller study of human character and behavior in general. Yet it was the earlier plays that she herself mainly discussed, her gift for descriptive linguistics, sociolinguistics, rhetorical studies and stylistics standing her in excellent stead. When Shakespeare's philologizing also offered a more complex literary critical challenge, her own philologizing seems to have pulled up short.

This, though, is something a more comprehensive philology can now try to improve upon. A greater stumbling block, perhaps, is that many present-day scholars would find Willcock's linguistic concerns and, to the extent that it does emerge, her paradigm for literary criticism very strange bedfellows. If her focus as a linguist was firmly on interaction within social contexts, as a literary critic she would apparently have been almost as concerned as Coleridge or Bradley to emphasize Shakespeare's own authorial independence and the individualities of his created characters. In present-day linguistic approaches such as critical discourse analysis, by contrast, the emphasis on social contexts can come close to a kind of sociocultural determinism, which reduces the scope of human beings as autonomous free agents, and the same kind of thing can also happen within historicist schools of literary criticism. Most typically with an appeal to post-structuralist theory, critics sometimes offer an account of the human subject that is strongly de-centering. New historicists and cultural materialists, for instance, can be so concerned to counteract the nineteenth-century liberal humanist idea of the free human subject who partakes in a timelessly universal human condition, that they describe history as an endless power struggle which shapes people and their lives quite inexorably.[6] All social discourse is seen as enacting an endless ideological battle, by which a dominant order consolidates its power, subjecting any potentially subversive threats to processes of containment. Such a view transfers agency from human beings themselves to a kind of timelessly universal mechanism, a mechanism referred to by such critics as history, but sometimes not very historical at all. When it comes to particular periods, persons, chains of events or texts, the reduction of all history to the single pattern can actually be historically inaccurate. Some critics even claim that historical accuracy in, say, the interpretation of a writer's words is both impossible and undesirable, an attitude which can only reopen the old rift between literary criticism and language history.

Take Terence Hawkes, for instance.[7] Hawkes is a wonderfully suggestive critic and a lively and amusing writer. To even the most reluctant of today's younger readers, he must seem to write about Shakespeare in a way which brings him alive. But "brings him alive" is not an encomium Hawkes would relish, and some of his pronouncements would fall very foul of anyone not wishing to read the past entirely through the present's spectacles. Presentist readings are exactly what Hawkes would claim to be giving all the time, deliberately and openly, in conformity with an extremist post-structuralist de-centering of the human subject. On this basis, he denies Shakespeare's texts even the slightest authority or authenticity as the words of somebody called Shakespeare. In effect, he seems to regard them more as if they were a kind of anonymous ballad, welling up from a virtually oral tradition through a collaboration of the folk.

In so clearly highlighting the relationship between the human being and the social community, Hawkes and others like him have performed a service which earlier generations of literary scholars sometimes neglected. Certainly any present-day account of communication, literary or other, will have to deal with this far more explicitly than Willcock did. Yet Willcock's relative individualism as a critic and her social orientation as a linguist were not necessarily in contradiction. The fact is that thoughts and behaviors which are really fairly personal can go hand in hand with traits that are far more historically representative. This was perfectly obvious to Dryden and his contemporaries, whose literary criticism moved between the "individual" and the "type" with no difficulty at all. Now, too, the point is once again becoming very clear, in branches of knowledge including not only linguistic and literary scholarship, but psychology, sociology, and cultural studies. As a result, paradigms involving socio-determinism and post-structuralist de-centering are coming in for some searching critique.

As Raymond Tallis points out, what they have basically ignored is the following statement of de Saussure's, who is so often paid tribute as a founding father:

> Language [*langue*] is not a function of the speaker; it is a product that is passively assimilated by the individual. . . . Speech [*parole*], on the contrary, is an individual act. It is wilful and intellectual.[8]

No matter whether the structured system be that of the psyche, language, society or culture, human beings *operate* the system, and are not to be conflated with it. Even if there can be no reinstatement of the transparent, self-possessed, controlling Cartesian *cogito*, what Tallis does object to is Lévi-Strauss's enormously influential talk of myths "think[ing] themselves out in the men and without men's knowledge."[9] Tallis's own project is to reassert

> the centrality of individual consciousness, of undeceived deliberateness, in the daily life of human beings. We are not absolutely transparent to ourselves but we are not utterly opaque either; we are not totally self-present in all our actions but nor are we absent from them; we are not complete masters of our fates, shaping our lives according to our utterly unique and original wishes, but neither are we the empty playthings of historical, political, social, semiological or instinctual forces.[10]

If liberal humanism could go too far in its idea of the human subject's autonomy, in other words, then the socio-determinist and post-structuralist corrections have sometimes been overcorrections. However paradoxically, *homo sapiens* is a social being, but a social individual. Shakespeare was much more of his time than many older critics used to allow, but was still identifiably Shakespeare.

So on the one hand, society certainly is the element in which we live and move and have our being. Within any social context, there are: certain ways of thinking, feeling and acting which are more or less prescripted; a certain range of encyclopedic knowledge; a certain set of values; and as a result of all this, certain ways of relating to each other the two halves of the linguistic sign, the signified and the signifier, in order to create, understand and respond to meanings. That is why people who do not share the same social context can experience problems in communication, though as a matter of fact no two communicants ever share exactly the same context, which is what makes communication so worthwhile and exciting. Communication can be partly thought of as a process by which different contexts become somewhat more isomorphic. And the contextual differences from which it starts out can be either in the synchronic dimension, between different cultural groupings coexisting in time, or in the diachronic dimension, between different historical phases, often within one and the same cultural tradition.

Yet on the other hand, society does not completely tie us down. We are capable of a certain mental and imaginative flexibility. Without this, we should not stand the slightest chance of communicating with somebody whose social world is different from our own—or with anyone at all, in the last analysis. Communication cannot take place without a movement of empathy. With greater or lesser success and patience, communicants try to enter into each other's life-world, in order to know how words are being used. At the same time, and by a kind of parallel processing, they may also find themselves disagreeing with each other. But here I should perhaps insert a hyphen: "dis-agreeing." Dissent presupposes a heuristics of consent, a kind of imaginative self-projection into the other person's meanings in order to try them on for size, as it were. As Habermas has suggested,[11] this movement of empathy is fundamental to communicative ethics, as something we owe each other as a matter of good faith, even though, when necessary, an agreement to "disagree" is no less mandatory. In genuine and unconstrained communication, we are all each other's equals.

From this it follows that an account of communicative pragmatics, literary or otherwise, must be not only historical but humanizing: historical enough to recognize the facts and implications of different sociocultural situationalities, yet humanizing enough to recognize the relative mental autonomy by which a communicant can seek to negotiate them. This is by no means the heady kind of autonomy envisaged in some versions of liberal humanism, which is why I call my account, not humanist, but merely humanizing. At the same time, I am certainly not viewing human beings as just social automatons.

Indeed, our relative independence also has a moral dimension, and the account of communicative pragmatics will need to retain a clear memory of the Greek root *pragma* (= "deed"). *Logos* is *pragma*, and that is ultimately why a comprehensive philology must include pragmatics. As a result of communication, the world may be changed, because people can stand back from their situation and view it in a new light. What happens in such a case is that social and individual features enter into a kind of coadaptation. The persuasive speaker adapts to society in order to be listened to and understood, but with the further motive of adapting society to the speaker's own project. Successful rhetoric is always coadaptive in this sense. As Aristotle explained, even if the truth is always the truth, orators may have to help it, so to speak, by meeting their audience halfway. To take a familiar and non-Shakespearean literary example, Dickens's *Dombey and Son* certainly kowtowed to Mrs. Grundy's notions of decorum. To the cheek of the Victorian young person it can have brought not the slightest blush. Yet in point of fact, it dealt with poverty, prostitution, adultery and marital rape, and was in the long run cutting the ground from under Mrs. Grundy's feet. This already begins to suggest how words, including the words of literature, can amount to deeds.

So much for words' strength. But there is a weakness to words as well, Shakespeare's just as much as anyone else's. Shakespeare's relative autonomy has never given him a huge amount of power over other people, partly because other people have a relative autonomy of their own. From his own contemporaries onward, people have been free to refuse him the humanly mandatory empathy. As speech act theorists would express it, illocutionary intent bears no necessary relation to perlocutionary effect.

Then again, to insist on the human being's relative autonomy and agency is in no way to deny the obvious: that when a person's words are reported, transmitted or interpreted, that person's own intention is not the only intention which will affect the words' current impact. When we go to see a play by Shakespeare, the chain of mediation is long and complicated. At the very least it includes: the actors, scene and costume designers, the director, earlier productions and critical discussion, scholarly editions of the text, and the earliest editions of all, which offer variant readings and are of varying degrees of closeness to anything Shakespeare himself may have put on paper. As time moves on, Shakespeare's control over the impact of his words can in many ways only diminish. Because he is dead, he himself cannot try to reassert it, and the number of mediators with whose intentions his own become interwoven gets steadily greater, sometimes with major ideological repercussions. On top of which, the historical situationalities within which his words are received are always changing as well.

All this, however, is not at all the same kind of cultural phenomenon as an oral tradition. Because Shakespeare was already working within a literate culture which has only spread more widely since his death, and because one of the great blessings of literacy has also been the growth of a reasonably reliable and accessible philology, his words still come down to us as his, so obligating us to the movement of empathy, which we can enter into with a certain confidence, and which is presupposed even by any ultimate "disagreement." Especially Shakespeare scholars, but also other theatergoers as well, actually take an interest in the way a current production itself seems to "dis-agree" with Shakespeare, or with previous understandings of him. Interpretations agree and "disagree," both with Shakespeare and each other, in ways that are typical of the interpreters themselves and their own sociocultural formations. But within a literate culture there will always remain a sense that what is at issue really is the mediation of *Shakespeare*, and that Shakespeare's written words can at least to some extent still act upon, and even change us today. In fact the empathetic effort is something we owe not only Shakespeare, but ourselves, as a way to enrich our own lives, as in all communication, through dialogue with otherness.

This is what Hawkes roundly denies. From his post-structuralist de-authorizing of Shakespeare's texts he draws the conclusion that their meaning has always been a kind of free-for-all. Mainly appealing to American philosophical pragmatists (William James, John Dewey, Richard Rorty), he says that readers, directors, actors, spectators, and critics are themselves pragmatists, who construct from a Shakespeare play the meaning which works best for them personally. "By" (i.e., by using) the Shakespeare play, they in fact make meanings of their own. Put another way, the play's meaning is "by" them (i.e., provided by them), in the same sense that a theater program might list "Cigarettes by Abdullah, Costumes by Motley, Music by Mendelssohn."[12] The final step in Hawkes's argument is to say that this meaning which readers construct is determined by their own ideological situationality, within "the large-scale and continuing cultural dialogue or "conversation" which constitutes the very precondition of democracy."[13] Hence his programmatic summary:

> What passes amongst some literary critics for a text's "real" meaning can only be a temporary pause in this otherwise healthy process [of cultural dialogue or "conversation"]. And . . . [a] text is surely better served if it is perceived not as the embodiment of some frozen, definitive significance, but as a kind of intersection or confluence which is continually traversed, a no-man's land, an arena, in which different and opposed meanings, urged from different and opposed political positions, compete in history for ideological power: the power, that is, to determine cultural meaning—to say what the world is and should be like. We try to make *Hamlet* mean for our purposes now: others will try to make it mean differently for their purposes then (or now). . . . [T]here is no final, essential or "real" meaning at the end of it. There is no end. There is only and always the business of "meaning by."[14]

In other words, Hawkes compounds his extremist post-structuralism with a theory of literary communication which is *not* actually a theory of communication. He may well be aware of this, since he christens it, not literary pragmatics but "literary pragmat*ism*."[15] The philosophical pragmatism he invokes is an epistemological theory, having to do with the truth or otherwise of our ideas about the world. And admittedly, the business of constructing what we hope will be true ideas about the world does involve processes of inferencing within context which resemble the ones we use in constructing meanings from other people's words. The cardinal difference, however, is that in truth-making only a single subjectivity is involved, whereas in meaning-making at least two subjectivities are in relationship. Even if communicants end up "dis-agreeing" with each other, they are humanly obliged to try and negotiate their meanings through empathetic understanding. Even if the significance and value a recipient places on an utterance can never be exactly the same as that placed on it by its producer, the recipient is still in fairness bound to consider what the producer meant by it, simply in order to be able to relate to it in the first place. Hawkes's professed concern to do justice to a *text* ("[a] text is surely better served if . . .") deprives human beings of a basic human right, the right to a fair hearing. This right he awards instead to the inanimate text, as a way of refusing the reader's obligation towards the text's known human writer. Hawkes speaks of democracy. But his account of readers simply imposing their own meanings is a travesty of democratic justice, because such justice can only obtain in a world of human interpersonality. For Hawkes here, reading is nothing but an occasion for solipsistic ego trips.

Unless I am mistaken, the irony is that Hawkes has an extremely sharp instinctive feel for communicative realities. Few critics have written with such insight into those textual "silences"—say, the loose-ended treatment of Hamlet's love of Ophelia—which actually baffle a spectator's movement of empathy, though Hawkes also shows how Shakespeare, in the "O" of the dying Cleopatra's "O Antony!", arouses an empathy with the character, and with all her creator's verbal and visual meanings, that is quite momentous.[16] As his theory would lead us to expect, he is especially astute on the links between a particular interpretation and the larger social and ideological ambience in which it is made. But theory is not his work's be-all and end-all, and in the old days he might well have been praised for very faithful readings. Given his theory, his understanding of early modern English is not something he flaunts. Yet it might be difficult to trip him up on it, and in practice, I think, he does see an interpretation of Shakespeare as potentially a "dis-agreement" with a Shakespeare who still has a relative autonomy, and whose meanings can still be approximated with the help of philological and other historical knowledge. Despite the long and complicated chain of mediation which he so tellingly analyzes, he time and time again bears witness that Shakespeare can, in the carefully qualified senses I am trying to suggest, act upon and change us even today.

I had better repeat: this is how Hawkes's work seems to me. This is why I personally return to it. Some of his other readers may find his practical criticism more consistent with his theory. As a result, they may also find it even more valuable—or far less valuable, of course.

What seems certain is that Hawkes himself could never enter into a debate about this without surrendering his theory's first premise. If he were to say that my argument is wrong, he would be authorizing my text as that of a subject whose meanings can be both empathetically known and critically "dis-agreed" with. If he were to say that I have misread him, he would be doing the same thing for his own text. And from this point of view, the only difference between Shakespeare's texts and and texts such as Hawkes's or mine is that Shakespeare's come to their recipients through a longer and more complicated chain of mediation.

In the theorizing of less extremist historicist critics, the communicative facts which Hawkes perhaps knows in his bones are sometimes squarely stated. John Turner writes:

> Two things . . . happen together in the course of reading or watching a play—two different things, which it is important to try to keep separate, even though the boundary-line is always lost between them: we re-create the work in our own language in order to claim acquaintance with it, to give it symbolic meaning in our own world, while at the same time we grapple with the language in which it was originally written in order to know it in its history. These two activities have tended in their extremes to produce what Brecht called empathic [*sic*] and critical approaches to literature, traditional criticism tending towards the former and post-structuralism towards the latter. But, as Brecht saw, both are necessary, each complementing the other: and indeed both activities are perhaps necessarily and ordinarily involved in the complex shuttling back and forth between self and other which constitutes the apparently simple act of understanding.[17]

But Turner's communicative pragmatics would have been even richer for a stronger sense of *logos* as *pragma*. As things are, he is taken up with his interesting perceptions of writing's playfulness, which in the present connection seems rather curious, since the texts he is studying are Shakespeare's history plays. No corpus of dramatic writing could ever be more about the interrelationship between words and real power. And few other plays have themselves transmitted such powerful agency—their author's and other people's, as I have explained—within history. In both respects, *Henry V* is particularly noteworthy, well suggesting some of the scope for a comprehensive philology.

As for the play's own communicative history, many of Shakespeare's other works have been much more widely performed and admired, and have doubtless had more impact on the way people have thought, felt and behaved. But no reading or performance can fail to acknowledge *Henry V*'s concern with politics and military conquest, and there has always been an open invitation to apply this to a current phase of history, and indeed to perceive the play and contemporary history in each other's light. To take a fairly recent juncture, Laurence Olivier's famous film version of 1944 was dedicated to the commandos and airborne troops of Great Britain, "the spirit of whose ancestors it has been humbly attempted to recapture."[18] To go back to the first performance of 1599, there is much we shall never know. But the Chorus's comparison of Henry's triumphant homecoming with a possible future return of the Earl of Essex from Ireland, "Bringing rebellion broachèd on his sword" (5.0.32),[19] had a far more explicit reference to the present moment than even *Richard II*'s deposition scene, through a staging of which Essex's supporters may later have tried to serve his cause against the queen. So precisely topical was the Chorus's semi-prophecy that any performance soon after Essex's disgrace would presumably have left it out, for fear of official reprisals.

As for communicative interaction within the play itself, Shakespeare's linguistic interests are even more obvious than in *Love's Labour's Lost*. As Andrew Gurr notes:

> No play of Shakespeare's makes so much use of differences in language and has more language barriers. With one entire scene in French, another half in French, and the French nobles regularly starting their scenes by making use of French phrases, plus Llewellyn's, Macmorris's and Jamy's non-standard English, Pistol's theatrical and old-fashioned quasi-verse, together with Mrs. Quickly's malapropisms, the play puts up a considerable show of non-communication.[20]

This is only the beginning, and none of it is merely on the surface. As Willcock hinted, by the midpoint of his career Shakespeare's philologizing was already moving wide and deep.

No less obviously, the play is also about getting things done. Dowden was neither the first nor the last to find it "clear and unquestionable that King Henry V is Shakspere's [*sic*] ideal of the *practical* heroic character. He is the king who will not fail."[21] The point is, though, that extremely high dramatic salience is given to those of the king's actions which take the form of words. He may tell Katherine that he is a rough soldier, ungifted in eloquence. But this speech itself is very long, and achieves precisely the required effect on her.

Indeed, if we look for signs of the practical hero's more hands-on practicality, we shall draw a blank. Where, for instance, is his genius as an inventor of military strategem?—his brilliant deployment of archers, his revolutionary use of the hedge of stakes to protect them against French cavalry? (Both these details were mentioned twice in the anonymous *Famous Victories of Henry the Fifth* of the previous year.) And when, *coram populo*, does the rough soldier hero actually get round to using a sword? The only time he even comes close to it is in connection with the duel he promised Williams, who is not even a Frenchman. In the event, he passes on the gage to the bellicose Llewellyn, who in his physical assaults on both Williams and Pistol is the only character really seen to do violence on stage, and who is in any case mainly comic, just as are Pistol and Nym or Pistol and Le Fer in the only other scenes where violence is even a remote possibility (2.1, 4.4).

The Chorus warns all along that the theatrical representation will give a very poor idea of the story's mighty events. But the spectacle is even more scanty than this leads an audience to expect. The only truly heroic deaths in battle are those of Suffolk and York, which happen offstage and are narrated by Exeter, as if by a messenger in Greek tragedy. The kind of thing Shakespeare does offer is: Henry giving the papers to Cambridge, Gray, and Scroop in which they read words tantamount to a death sentence; Henry inciting his men once more unto the breach at Harfleur; Henry raising Westmoreland's spirits with the Saint Crispian speech; and Henry reacting to a change in the state of battle with a lightning-swift imperiousness of speech:

> But hark, what new alarm is this same?
> The French have reinforced their scattered men.
> Then every soldier kill his prisoners.
> Give the word through.
>
> (4.6.35–38)

According to most editors (though not to Taylor),[22] not even this command is obeyed on stage,[23] and there is a pervasive sense that words are decidedly more important than actions, almost as if they have a power of their own. This is not just because of the paucity of visible violence. Time and time again the play's own wording draws attention to it, and from the very beginning, as when the Archbishop of Canterbury remarks that if Henry speaks,

> The air, a chartered libertine, is still,
> And the mute wonder lurketh in men's ears
> To steal his sweet and honeyed sentences,
> So that the art and practic part of life
> Must be the mistress to this theoric.
>
> (1.2.48–52)

Shakespeare makes His Grace an observant communicative pragmaticist. He appreciates that Henry is a great rhetorician, and that such a person's words can truly affect the world of human reality. His words have strength.

Here there are already considerations which are somewhat overlooked in recent historicist criticism. Not that critics have ignored relationships between communication and context. On the contrary, Stephen Greenblatt's brilliant account of *Henry IV 1 & 2* and *Henry V* draws parallels between literary and nonliterary texts as a way of suggesting literature's implication in ongoing ideological processes. No less than Thomas Harriot's *A Briefe and True Report of the New Found Land of Virginia* (1588), Shakespeare's plays are seen by Greenblatt as testing the limits of political power, as recording the way in which challenges to it can be negotiated or assimilated, and as offering convenient interpretations of events or phenomena which do not quite fit in with official dogma. This leads him to speak of a poetics of Elizabethan power, which is in turn bound up with a poetics of the theater.

> Testing, recording, and explaining are elements in this poetics that is inseparably bound up with the figure of Queen Elizabeth, a ruler without a standing army, without a highly developed bureaucracy, without an extensive police force, a ruler whose power is constituted in theatrical celebrations of royal glory and theatrical violence visited upon the enemies of that glory. . . . Elizabethan power . . . depends upon its privileged visibility. As in a theatre, the audience must be powerfully engaged by this visible present while at the same time held at a certain respectful distance from it. "We princes", Elizabeth told a deputation of Lords and Common [*sic*] in 1586, "are set on stages in the sight and view of all the world."[24]

Yet as a gloss on *Henry V* this is surely not quite right. "Theatrical violence visited upon the enemies of . . . [royal] glory"? It is not *vio-*

lence that is staged, and many critics, taking their cue from the Chorus, have argued that no theatrical representation could ever have bodied forth the English victories. According to J. H. Walter, Shakespeare's task was "to extract material for a play from an epic story" and to give "within the physical limits of the stage and within the admittedly inadequate dramatic convention . . . the illusion of an epic whole."[25] If spectators do carry away an impression of a "brave fleet / With silken streamers the young Phoebus feigning," or of "ordnance on their carriages / With fatal mouths gaping on girded Harfleur" (3.0.5–6, 26–27), it is because they themselves have imagined this in response to the play's own words, as the Chorus continuously and very exactly urges. "Think when we talk of horses that you see them / Printing their proud hooves i' th' receiving earth" (1.0.26–27). "Work, work your thoughts, and therein see a seige" (3.0.25). Right from the play's opening lines, themselves so memorable, Shakespeare is meta-theatrically foregrounding his own word-power over his audience, and Henry is a hero who—far more than Richard II, a poet-king whose solipsistic poetry only causes his downfall—resembles Shakespeare. Physical violence is merely secondary and almost incidental here, mere noises off. It is words that count.

Then again, if violence wrought on the monarch's enemies is not actually shown, how much regal awesomeness is left? Henry may be a sovereign lord of language, and very good at cheering people up. But what about Greenblatt's phrase, "theatrical celebrations of royal glory"? Does even this apply?

How much, for instance, does the play resemble a coronation, or a royal pageant or progress? Most of all, I suppose, in act 1, scene 2, where Henry, often positioned center stage upon his throne, confers with his advisers and receives the French ambassadors. But what happens next? The ambassadors perpetrate a carnivalistic hoax. Their diplomatic tribute turns out to be an egregious insult: the gift of the tennis balls. In the long term, the incident may redound to Henry's favor. In France he can show how mistaken the Dauphin was to see him as a frivolous ne'er-do-well. More immediately, though, the impact is, first, to remind everyone on stage and in the audience of his misspent youth, discussed in the previous scene by Canterbury and Ely, and secondly, to send Henry himself huffing and puffing into the first of the play's long series of imprecations—"tell the pleasant prince this mock of his / Hath turned his balls to gun-stones" and so on (1.2.281–82). That this brings even Henry's eloquence to the verge of the ridiculous is hinted by what is hardly a very gross parody in act 2, scene 1, in which Pistol lets fly his preposterous verbal batteries at Nym, a scene which Pope very sensibly placed *immediately after* the court scene, and *before* the Chorus's second speech.[26]

Even when Henry is on the warpath, just how awesome is he? To use Greenblatt's phrases, how likely is his "visible presence" to cow beholders to "a certain respectful distance"? The rhetoric of the "unto the breach" speech and the Saint Crispian speech is wonderful beyond praise. But Henry knows exactly what Aristotle meant: great orators coadaptively *diminish* their distance from their hearers. At Harfleur:

> Once more unto the breach, *dear friends*, once more,
> . . . . [T]here is none of you so mean and base
> That hath not noble lustre in your eyes.
> (3.1.1, 29–30, italics mine)

At Agincourt:

> We few, we happy few, we band of brothers—
> For he today that sheds his blood with me
> Shall be my brother; be he ne'er so vile
> This day shall gentle his condition. . . .
> (4.3.60–63)

In the Harfleur speech, Henry positively demythologizes the fearsome wrath with which great warriors scare their enemies. He tells his common soldiers how to do it!

> Then *imitate* the action of the tiger:
> . . . *Disguise* fair nature with hard-favoured rage.
> Then *lend* the eye a terrible aspect.
> (3.1.6, 8–10, italics mine)

And although, before Agincourt, the Chorus urges the audience to imagine the king "[w]alking from watch to watch, from tent to tent" in order to show a "royal face" without "a note / How dread an army hath enrounded him," this, too, involves a bluff, which even the enthusiastic Chorus frankly mentions: Henry "overbears attaint / With cheerful semblance" (4.0.30, 35–36, 39–40). In his inner man, he is still closer to his "brothers, friends and countrymen" (4.0.34) than he encourages them to believe, and this is something the audience will again realize when, having cast aside all visible marks of kinghood, he says to Bates, "I think the king is but a man as I am" (4.1.97), words whose force as dramatic irony is curiously twofold:

Bates does not know that the person before him *is* the king; yet perhaps Bates is *right* to think him just a man. Henry even says that

> no man should possess him [the king] with any appearance of fear, lest he [the king] by showing it should dishearten his army,

by which time Bates is on just the same wavelength: the king

> may show what outward courage he will, but I believe, as cold a night as 'tis, he could wish himself in Thames up to the neck.
> (4.1.104–6, 107–9)

During this highly charged lull before the storm, then, the king is somebody whom Bates cannot find it in his heart to envy or even much respect. If anything, he feels sorry for him; if the king's cause is unjust, the blood of many men will be upon his conscience. Henry may testily counter that every man dying in battle will still have to pay for his own sins. But Bates has only repeated what Henry himself said to Canterbury at the beginning—"May I with right and conscience make this claim?" (1.2.96)—and when Bates and Williams have moved away, Henry's soliloquy on ceremony is ruthlessly honest, not only with himself but, of course, toward the audience. The kingly role is hugely oppressive. The responsibility and the scope for failure hardly bear thinking of. Far from being a "theatrical celebration of royal glory," the play is a step-by-step demonstration of royal glory's fundamental and very burdensome theatricality.

The value of recent historicist criticism is not in question. In exploring power in Shakespeare's England and Shakespeare's plays, Greenblatt and others have shown power and its attendant ideology, discourse, roles and ceremonies to be of pressing relevance. In any society, they never simply go away. Henry may tell the Dauphin's messengers that up until now "I have laid by my majesty / And plodded like a man for working days" (1.2.276–77). He may tell Bates that when "[the king's] ceremonies [are] laid by, in his nakedness he appears but as a man" (4.1.99–100). But not even Lear's madness or Richard II's deposition is a complete laying-by. The royal function is still ideologically in place, and includes a sense of "once a king, always a king." Lear is still restorable to the throne, and Bolingbroke can never shake off his usurper's guilt. Even his victorious son still does expensive penance, and still hopes for a son of his own to beard the Turk and generally patch things up. His main point to the Dauphin's messengers is about the great expectations that in any case surround his position, and his determination to live up to them. When he speaks the words to Bates, similarly, he is not actually naked, either literally or metaphorically, but disguised. The prescribed kingly role still persists for himself and for the audience, and throughout the play is absolutely central to his own and their perceptions of everything he says and does.

Nor can he be immune to the human pain of yielding to such a mold. Given the play's explicit demythologization of royalty, certain configurations of events carry a poignant subtext. Closest to deciphering this is Llewellyn:

> As Alexander killed his friend Cleitus, being in his ales and his cups, so also Harry Monmouth, being in his right wits and his good judgements, turned away the fat knight with the great belly doublet. . . . I'll tell you, there is good men porn at Monmouth.
>
> (4.7.36–43)

Nowhere in either *Henry IV, Part 2* and *Henry V* themselves or any of the subsequent critical commentary is the rejection of Falstaff mentioned with warmer approbation. Not even Canterbury and Ely are more impressed. Yet even Llewellyn underlines Henry's appearance of coolness, and the question is: What if it really is just an appearance? What if the coolness is no less a part of the royal theatricals than we know the courage to be? Graver still, Llewellyn's words come very shortly after Henry's brusque order that the prisoners be killed, thus half recalling Nym and Pistol's diagnosis of Falstaff's mortal ailment: "The king hath run bad humours on the knight. . . . [H]is heart is fracted" (2.1.97–100). Nor is this the only hint that Henry's own subjection to the kingly role turns him into his friends' virtual murderer. Scroop, one of the traitors he impassively delivers to the laws of the land, was, as Exeter remarks, his bedfellow. He knew, Henry himself says, "the very bottom of my soul" (2.2.94). But Scroop could never have betrayed anyone but a king so very completely. And who but a king could lead his loving York and Suffolk to their end? After Exeter's beautiful narration has squeezed every last drop of pathos and moral significance from this, is there any reason for not believing Henry's awkward remark that he "must perforce compound" with his eyes to prevent them from weeping (4.6.33)? Could it be that the immediately subsequent order to kill the prisoners is part of the same occupational reflex? Does he have to keep on steeling himself? Or if he really is hardhearted now, how much pleasure can he be getting from his progressive isolation? Once again there is the parodic parallel with vainglorious Pistol, who also loses Falstaff, plus Bardolf, Nym, the

Boy and Nell. Nor is it very likely that the conqueror of France will find a new soul mate in the French princess. Of which, more below.

Yet the fact remains: the social and the individual can enter into coadaptation. Although the kingly function is deeply entrenched, although Henry pays an enormous human price in adapting to it, he still has the option of somewhat adapting it to himself, and he knows it. When it suits him, he even appeals to his powerful social role in the course of bringing about social change. Hearing from Katherine that "[i]t is not a fashion for maids in France to kiss before they are married," he counters: "O Kate, nice customs curtsy to great kings. . . . We are the makers of manners . . ." (5.2.240–45). He clearly experiences himself as reasonably autonomous, and the political machinery does not entirely sweep him along with its physical and ideological force. The violence or the celebration normally prescribed to bolster royalty does not entirely determine the course of events. His great achievements spring from the extraordinary force of his own speech, which itself involves that coadaptive shortening of the distance between his kinghood and humanity in general. As for the pomp and circumstance, it is a facade behind which we see him trembling, a facade that he himself actually has to work to keep up. As Alexander Leggatt remarks, what Shakespeare's history plays really show is the social symbolism of kinghood becoming less effective.

> What matters now is the individuality of the man who wears the crown: the neurotic self-destructiveness of Richard II, the practical competence and panache of Henry V. The latter can rescue kingship for a while, but only by turning it into leadership; and that means that kingship is a diminished thing.[27]

It means, in short, that the king will have to be a communicator, and Shakespeare has a very clear view of how the relationship between *logos* and *pragma* actually works.

❧

When the communicative king is persuading other people to do things, his most successful strategy is the one already noted: a coadaptation by which the king meets other people halfway. Altogether more problematic are his attempts to influence people by undertaking to do something himself.

This can never be the slightest bit effective unless his hearers have the feeling that the words will be backed up with deeds—that the king will be "as good as" his word. Henry is obviously at a huge disadvantage here. Far from having a splendid track record to point to, he knows perfectly well that everyone, both at home and abroad, is still gossiping about his misspent youth. On top of which, the French are increasingly unimpressed by the size, equipment and medical condition of his army.

Even so, he may still manage to be convincing by the sheer intensity of his words, and by the kind of theatrical bluff he is so good at. For a warrior king, it is vital that both his own men and the enemy should feel him capable of great bravery and bloodshed. Here, then, there is a paradox. On the one hand, Shakespeare suggests the strength of Henry's words by never staging him in the act of slaughter. On the other hand, Henry's words themselves often prophesy slaughter, and he is obliged to support them with a matching impression of physical prowess. In his own body, he has to suggest a capability to "imitate the action of the tiger." To add to the terminology of Austin[28] and Searle,[29] what Shakespeare demonstrates is that certain speech acts cannot be successfully carried out unless a kind of corporal felicity condition is fulfilled. Conversely, if this condition is patently not fulfilled, words lose their weight.

Theobald, in that most celebrated of emendations, was, I believe, accutely sensitive to Shakespeare's discourse-analytical insight here. To spell out the familiar details, when the Hostess describes the death of Falstaff, the Folio has her saying:

> . . . I knew there was but one way. For his nose was as sharp as a pen, and a Table of greene fields.

Instead of this last phrase, the Quarto has ". . . and talk of floures." Something to do with talking would certainly help to make sense, and "talkd" was itself suggested to Theobald by an anonymous "gentleman sometime deceased." But the Quarto's "floures" could merely be a mistaken recapitulation of the Hostess's slightly earlier mention of Falstaff playing with flowers, and "talk" seems rather un-Shakespearean in its connotational poverty. Theobald's own suggestion was of course

> . . . his nose was as sharp as a pen, and a babbled of green fields
> (2.3.14, Gurr's text of 1992)

and according to the latest paleographical and bibliographical wisdom, the choice between "babbled" and "talked" can only be decided on aesthetic grounds.[30] Well, one aesthetic detail surely worth pointing out is that "babbled" anticipates Llewellyn's description of words without substance:

> If you would take the pains but to examine the wars of Pompey the Great you shall find, I warrant you, that there is no tiddle taddle nor pibble pabble in Pompey's camp.
>
> (4.1.66–69)

Throughout the play a simple chiasmus operates: a person without physical thrust is likely to be or to seem a babbler, and a babbler is unlikely to have much physical thrust. The Hostess goes on to report Falstaff's last effective words as a request that she lay more clothes upon his feet. Then:

> I put my hand into the bed, and felt them, and they were as cold as any stone. Then I felt to his knees, and so up-peered and upward, and all was cold as stone.
>
> (2.3.19–22)

After which, even the babbling had to stop.

Llewellyn thinks of the French enemy as "an ass and a fool and a prating coxcomb"—quite weightless as a word-user (4.1.74–75). This is a bit unfair on the French king, but Bourbon's sonnet to his horse ("Wonder of nature!" [3.8.37]) certainly points in the same direction as Constable's remark behind his back:

> *Orléans:* I know him to be valiant.
> *Constable:* I was told that, by one that knows him better than you you.
> *Orléans:* What's he?
> *Constable:* Marry, he told me so himself, and said he cared not who knew it.
>
> (3.8.92–97)

Not that Constable himself is a weighty speaker. Urging his companions into battle, he exclaims:

> . . . Let us blow on them [the English],
> The vapour of our valour will o'erturn them.

But given the audience's prior knowledge of the impending debacle, his words can only boomerang. He may boast

> . . . What's to say?
> A very little little let us do
> And all is done.
>
> (4.2.23–24, 32–34)

But the dramatic irony coolly underlines that there is much more saying than doing here.

Pistol, too, has "a killing tongue but a quiet sword," as the Boy says (3.2.29). Even Llewellyn is impressed at first:

> There is an anchient lieutenant there at the pridge. I think in my very conscience he is as valiant a man as Mark Antony, and he is man of no estimation in the world, but I did see him do as gallant service.
>
> (3.7.10–13)

See him do? Llewellyn has for the moment allowed Pistol's words to have the same imaginative effect on him as the Chorus hopes to have on the audience. By the time he has been exposed to a bit more of Pistol's language—"I do partly understand your meaning," he says—and has realized that Pistol wants him to help Bardolf escape being hung for pilfering a church, what he saw is no longer quite so clear:

> I'll assure you, a uttered as brave words at the pridge as you shall see in a summer's day.
>
> (3.7.41–42, 53–54)

Seeing words just about sums it up! In the case of Pistol, physical bravery is conspicuous by its absence. This makes it only the more amusing that even he himself imagines that a person with no verbal dash at all, a Welshman who laboriously tries to interpret Pistol's own Marlovianisms like a grammar school pedagogue on an off day—

> By your patience, Anchient Pistol, Fortune is painted plind, with a muffler afore her eyes to signify to you that Fortune is plind,
>
> (3.7.25–27)

—will simply have no clout. Gower's comment on Pistol's rude disillusionment is very much part of Shakespeare's study of communication:

> You thought because he could not speak English in the native garb he could not therefore handle an English cudgel.
>
> (5.1.66–68)

Llewellyn is unusual in the play for packing *more* of a punch than his words suggest. Pistol's own last words are much more typical. Solitary and deflated, back in England he will still go on boasting, swearing that he got his "cudgelled scars" in the "Gallia wars" (5.1.78).

One of the play's key moments is when Pistol and Henry's paths finally cross. Henry is disguised still, and they exchange names:

> *Pistol:* What is thy name?
> *King:* Harry *le roi*.
> *Pistol:* Leroy? A Cornish name. . . .
>
> *Pistol:* My name is Pistol called.
> *King:* It sorts well with your fierceness.
>
> (4.1.46–49, 61–62)

Pistol's mastery of Romance philology is not what it might be, and he has no idea that the man in front of him may be more than he appears, not only by title but as a person who gets things done. Henry's etymological gloss is marginally better scholarship. But does he really think Pistol's name fits? Or would he already be unconvinced by Pistol's earlier threat against Nym—"Pistol's cock is up, and flashing fire will follow!" (2.1.43)?

Either way, the doggedness with which the parodic Pistol shadows the royal footsteps—a plot device which may have taught Dickens something of his trade[31]—draws particular attention to Henry's own pledges of future action. At one point the Boy describes Pistol as no more valorous than a roaring devil in an old play (4.4.56). The question is: Doesn't Henry sometimes come close to being just a roaring stage king?

After his victory at Agincourt, admittedly, he is hyperbolically modest: "be it death proclaimèd through our host / To boast of this" (4.8.106–7). Whereas at the outset of the play no less a person than the Archbishop of Canterbury had said that "miracles are ceased" (1.1.67), Henry will now accept no other explanation for his success than divine intervention. Llewellyn, who has obviously done a lion's share of the real fighting, slightly dents the royal sanctimoniousness, ruefully asking: "Is it not lawful, an't please your majesty, to tell how many is killed?" But Henry hardly budges—"Yes captain, but with this acknowledgement / That God fought for us"—and the Chorus later drums this in still harder: Henry, "free from vainness and self-glorious pride," as little like Pistol as possible, in other words, gives "full trophy, signal and ostent / Quite from himself to God" (4.8.109–10, 111–12; 5.0.20–22).

This saintliness has not been his usual tune, though, and could be just another example of his adopting a pose for the occasion. Before

Agincourt, he actually asks God's forgiveness for bragging to the French envoy (3.7.131–32), a pattern which began, we have seen, with his reaction to the tennis balls. The Chorus's opening speech encourages the audience to imagine

> . . . the warlike Harry, like himself,
> Assume the port of Mars, and at his heels
> (Leashed in, like hounds) . . . famine, sword and fire
> . . . [crouching] for employment.
>
> (Prologue 6–9)

What Henry usually threatens is to let the hounds off the leash, and with dreadful consequences which he is far from euphemizing away as collateral damage. Shakespeare traces the repetition and escalation of invective very closely. The Dauphin's practical joke, Henry tells the ambassadors, will mock

> . . . many a thousand widows
> . . . out of their dear husbands,
> Mock mothers from their sons, mock castles down,
> And some are yet ungotten and unborn
> That shall have cause to curse the Dauphin's scorn.
>
> (1.2.285–88)

Exeter's embassy to the French king resumes the theme:

> . . . take mercy
> On the poor souls for whom this hungry war
> Opens his vasty jaws. . . .
> [Think of] . . . the widow's tears, the orphan's cries
> The dead men's blood, the privèd maiden's groans.
>
> (2.4.104–8)

And in urging the defenders of Harfleur to yield up their city, Henry's promises of impending horrors are even more intense. The reasons maidens might have for groaning become more explicit, and are mentioned no fewer than three times:

> . . . the fleshed soldier, rough and hard of heart,
> In liberty of bloody hand shall range
> With conscience wide as hell, mowing like grass
> Your fair virgins . . . ;
>
> What is't to me . . .
> If your pure maidens fall into the hand

> Of hot and forcing violation?;
> . . . look to see
> The blind and bloody soldier with foul hand
> Defile the locks of your shrill-shrieking daughters.
> (3.3.11–14, 20–21, 34–35)

There is one scene in which Henry's threats are successful. This, though, is when they are veiled in his special brand of humor, and transferred from war-making to lovemaking, if "love" is the word. The interview with Katherine is less a question of courtship than continued conquest, Shakespeare now giving Henry, as Johnson remarked, "nearly such a character as he made him formerly ridicule in *Percy*."[32] This is Henry's way of preparing Katherine for her transfer from the rule of a father to the rule of a husband, who is going to take over her father's kingdom, and requires of her a son who will lead a new crusade. Very intelligently, Katherine asks whether it is possible that she should love the enemy of France. In reply, Henry mixes pleasantry and malice à la Uriah Heep: "I love France so well that I will not part with a village of it" (5.2.161). Similarly, when she finally says that she will have him if it pleases her father, he gives her a crash course in political necessity: "Nay, it will please him well, Kate; it shall please him, Kate" (5.2.225). In view of the deal Henry's diplomats are at this very moment forcing on Katherine's father, the semantic progression from "will" to "shall" probably carries a sinister echo of the old sense of "shall" as entailing obligation.[33] Certainly in Henry's subsequent bawdy conversation with her father and Burgundy, the memories of the seige of Harfleur are sufficiently strong—both the threats to penetrable virgins and the spectacle of the English army finally penetrating the central door or discovery-space in the tiring-house.

> *King:* . . . And you may, some of you, thank love for my blindness, who cannot see many a fair French city for the one fair French maid that stands in my way.
> *French King:* Yes, my lord, you see them perspectively, the cities turned into a maid, for they are all girdled with maiden walls that war hath never entered.
> (5.2.283–88)

Obviously, the threats Henry directed at Harfleur were quite enough to send a shiver down a father's spine. Not even the hippophile Bourbon wants to be a base pander, cap in hand, holding

> the chamber door
> Whilst by a slave, no gentler than my dog,
> His fairest daughter is contaminate.
>
> (5.5.15–17)

But when, exactly, does this self-knowledge dawn on him? Not until he and his fellow countrymen are already well on their way to losing the final battle. Up until the siege of Harfleur, Henry's threats have not made the slightest impression on the French, and perhaps not even then. The Governor gives a perfectly plausible reason for his surrender: the Dauphin has let him down. Oddly enough, Pistol will be far more visibly successful in scaring Le Fer, and Henry's very repetitiousness here may suggest an underlying desperation on his part, as if he simply cannot think of anything else to say or do. Certainly Shakespeare shows that the relationship between saying and doing has become very precarious. One of the things Henry does say is:

> . . . Therefore, you men of Harfleur,
> Take pity of your town and of your people
> Whiles yet my soldiers are in my command,
> Whiles yet the cool and temperate wind of grace
> O'erblows the filthy and contagious clouds
> Of heady murder, spoil and villainy.
>
> (3.4.27–32)

At one and the same time he uses images of future violence as a threat to his enemy, and confesses that his verbal hold on his men, his true forte, could come to an end. This in itself is perhaps the most terrifying of all his threats. Yet how can he contemplate such an access of verbal weakness without being terrified himself?

So how communicative a king is Henry overall? How much did his words change the world? And how, in consequence, will words be used *about* him afterward? Not least, what about Shakespeare's own words, and the way they have been taken?

Is Henry a better communicator than a woman would have been, for instance? Well, with men so boastful and power hungry and women so much their pawns and targets of battery, the only thing women can do is to try to calm things down and work for peace. At the beginning of the play, the Hostess, herself newly wrested from Nym by Pistol, pleads for what the audience may recognize as the

Falstaffian variant of valor: "Good Corporal Nym, show thy valour, and put up thy sword" (2.1.36–37). In the last scene, the Queen, too, knows her role. Going off with the diplomats who are to settle the final terms of the deal, she says

> Happily a woman's voice may do some good
> When articles too nicely urged be stood on.
>
> (5.2.93–94)

She also makes the scene's penultimate speech, in which she warns against any "divorce of . . . [the] incorporate league" between the two kingdoms (5.2.329). But how much power does her language harnass? The Chorus's final speech follows closely on her words, and is terse and very grim. Henry, "[t]his star of England," ruled "[s]mall time," and left a son, Henry VI, "Whose state so many had the managing / That they lost France and made his England bleed" (5.3.5–6, 11–12). The divorce came soon enough, and in the worst possible way.

But then again, is a woman's voice any more powerless than a man's? As a man, Henry can be a major player in his time's power politics, and may also better fulfill the corporal felicity condition which applies to threats. Yet apart from in his sexual conquest, his threats are not demonstrably productive. And although his more coadaptive rhetoric of encouragement gets his men to win his battles for him, that, it would seem, is that. The Chorus does not let the audience leave the theater thinking that the whole future course of history was changed.

So if Henry is remembered, one might almost ask why. Some of Shakespeare's most fascinating insights into the relation between *logos* and *pragma* are tied up with Henry's own thoughts on just this matter. In his threats, we have seen, he uses the prospect of future action as a way of trying to influence the present. But sometimes, his incitements go one step further still into the future, to a point from which later generations are *looking back* on deeds which at the time of his speaking have still not been performed.

At the beginning of the play, for instance, he characteristically boasts that he will "bend . . . [France] to our awe / Or break it all to pieces" so as to achieve a "large and ample empery." Then, however, he suddenly conjures up the possibility of failure, and in the following terms: he would be tombless; there would be no remembrance over his bones; his history would not "with full mouth / Speak freely of" his acts; his "grave / Like a Turkish mute shall have a tongueless mouth" (1.2.224–32). His verbalized prospect of such verbal desolation is what gives him a final adrenalin kick before receiving the French ambassadors.

Another example works rather differently. Just before Agincourt, when the chance of failure seems very real, Henry again verbalizes it in order to inspire forthcoming action, and again by taking that extra imaginative step into the future. This time, though, he can conceive of posterity glorifying failure itself:

> This story shall the good man teach his son . . .
>
> Dying like men, though buried in . . . [French] dunghills,
> They shall be famed, for there the sun shall greet them
> And draw their honours up to heaven.
>
> (4.3.56, 88–101).

Now if their dream of being remembered either for breaking France to pieces or for dying bravely inspires Henry and his fellow soldiers in their efforts now, then future generations, if such memories really do come about, will themselves be inspired by them. Such ancestral memories figured in the powerful words of persuasion used by Canterbury and Ely:

> Awake remembrance of these valiant dead,
> And with your puissant arm renew their feats.
>
> (1.2.115–16)

And this, we saw, is how Henry himself is remembered in the Olivier film.

Shakespeare's meta-theatricality extends to actually foregrounding the audience's own reception of the national memory of Henry. The Chorus conveys a clear sense of the story as a narrative tradition already existing in written form ("Vouchsafe to those that have not read the story / That I may prompt them" [5.0.1–2]), which the author of the present play has adapted ("with rough and all unable pen / Our bending author hath pursued the story" [5.3.1–2]). At the end of his first speech he entreats the audience:

> Admit me Chorus to this history,
> Who, Prologue-like, your humble patience pray,
> Gently to hear, kindly to judge our play.
>
> (Prologue 32–34)

Notice what the Chorus does *not* say: "Who, Prologue-like, your patience humbly pray." With the very best of manners, he is asking the audience to make a truly humble effort of empathy: not to exalt themselves over the story—not to engage in the solipsistic type of reading described by Terence Hawkes. Yet at the same time, he so constantly harps on the need for the spectators' own generous imagination, on the sheer despicableness of the things actually shown *coram populo* ("four or five most vile and ragged foils / Right ill disposed in brawl ridiculous" [4.0.50–51]), that the audience's disbelief, if it is not completely disarmed, may take a rather disrespectful tack. What if the "true things" of Agincourt were not really much better than the theatrical "mockeries" of them (4.0.54)? For the time being, the audience hears of Henry and his men's valor only from the Chorus himself, who so pointedly draws attention to his own powers of verbal deception. Spectators in the theater, like Llewellyn as he comes to know Pistol better, will perhaps get tired of having to "see" nothing but words all the time. Resisting the Chorus's appeal for empathy, they may even begin to suspect that Granpré—no less a part of Shakespeare's play than the Chorus, after all—comes closer to the mark:

> Description cannot suit itself in words
> To demonstrate the life of such a battle,
> In life so lifeless as it shows itself.
>
> (4.2.52–54)

Granpré is saying that no words are powerful enough to describe the utter powerlessness of the English army. Even the Chorus's own final speech not only contains all the usual apologies for "confining mighty men" in "little room," but brings about that crushing anticlimax after the Queen's final words (5.3.3). There is no covering up the short time span of Henry's empire. His end sounds almost as ignominious as the sight of Pistol slinking back to London with his "cudgelled scars." And the play's very last lines do not even make sense: "so many had the managing" of Henry VI's state

> That they lost France and made his England bleed,
> Which oft our stage hath shown—and for their sake,
> In your fair minds let this acceptance take.
>
> (5.3.12–14)

For *whose* sake? For the sake of the bunglers who lost France and made England bleed? For the sake of productions of earlier plays? Well, perhaps. But in that case, this is the Chorus's way of confessing that the "Muse of fire" he summoned at the beginning of the play (Prologue 1) has finally been extinguished. For a disaffected spectator, there may be more than a hint that the theatrical mockery of true things was not such a mockery after all. It may even have been a mite too flattering. On Shakespeare's showing, Henry was not a great practical handyman; his army was pathetic; and his *non nobis* humility is perhaps ingenuous after all. That the Dauphin did not relieve Harfleur, that the French made such a cock-up of Agincourt, was hardly Henry's doing.

Shakespeare knows that communication is always touch and go. Either his audience will empathize as he humanly deserves or they will not. But even if they do empathize, John Turner is right: their response will be mixed with criticism as well. In this play so centrally *about* communication, Shakespeare often shows characters going through the motions of philological interpretation—Henry and Pistol's onomastic speculations are part of this large pattern. Canterbury gets things off to a good start with his speech on Salic Law, which reads rather like some learned article on, say, the identity of the Eotenas in *Beowulf*. Other instances include Katherine's English lesson, and the Boy's translations of Le Fer for the benefit of Pistol. And in every case, Shakespeare draws the audience into the characters' philological efforts, highlighting, above all, the scope for both error and "dis-agreement." We are alerted to the fact that Canterbury's philology is itself a power of words, strongly underwritten by the church's temporal interests, and directed toward getting Henry off to battle. As a result, we cannot help wondering whether the scholarship is as unimpeachable as Henry says it has got to be. If we try to unravel it, we are probably nonplussed. During Katherine's French lesson, again, spectators ignorant of French may find themselves starting to learn the French words for finger, hand and so on, while Alice's pronunciation of English may make some members of the audience feel amusedly superior—and Katherine's imitation even more so. As for the Boy's glossings of Le Fer, one extraordinarily insightful passage highlights the sheer one-sidedness of Hawkes's notion of "meaning by":

> *[Le Fer] . . . je m'estime heureux que je suis tombé entre les mains d'un chevalier, je pense, le plus brave, vaillant, et très distingué seigneur d'Angleterre.*
> *Pistol:* Expound unto me, boy.
> *Boy:* . . . he esteems himself happy that he hath fallen into the hands of one (as he thinks) the most brave, valorous and thrice-worthy signieur of England.
>
> (4.4.43–50)

In "(as he thinks)," the genuine interpretation's inevitable interplay of criticism and empathy is definitively registered.

Shakespeare, we can therefore assume, knew the exact limits of his own words' power. He could do nothing to stop Laurence Olivier from leaving out almost seventeen hundred lines—including the hint that Canterbury has cooked the philology, Henry's appalling threats to Harfleur, and the concluding mention of his disastrous successor. He may even have calculated that, if some of the first spectators would admire Henry immensely, and admire Essex by association, others might be less than thoroughly convinced by the Chorus's panegyrics. He would certainly have realized that the Chorus's own meta-theatrical apologies were a bold artistic gamble. Either they would boost the power of poetry—his own power. Or they would backfire, in which case neither Henry nor Essex would seem quite so wonderful after all.

True, Henry's achievements, even on the least favorable view of them, gave "much more, and much more cause" to Londoners to turn out for him than could Essex's possible subjugation of Ireland. But perhaps Shakespeare hedged his bets. Perhaps he wasn't even sure what he thought himself. If Essex succeeds, all well and good, and *Henry V* gives ample pretext for patriotism. If Essex fails, look again, and you may find that *Henry V* is saying, "I told you so!" This would certainly help to account for the later swing from, say, Dowden's idealization of Henry the practical hero to Gerald Gould's indictment of Henry the cold-blooded, lying cynic.[34] The text as a whole, I mean, may be fundamentally ambivalent. Just because it is authored by a relatively autonomous and identifiable human being, it will not necessarily be completely intelligible and coherent—not more coherent than is humanly possible, anyway. Intellectual coherence, we should remember, does not always chime with real-world complexity, and may even be the result of a total misunderstanding. As Hawkes so well shows, there are things in Shakespeare's plays which resist empathy and baffle explanation. Shakespeare was a great enough writer to let the "the art and practic part of life" be the mistress of the "theoric" in a far less submissive sense than that intended by Canterbury. Words, he knew, cannot net everything in. If they could, communication would have come to an end long ago.

But even if his words give warrant for both Dowden and Gould's readings, Shakespeare, no less than Hawkes, would have recognized that readings are very much linked to their particular context, just like Canterbury's possibly tendentious interpretation of Salic Law. Dowden was writing in the age of empire-building. Gould was traumatized by the war that brought it to an end.

What, then, if Shakespeare could have seen Phelps's or Macready's or Kean's lavishly spectacular stagings, with their vast hordes of actors, their pageantry, their realistic medievalism—their attempt, in short, to make the Chorus's descriptions redundant? On the one hand, their emphasis on action and ceremony *coram populo* would certainly have registered with him. Oddly enough, this made the Victorian theater a bit like the Elizabethan theater as seen by Greenblatt. Shakespeare's own focus, I have suggested, was much more on the king's use of language. On the other hand, there was probably enough of the Chorus in him to have enjoyed his continuing appeal to the public imagination, and he would certainly have recognized later generations' right to adapt his words to their own ends, just as he himself left out the archers and the hedge of stakes. To the philological intelligence that produced the Boy's "(as he thinks)," the Victorians' combination of empathy and "disagreement" with his texts would have seemed quite inevitable. Indeed, the fidelities and infidelities of the entire tradition of reception would probably have struck him as just one more illustration of, respectively, the strength and the weakness of a human being's words.

Notes

This is a revised version of an essay which first appeared in *Neuphilologische Mitteilungen* 100 (1999): 535–63. Grateful acknowledgment is due to that journal's editors.

1. See, e.g., D. J. Palmer, *The Rise of English Studies: An Account of the Study of English Language and Literature from its Origins to the Making of the Oxford English School* (Oxford: Oxford University Press, 1965).

2. Konrad Ehlich, "On the historicity of politeness," in Richard J. Watts et al., eds., *Politeness in Language: Studies in its History, Theory and Practice* (Berlin: Mouton de Gruyter, 1992), 71–107; Roger D. Sell, "Literary texts and diachronic aspects of politeness," in Watts, *Politeness in Language*, 109–29; Roger D. Sell, "Postdisciplinary Philology: Culturally Relativist Pragmatics," in Francisco Fernández et al., eds., *English Historical Linguistics, 1992: Papers from the 7th International Conference on English Historical Linguistics.* (Amsterdam: Benjamins, 1994), 29–36; Andreas J. Jucker, ed., *Historical Pragmatics: Pragmatic Developments in the History of English* (Amsterdam: Benjamins, 1995).

3. Cf. Roger D. Sell, "Literary pragmatics and speech act theory of literature," in Světla Čmejrková et al., eds., *Writing vs Speaking: Language, Text, Discourse, Communication,* (Tübingen: Gunter Narr, 1994), 127–35, and *Literature as Communication: The Foundations of Mediating Criticism*, Pragmatics and Beyond, n.s., vol. 78 (Amsterdam: Benjamins, 2000), 29–75.

4. Roger D. Sell, *Literature as Communication,* and "A historical but nondeterminist pragmatics of literary communication," *Journal of Historical Pragmatics* 2 (2001): 1–32.

5. London: Oxford University Press. See also Willcock, "Shakespeare and Rhetoric," *Essays and Studies* 29 (1943): 50–61, "Shakespeare and Elizabethan

Rhetoric," *Shakespeare Survey* 7 (1954): 12–24, and "Language and Poetry in Shakespeare's Early Plays," *Proceedings of the British Academy* 40 (1954): 103–17.

6. See Jonathan Dollimore, "Introduction: Shakespeare, cultural materialism and the new historicism," in Jonathan Dollimore and Alan Sinfield, eds., *Political Shakespeare: New Essays in Cultural Materialism* (Manchester: Manchester University Press, 1985), 2–17.

7. Terence Hawkes, *That Shakespeherian Rag: Essays on a Critical Process* (London: Methuen, 1986), and *Meaning by Shakespeare* (London: Routledge, 1992).

8. Ferdinand de Saussure, *Course in General Linguistics* [1916] (London: Fontana, 1974), 14.

9. Claude Lévi-Strauss, "Overture to Le Cru et le Cuit" [1964], in Jacques Ehrmann, ed., *Structuralism* (Garden City, NY: Anchor-Doubleday, 1970), 31–55, esp. 46.

10. Raymond Tallis, *Enemies of Hope: A Critique of Contemporary Pessimism, Irrationalism, Anti-Humanism and Counter-Enlightenment* (Basingstoke: Macmillan, 1997), 228.

11. Jürgen Habermas, *Justification and Application: Remarks on Discourse Ethics* (Cambridge, Mass.: MIT Press, 1993).

12. Hawkes, *Meaning by Shakespeare*, 3.

13. Ibid., 7.

14. Ibid., 7–8.

15. Ibid., 6, italics mine.

16. Hawkes, *Shakespeherian Rag*, 27–50, 79–85.

17. John Turner, "Introduction," in Graham Holderness et al., eds., *Shakespeare: The Play of History* (Basingstoke: Macmillan, 1988), 1–9, esp. 5–6.

18. Harry M. Geduld, *Filmguide to "Henry V"* (Bloomington: University of Indiana Press, 1973), 48.

19. All quotations are from Andrew Gurr, ed., *King Henry V,* the New Cambridge Shakespeare edition (Cambridge: Cambridge University Press, 1992), to which parenthetical act, scene and line references are given.

20. Gurr, *Henry V*, 36.

21. Edward Dowden, extract from his *Shakespeare: His Mind and Art* [1875], in Michael Quinn, ed., *Shakespeare: Henry V: A Casebook* (London: Macmillan, 1969), 42–47, Dowden's italics.

22. Gary Taylor, *Henry V,* the Oxford Shakespeare edition (Oxford: Clarendon Press, 1982), 65.

23. Cf. Gurr, *Henry V*, 177.

24. Stephen Greenblatt, "Invisible bullets: Renaissance authority and its subversion, *Henry IV* [*sic*] and *Henry V*," in Dollimore and Sinfield, *Political Shakespeare*, 18–47, esp. 44. Greenblatt annotates the last sentence of the passage quoted here with a reference to J. E. Neale, *Elizabeth I and her Parliaments, 1584-1601*. 2 vols (London: Cape, 1965), 2: 119.

25. J. H. Walter, *King Henry V,* the Arden edition (London: Methuen, 1954), xv.

26. The main advantage of Pope's arrangement is usually said to be that it allows the Chorus's speech to provide a direct run-in to act 2, scene 2, set in Southampton. The Chorus announces Henry's arrival in Southampton, but act 2, scene 1 is still set in London. See Gurr, *Henry V*, 90.

27. Alexander Leggatt, *English Drama: Shakespeare to the Restoration, 1590-1660* (London: Longman, 1988), 44.

28. J. L. Austin, *How To Do Things With Words* (Oxford: Clarendon Press, 1962).

29. John Searle, *Speech Acts: An Essay in the Philosophy of Language* (Cambridge: Cambridge University Press, 1969).

30. Gary Taylor, *Henry V*, 295.

31. As when he has David Copperfield shadowed by Uriah Heep, for instance. See Roger D. Sell, *Mediating Criticism: Literary Education Humanized* (Amsterdam: Benjamins, 2001), 281–86.

32. Samuel Johnson, extracts from his Shakespeare criticism [1765], in Quinn, *Shakespeare: Henry V,* 32–34.

33. Cf. Norman Blake, *The Language of Shakespeare* (Basingstoke: Macmillan, 1989), 93–94.

34. Gerald Gould, "Irony and Satire in Henry V" [1919], in Quinn, *Shakespeare: Henry V*, 82–94.

Notes on Metrical and Deictical Problems in Shakespeare Translation

CLAS ZILLIACUS

THE TOPIC OF THIS ESSAY IS THE PURSUIT OF EQUIVALENCE IN SHAKESPEARE translation. I propose to look at a few concrete problems involving metrics and deictics respectively, my point being that in theater translation no element is small enough to be of no consequence for the pragmatics of the stage. All of them involve decision making; at least they will emerge as having done so. And even if one tries to scrap the concept of equivalence for the less emphatic one of adequacy, the pursuit remains.

My field of choice is Shakespeare in Swedish, but I trust that the problem areas which I shall be focusing on are common to most Germanic languages. These are all basically amenable to blank verse: they are ready, if not uniformly willing, to play by the rules of that particular game. It seems to me that the recent upsurge of new Swedish translations—caused, I think, by box office considerations and directors' vanity as much as by an acute demand for actable versions—has brought a kind of normalization pressure to bear on Shakespeare: iambic pentameters should be very recognizably just that, an even five-foot measure. That is how a translator documents his proficiency. The result is that Swedish Shakespeare invariably sounds like early Shakespeare.

There are, however, licenses subject to laws. Jiří Levý, in his theory of literary translation, pairs off three basic opposites.[1] One is syntactical (end-stopped as opposed to run-on), two are metrical (iambic versus dactylic line beginnings, and masculine versus feminine endings). Beyond these confines of alternatives, translators find that no recognition of their professional skill is forthcoming, even if the original material may have been much craggier. But within the set of legitimate options all six are considered to be freely available.

The main difference between English and Swedish blank verse lies in the latter's frequent hypercatalectic, hendecasyllabic, weak-stress endings. There are various reasons for these supernumeraries. Swedish prosody calls for them: trochaic verbs and verb forms abound; the definite article is suffixed to the noun. Feminine verse endings were more reminiscent of the alexandrine traditionally used in Swedish; hence it was easy to consider them more mellifluous than decasyllabics, which were perceived as curt and chopped off.

Translators into Swedish, then, seem to have regarded the choice between masculine and feminine endings as a nondistinctive issue. It often is. At times it does matter, and not just because a consistent use of the latter might make a play ten percent longer, but rather because it may end up having built an accumulative effect. In that case the resonance of the lines will counteract or deflate what the lines were constructed to convey.

I shall pick an instance from *The Taming of the Shrew*. It is a passage which exposes the technical terms of masculine and feminine as something rather more than that. Bianca's suitors have addressed the question of what a vixen Katherina is. Petruchio counters with a very macho exposition of what he has been up to in his days. It is an enumeration of feats devised to persuade, verbally and phonically, by sheer force. Petruchio's purpose is no other than to woo the shrew:

> Why came I hither but to that intent?
> Think you a little din can daunt mine ears?
> Have I not in my time heard lions roar?
> Have I not heard the sea, puff'd up with winds,
> Rage like an angry boar chafed with sweat?
> Have I not heard great ordnance in the field,
> And heaven's artillery thunder in the skies?
> Have I not in a pitched battle heard
> Loud 'larums, neighing steeds, and trumpets' clang?
> And do you tell me of a woman's tongue,
> That gives not half so great a blow to hear
> As will a chestnut in a farmer's fire?
> Tush, tush, fear boys with bugs![2]

(1.2)

Petruchio's tirade runs for thirteen lines, and its medium is a palpable part of its message. The lines all have emphatic endings; he whips them into place, as he will Katherina. A glance at the corpus of Swedish translations indicates that they dilute at least one-third or even half of the lines by feminine endings. Unstressed syllables in the wrong place, particularly if they are consistently applied, produce an elegiac cadence. They eat away at the rhetoric, and proceed by gnawing at semantic content. (Male and other chauvinisms are curiously alike in this respect. Kornei Chukovsky, the Russian advocate of translation as a high art, found one of his keys to Kipling in an emphasis on jingoistic masculine line endings.)[3]

This is to say that, in the last analysis, adequacy in verse translation for the theater cannot be achieved by checking the sum total of solutions. It has to be got at in each specific case if it is to be found where needed. The repertoire of "legitimate" solutions in blank verse translation is not an abstract set. All solutions have to be made in situ; there is no line, whether verse or prose, that is not to be carried by a voice, uttered. That goes for the strictly metrical pair of opposites, masculine versus double endings; it applies in equal measure to the syntactical pair of end-stopped versus run-on lines.

Shakespeare is commonly credited with having broken the confines of the line unit: he expanded the set of acceptable strategies to the point where non-enjambment came to be recognized as a solution on a par with the run-on line. Both are of the game; both are audible, as devices or minus-devices. There is a celebrated passage in *As You Like It* which is, by a daringly duplex maneuver, an instance of both. I have, for purposes of clarity, slashed Jaques's tirade on the ages of man into acts, as he has.

All the world's a stage,
And all the men and women merely players.
They have their exits and their entrances,
And one man in his time plays many parts,
His acts being seven ages. / At first the infant,
Mewling and puking in the nurse's arms. /
Then, the whining school-boy with his satchel
And shining morning face, creeping like snail
Unwillingly to school. / And then the lover,
Sighing like furnace, with a woeful ballad
Made to his mistress' eyebrow. / Then, a soldier,
Full of strange oaths, and bearded like the pard,
Jealous in honour, sudden, and quick in quarrel,
Seeking the bubble reputation
Even in the cannon's mouth. / And then, the justice,
In fair round belly, with good capon lin'd,
With eyes severe, and beard of formal cut,
Full of wise saws, and modern instances,
And so he plays his part. / The sixth age shifts
Into the lean and slipper'd pantaloon,

With spectacles on nose, and pouch on side,
His youthful hose well sav'd, a world too wide
For his shrunk shank, and his big manly voice,
Turning again toward childish treble, pipes
And whistles in his sound. / Last scene of all,
That ends this strange eventful history,
Is second childishness and mere oblivion,
Sans teeth, sans eyes, sans taste, sans everything.

(2.7)

There is very little in this speech that insists on syntactical completion when the line is up. The dynamics of it are found elsewhere, in the movement from one line to the next. There are seven acts, that is, six cuts, and they cue each other as filmically as Shakespeare's scene changes generally do. Only one act, the first, ends where a line ends, in the infant's "nurse's arms." All the others begin within lines.

Shakespeare translators as a rule are sensitive to enjambment but this kind of end-stopping in mid-line, a kind of monological stichomythia, seems easier to overlook. The most recent Swedish translation of *As You Like It*, for instance, portions out the last four ages in end-stopped chunks, and the flow of acts is weakened in the process. The overall end-stoppedness of the lines in Jaques's tirade provides for a shift of focus to the in-stoppedness of the ages they depict. Much like my previous example of hypercatalectics in *The Taming of the Shrew,* this is no merely formal matter. Life, according to Jaques, is over and done with before we know it. Our ages cue each other at a rapid pace. Life is no pompous procession; it is a relay race.

Deictics, with the present surge of interest in the pragmatics of verbal interaction on the stage, is a very active field of research. I wish to take a quick look at a narrow sector of it of it, namely, the use of the second person singular, with specific reference to *Hamlet.* I shall use my example as a case for doggedly verbatim translation. The idea is not even mine: it has been put to the test by Benno Besson, the Swiss-born director, in translations commissioned for his German, French, Swedish and Finnish productions of the play. (I was involved in the making of the Swedish version; hence my loyalty.)[4]

A great deal of printer's ink has been spilled on the difference between *you* and *thou* in Elizabethan English. Most of it has been spilled in English, which goes to show that the feeling for this extinct distinction has gone numb. E. A. Abbott, providing the bard with a grammar in 1869, tried to make clear what *thou* stood for: it was "the pronoun of (1) affection towards friends, (2) good-humoured superiority to servants, and (3) contempt or anger to strangers. It had, however, already fallen somewhat into disuse, and, being regarded as archaic, was naturally adopted (4) in the higher poetic style and solemn prayer."[5] After a wealth of examples, many of which give instances of pronoun shifts in mid-speech, Abbott concludes: "In almost all cases where *thou* and *you* appear at first sight indiscriminately used, further considerations show some change of thought, or some influence of euphony sufficient to account for the change of pronoun." Shakespeare's usage in fact indicates that these wordlets are much more than mere stand-ins for nouns. They are deictic markers that alter the dynamics of the discourse. They recharge the relationships between the *dramatis personae,* and in so doing become part of the action.

How is the *you/thou* problem to be tackled in translation? In Swedish the distinction is extant. Swedish pragmatics, however, knows few of the nuances discussed by Abbott, and certainly does not know how to mix the two or how to exchange one for the other profitably: vacillation creates anomie, unease. One option would be to decide once and for all upon the pronominal level on which a certain character confronts another, and to consider that what is lost in the process is dispensable. This is the way Swedish translators tend to go about it. There seems to be a fairly strong preference for *du*. This solution tends to inform court dramas such as *Hamlet* with a kind of homely intimacy that forestalls any sense of things capital, such as heads, being at issue. Another possibility would be to take care of the source-text nuance by other, indirect means; but the verse rarely parts with the syllables necessary for such detours. Alternatively, one could decide that *you* is *ni* and *thou* is *du*, literally and intransigently. This has been the solution opted for in the translation made for Besson's *Hamlet*. I venture to suggest that it has proved its viability on the stage, even if it does look confusing on the page.

The Elizabethan manner of oscillating between *you* and *thou* is, among other things, a way of keeping uncertainty alive. The characters enter into relations with each other which are unstable; their status may be revoked, altered, up- or downgraded. Characters are built by being maneuvered into relations; thus they are, in part, constituted by the deictics they use, or are made objects of.

I may be overstretching my point but I seem to have noticed when reading Swedish versions of *Hamlet* that the text and what takes place in it is lulled into a false sense of security by making these pronominal deictics unequivocal instead of using the gamut. I seem, moreover, to espy greater dangers ahead. By affixing an unvarying mode of address—for example, opting for *du* when Hamlet talks to Horatio; this is the regular Swedish solution—the relationship freezes into a *donné,* the dialectics are lost. Horatio becomes "friend to Hamlet," as he is usually characterized in the list of *dramatis personae.* There can be little doubt that Horatio is, has become, friend to Hamlet when the play is over. But this is no established fact when the two first meet. The building of this friendship, the whys and wherefores and the context of its coming about, are an integral part of what happens in *Hamlet.* It is conveyed on many levels, one of them being deictics. Hamlet first says *you* to Horatio but he dies saying *thou.* The change to *thou* in this case is an audible, one might say dramatic, nonoccurrence of *you.* But it is audible only if the pronominal pair has been taken over into the target text.

Notes

This essay was first printed in a slightly different form in Bo Göranzon and Magnus Florin, eds., *Dialogue and Technology: Art and Knowledge* (London: Springer-Verlag, 1991). It is reproduced here with the permission of the editors and publisher.

1. Jiří Levý, *Die literarische Übersetzung: Theorie einer Kunstgattung*, trans. Walter Schamschula (Frankfurt: Athenäum, 1969), 258ff.
2. Quotations from plays follow the Arden edition throughout.
3. Lauren G. Leighton, trans. and ed., "The translator's introduction" in *The Art of Translation: Kornei Chukovsky's "A High Art"* (Knoxville: University of Tennessee Press, 1984), xxii.
4. *Den tragiska berättelsen om Hamlet, prins av Danmark,* trans. and postscript by Clas Zilliacus (Helsingfors: Schildts, 1983).
5. E. A. Abbott, *A Shakespearian Grammar* (London: Macmillan, 1929), 153f.

Observations on Georg Brandes's Contribution to the Study of Shakespeare

NIELS B. HANSEN

> It is one of the minor consolations which a patriotic Briton may justly feel, that Shakespearian criticism is no longer made in Germany. For years there was a prevalent impression that the Elizabethan dramatist, neglected by his own countrymen, had been practically re-discovered by Teutonic commentators.

THUS BEGINS A BOOK REVIEW BY W. L. COURTNEY WHICH APPEARED IN *The Daily Telegraph* on Wednesday, February 23, 1898. The occasion was the publication in English of Georg Brandes's *William Shakespeare, A Critical Study,* a large work in two volumes running to a total of some eight hundred pages. After a longish and rather biased description of "your Shakespearian scholar, when bred in a Teutonic school," the review continues:

> Dr. Georg Brandes, of Copenhagen, is no mere German scholar. We know that he has devoted a life-time to the study of English literature, and has understood with rare critical insight the extraordinary combination of antagonistic elements which goes to make up our character. . . . When Dr. Georg Brandes writes about Shakespeare he seems to understand better than any foreign commentator of recent times how all these discordant trains of thought and feeling were united in our great representative poet.

The reviewer has reservations about the biographical and historical interpretation of Shakespeare's plays, which is also Brandes's approach in this book, but even so the review is a highly appreciative tribute to the Danish critic's insight and the tact with which he applies the method.

William Shakespeare, A Critical Study had appeared simultaneously in Danish and German two years earlier, in 1896. The English translation was widely noted in newspapers and scholarly journals on both sides of the Atlantic. It was acclaimed as a major work of criticism, but also frequently subjected to strictures for its imaginative and sometimes rather fanciful attempts to construct the mind of the bard on the basis of his plays and poems.

In this article I shall discuss Brandes's position in relation to English and Continental Shakespeare studies toward the end of the nineteenth century, explain and comment on the ideas and procedures in his book on Shakespeare, and assess his contribution to the study of Shakespeare, at the time and later in the twentieth century.

Toward the end of the nineteenth century the Danish literary critic Georg Brandes had acquired a solid reputation, not only in his home country but also outside Denmark, largely in German-speaking countries. Born in Copenhagen in 1842, he graduated from Copenhagen University in 1864 and soon after went to France to study. On his return he earned his doctor's degree for a thesis on Taine (1870), and the major French critics of the day, Taine and Sainte-Beuve, exerted a considerable influence on Brandes's ideas and procedures. The following year he began to give the series of lectures which was to become his first major opus and his claim to international recognition, *Main Currents in Nineteenth Century Literature.* In spite of his obvious qualifications he was unable to obtain a post at the University of Copenhagen, and from 1877–83 he lived and worked in Germany. Back in Denmark he began lecturing on Shakespeare in the early nineties, and in 1896 his large book in three volumes on Shakespeare was ready for publication in Danish and German. An English translation in two volumes followed in 1898, *William Shakespeare: A Critical Study,* frequently reprinted in England well into the 1920s and in the United States long after that, the last reprint appearing in 1963.[1] Volume 4 of *Main Currents* had dealt with nineteenth-century English literature (first published in English in 1905 as *Naturalism in England).* Brandes's book on Disraeli (1878) had been published in England in 1880 (*Lord Beaconsfield, A Study),* but contrary to what Courtney claims in the section of his review quoted above, English literature had not been central to Brandes's interests, though he had written a fine essay on *Henry IV* in his youth. His radical outlook may have attracted him to the Renaissance period and his admiration for men of genius at this point in his career to the life and works of William Shakespeare.

Brandes had some literary contacts in Britain (for example, Edmund Gosse). He had spent about a month in England in 1895, working at the British Museum and also visiting Stratford-upon-Avon, but his reading and his critical orientation were predominantly Continental. Paul V. Rubow, sometime professor of comparative literature at the University of Copenhagen, has written a book in Danish, *Georg Brandes' Briller*[2] which explores the shaping of Brandes's critical orientation. Writing about Brandes's study of Shakespeare from his early student days, Rubow remarks that he depended on German translations along with the originals, and that he used the commentaries of German scholars. Rubow singles out the works of Ulrici and Gervinus as particularly influential in this early period. A more pervasive influence on his much later Shakespeare project was Hippolyte Taine, whose *Histoire de la littérature anglaise* Brandes knew well before he went to Paris. Taine influenced his general approach to the study of literature,[3] but there are also traces of direct, if not always acknowledged, indebtedness to Taine in Brandes's *William Shakespeare,* for instance the perceptive observation that when Hamlet complains about "the oppressor's wrong, the proud man's contumely," and so on, this is felt from below upward, so that the words are "improbable, almost impossible in the mouth of the Prince" (vol. 2:28).

Much of the scholarship and criticism that Brandes drew upon when working on his *William Shakespeare* was German; the majority of works he refers to in his notes are by German scholars, especially for comments on Shakespeare (as opposed to works on the historical context). This is not surprising, as German scholars had taken a lead in the study of Shakespeare during the nineteenth century, as a brief glance at Augustus Ralli's *History of Shakespearian Criticism* will make clear. In addition to Ulrici and Gervinus, Brandes shows familiarity with many other, more recent German critics such as Werder, Delius, Kreyssig, and Elze, even if painstaking and pedantic annotation was never Brandes's strongest point. Many of these works were translated into English in the 1880s and 1890s, but at the same time important work began to appear in England in the last quarter of the century. When Furnivall founded "The New Shakspere Society" in 1873, it was his hope and ambition to create a context for a book "which deals in any worthy manner with Shakspere as a whole." Two years later such a book appeared, Edward Dowden's *Shakspere: A Critical Study of his Mind and Art*. From time to time Brandes refers to and draws upon Dowden's work, but he does not explicitly acknowledge that it was a work that shared important assumptions and ambitions with Brandes's approach. Other contemporary scholars both on the Continent and in Britain aimed at a factual account of Shakespeare's life and works (for example, the Swedish scholar Henrik Schück, whose *William Shakspere: hans lif och värksamhet* appeared in 1883–84, and Sidney Lee in his *Life of William Shakespeare* [1898]), but Brandes and Dowden alike were happy to speculate on and construct the mind of the great man on the basis of his works. In the opening chapter of his *Shakspere* Dowden writes that "in such a study as this we endeavour to pass through the creation of the artist to the mind of the creator," and at the outset of Brandes's great project he premises his treatment of his subject in the following words: "Ranging the plays in their probable order of production, and reviewing the poet's life-work as a whole, he [the reader] feels constrained to form for himself some image of the spiritual experience of which it is the expression."[4] Brandes returns to this programmatic statement at the very end of his work, concluding that:

> It is the author's opinion that, given the possession of forty-five important works by any man, it is entirely our own fault if we know nothing whatever about him. The poet has incorporated his whole individuality in these writings, and there, if we can read aright, we shall find him.[5]

The kind of psychobiography which both these two talented critics practiced may be more or less outdated and discredited today, but undoubtedly they have both had a strong and long-lasting influence on the general climate of opinion even if their importance in the sphere of Shakespearean scholarship was never substantial. As their aims were comparable, it is illuminating to compare the results of their endeavors. The occasionally striking differences in their conclusions highlight the limitations of their procedures.

Most critics, whether of the nineteenth or the twentieth century, tend to find confirmation of what they look for, and Brandes is no exception. The case of Brandes is, however, exceptional in that the Shakespeare he looked for and found in the texts was a personality who in many ways reflected Brandes's concept of himself. In constructing the psychobiography of the Renaissance genius, he was in a sense working in an autobiographical vein, or at least engaged in a process of identification—a poetic rather than a scientific project. There is evidence that he was fully aware of this himself, for instance when he writes in a letter that he has written "a book about old Shakespeare, which hopefully resembles him, but which, I am afraid, resembles myself quite as fully."[6] Pursuing this idea Georg Brandes's most recent Danish biographer, Jørgen Knudsen, has wittily created a composite picture of a fictional character he calls

Branspeare, based on his intimate knowledge of Brandes and a mosaic of details from the latter's *William Shakespeare.* It is Branspeare who has written with so much empathy about Hamlet, and who has felt that "something is rotten in the state of Denmark."[7]

The very personal motives that guided Brandes in his reconstruction of Shakespeare's mind added to his project an implicit and indeed sometimes quite explicit identification with the subject of his investigation, the great creative genius as well as the characters who were the products of this genius, particularly the tortured minds of his tragic protagonists. It was above all Hamlet, the melancholy Dane, the outsider fighting against the masters of a powerful system, who appealed to Brandes's imagination. The eight chapters on *Hamlet* take up more pages than the combined chapters on *Macbeth, Othello,* and *King Lear.* A very striking example of Brandes's subjective approach occurs in the concluding paragraph of chapter 16 in "Book Second," in which Hamlet's relationship to Ophelia is compared to Faust's relation to Gretchen. This in its turn leads to a comparison of Hamlet and Faust, the latter described as the highest poetic expression of modern humanity. Brandes concludes:

> But none the less dear to us art thou, O Hamlet! and none the less valued and understood by the men of to-day. We love thee like a brother. Thy melancholy is ours, thy wrath is ours, thy contemptuous wit avenges us on those who fill the earth with their empty noise and are its masters. We know the depth of thy suffering when wrong and hypocrisy triumph, and oh! thy still deeper suffering on feeling that the nerve in thee is severed which should lead from thought to victorious action. To us, too, the voices of the mighty dead have spoken from the under-world. We, too, have seen our mother wrap the purple robe of power round the murderer of "the majesty of buried Denmark." We, too, have been betrayed by the friends of our youth; for us, too, have swords been dipped in poison. How well do we know that graveyard mood in which disgust and sorrow for all earthly things seize upon the soul. The breath from open graves has set us, too, dreaming with a skull in our hands![8]

The highstrung and highly personal note in this quotation may be characteristic of the best and the worst in Brandes's critical manner, but seen in isolation it gives a somewhat distorted and unfair impression of what his book has to offer. His sixty-page section on *Hamlet* is a wide-ranging and factual discussion drawing on many sources. It deals with the sources of the play, its literary antecedents and indebtedness to contemporary writers (Bruno, Montaigne), and its use of (Danish) local color. Brandes also speculates on the inspiration which Shakespeare may possibly have drawn from contemporary historical characters and events, but is careful to distance himself from crude and naive insistence on topical references. That is not, claims Brandes, how works of imagination come into existence. A play like *Hamlet* "has its origin in an overmastering sensation in the poet's soul, and then, in the process of growth, assimilates certain impressions from without."[9]

Brandes also addresses himself to the question of *Hamlet*'s influence on European literature and writes briefly about the dramatic aspects of the play, but his analysis tends to revert quickly to what interests him most, the psychology of the protagonist. In this area Brandes feels most at home and ready to hold his own in the contemporary critical debate. In this area his talents, his insight and literary acuity, his wide reading, and inspired and inspiring style are displayed most convincingly for the present-day reader. It is also in this area that his particular project finds expression: the endeavor to trace the personality and even the personal life of the writer in his works. The first Hamlet chapter begins, significantly, by reminding us that in 1601 Shakespeare lost his father. More importantly, in the short chapter 13 called "The personal element in *Hamlet*" Brandes makes the point very clearly and strongly that "in giving expression to Hamlet's spiritual life he was enabled quite naturally to pour forth all that during the recent years had filled his heart and seethed in his brain."

Hamlet's outward fortunes were, of course, different from his own, but even so he had lived through all of Hamlet's experience. The particular events were only "symptoms in the young man's eyes of the worthlessness of human nature and the injustice of life," of the kind of crisis Shakespeare himself had recently undergone.

> He merged himself in Hamlet; he felt as Hamlet did; he now and then so mingled their identities that, in placing his own weightiest thoughts in Hamlet's mouth, as in the famous "To be or not to be" soliloquy, he made him think, not as a prince, but as a subject, with all the passionate bitterness of one who sees brutality and stupidity lording it in high places.[10]

He goes on to quote the lines about "the oppressor's wrong, the proud man's contumely. . . . the law's delay, The insolence of office," which I referred to above, and to relate the thoughts contained in them to the bitter feelings and thoughts to which Shakespeare had recently given expression "in his own name" in Sonnet 66.

Hamlet was the fictional creation in whose makeup Shakespeare more than anywhere else gave voice to his own ambitions and frustrations. But he was by no means the only one. Writing about Richard III, a much simpler and more primitive character, Brandes speculates on Shakespeare's creative technique from an artistic rather than a personal viewpoint:

> Into this character Shakespeare transforms himself in imagination. It is the mark of the dramatic poet to be always able to get out of his own skin and into another's . . . How did he set about it? Exactly as we do when we strive to understand another personality; for example, Shakespeare himself. He imagines himself into him.[11]

Likewise we hear of Mark Antony that "There was a crevice in this antique figure through which Shakespeare's soul could creep in" (2:147), only in this case there was genuine identification, even if less so than with Hamlet. As suggested in the quotation about Richard III, this imaginative "creeping into" a character is a skill that the dramatist shares with the critic, or at any rate with Brandes. In his *Levned* (Autobiography) he explains how he previously strongly rejected the idea of writing his own life:

> It was in a very different way I then felt the urge to display my inner life, a way I had been using for many years, through the description of an impressive personality I could break into from some angle in order to immerse myself in this man. A condition of success was that this personality in some respect corresponded to the stage of my own development at the time and was spacious enough for me to move in.[12]

This was unquestionably a strong motive for Brandes to write his study of Shakespeare in the 1890s. We also learn from his *Levned* (3:386) that what attracted him to Shakespeare was the urge to describe the period of intense bitterness in his mind, rather than his finest and most famous dramas: "Had Shakespeare not written *Troilus and Cressida, Coriolanus,* and *Timon of Athens* he would not have fascinated me so absolutely that I had to bury myself in him" (my translation). This special, personal urge has left its very strong mark in the focus and emphasis given to these plays in Brandes's psychobiographical study of the life and works of William Shakespeare, and should by no means be ignored in a presentation of the critic and his project.

To assess Brandes's discussion of these plays, one must approach it within the context of his project as a whole. "Ranging the plays in their probable order of production and reviewing the poet's life work as a whole" was the programmatic statement with which Brandes opened his study of Shakespeare, so obviously a plausible chronology was highly important for his argument. It is not an issue he discusses much. Naturally he relied in the main on the comprehensive efforts to date and order chronologically Shakespeare's plays by metrical tests and other means which had occupied Shakespearean scholarship on both sides of the Channel so much in the second half of the nineteenth century. On the whole his datings are fairly orthodox, based on the existing consensus, and his deviations from it are not terribly significant. However, when it suits his argument he does not hesitate to adopt a controversial chronological order, the most striking example of this being his placing *Troilus and Cressida* in a group with *Coriolanus* and *Timon of Athens*, written after *Antony and Cleopatra.*

By and large the traditional division of Shakespeare's dramatic career into phases is reflected in the structure Brandes has imposed on his opus with a division of the material into three "Books." "Book First" traces Shakespeare's development from his Stratford years to the publication of *Twelfth Night,* in thirty chapters. The intended pattern is very clear in the description of the evolution not only of his dramatic skills but also of the overall mood in the plays as a reflection of a personal development. Brandes outlines a curve that climaxes in the chapters on *As You Like It* and *Twelfth Night*, entitled respectively, "The Interval of Serenity" and "Consummate Spiritual Harmony," leading to a concluding chapter that looks ahead to a period of increasing gloom: melancholy, pessimism, misanthropy, briefly traced in the sequence of plays from *Julius Caesar* to *Coriolanus.*

"Book Second" moves through the new decade, tracing Shakespeare's personal development first as reflected in the Sonnets (which Brandes dates at about 1601) and then in the succession of dark comedies and the major tragedies, ending with *Antony and Cleopatra*—"the picture of a world-catastrophe." The book begins by contrasting the public mood in Elizabeth's early years with the tiredness and gloom that marked the end of her reign, and moves on to the following opening of chapter 5:

> The turning-point in Shakespeare's prevailing mood must be placed in or about the year 1601. We naturally looked for one source of his henceforth deepening melancholy in outward events, in the political drama which in that year reached its crisis and catastrophe; but it is still more imperative that we should look into his private and personal experiences for the ultimate cause of the revolution in his soul. We must therefore inquire what light his works throw upon his private circumstances and state of mind during this fateful year.[13]

The gloom had not, however, reached its climax with *King Lear* and *Antony and Cleopatra*. The story Brandes has to tell falls into three acts, but they do not quite coincide with the three "Books." Only halfway through Book Third, in chapter 14 (out of a total of twenty-seven), does Brandes reach Shakespeare's "convalescence" and "transformation." The preceding chapters deal with conditions at the court of King James and the three plays that in accordance with Brandes's overview are placed together at this point in Shakespeare's career: *Troilus and Cressida, Coriolanus,* and *Timon of Athens*. Chapter 1 in this book, which sets the keynote for this sequence, is called "Discord and Scorn" and begins with these words:

> Out of tune—out of tune!
>
> Out of tune the instrument whereon so many enthralling melodies had been played—glad and gay, plaintive or resentful, full of love and full of sorrow. Out of tune the mind which had felt so keenly, thought so deeply, spoken so temperately, and stood so firmly 'midst passion's whirlpool, storm, and whirlwind.' His life's philosophy has become a disgust of life, his melancholy seeks the darkest side of all things, his mirth is grown to bitter scorn, and his wit is without shame.[14]

Though desirous to find an explanation of this change of mood in Shakespeare's life, Brandes finds himself unable to penetrate the darkness and find its cause. The prevailing disdain and cynicism toward life in general and women in particular seems, though, to have been growing on Shakespeare for some time. The overwhelming misogyny of *Troilus and Cressida* may well be the final stage in a development that can be traced back through the character of Cleopatra to the Dark Lady of the sonnets, a development from worship and celebration, complaint and grief, through the memory of enchantment to disillusionment and a sense of degradation to a "final and supreme relief in the outburst 'What a farce'!" which is in itself the germ of *Troilus and Cressida* (2:197).

So before discussing the misogyny and misanthropy that Brandes insists on in this phase in Shakespeare's life, we should look briefly at his observations on the sonnets as the potentially most personal and revealing expression of the poet, where Shakespeare—as Brandes suggested in the quotation about the personal note in "to be or not be"—speaks "in his own name." It is true that at the outset of his project he had expressed reservations about the use of the sonnets as autobiographical documents, but even so they are described in Book Second, chapter 5 as a work that enables us to look into his inmost soul.

Brandes writes at some length concerning the various theories about biographical evidence based on the Dedication that contemporary scholarship had made available, and he is prepared to follow Dowden, Tyler, and other specialists in identifying W. H. as Pembroke and the Dark Lady as Mary Fitton. When, however, *William Shakespeare* was reprinted a few years later in Brandes's *Samlede Skrifter* ("Collected Works," 1899 ff.), new evidence forced him to drop his theory about Mary Fitton, and more importantly to revise his identification of W. H. in the light of material published by Sidney Lee in his 1898 edition of *A Life of William Shakespeare.* It is not so much the identity of W. H. (Southampton rather than Pembroke) or the revised dating of the poems in the cycle that concerns Brandes as Lee's insistence, supported by other weighty scholars (Delius, Elze, Schück), that the sonnet genre is so full of conventions that these poems have no value as personal, biographical evidence. This strikes at the roots of Brandes's entire project. He is thus called upon to insist that although imitation is a factor in all poetic creation, past and present, and no sensible critic would accept lyric poems as autobiographical in a crude sense, even so first-rate art is bred from life, not from books; and lyric poetry in particular, where the poet speaks in his own name, must have its roots in personal experience, as we can see so clearly from the example of Goethe and other modern poets:

> He who works from the by no means fantastic assumption that there is a connection between Shakespeare's life and his life's work will thus remain unaffected by the numerous attempts to deny his sonnets all value as autobiographical material because of their frequent use of convention and imitation.[15]

What the sonnets add to the picture of the poet's personality that we can piece together from his plays is

> an emotional nature with a passionate bent towards self-surrender in love and idolatry, and with a corresponding, though less excessive yearning to be loved. We also learn from the Sonnets to what a degree Shakespeare was oppressed and tormented by his sense of the contempt in which the actor's calling was held. (1:347)

This second point in particular becomes a recurrent feature in the portrait of Shakespeare that Brandes goes on to develop toward a misanthropic climax in his trilogy of disdain for women, mobs, and man in general: *Troilus and Cressida, Coriolanus,* and *Timon of Athens.* Next to *Hamlet, Troilus* is the play Brandes writes most about. Much of it concerns the history of the Matter of Troy in an attempt to define and understand the reasons for Shakespeare's distorted travesty of the material in general and Cressida in particular. In Brandes's eyes Homer's *Iliad* contains some of the noblest, most perfect passages in all European literature. Not even the genius of Shakespeare can get away with denigrating these exquisite characters without tasting Brandes's indignation:

> In the *Iliad* these forms represent the outcome of the imagination of the noblest people of the Mediterranean shores, unaffected by religious terrors and alcohol; they are bright, glad, reverential fantasies, born in a warm sun under a deep blue sky. From Shakespeare they step forth travestied by the gloom and bitterness of a great poet of a Northern race, of a stock civilised by Christianity, not by culture; a stock which, despite all the efforts of the Renaissance to give new birth to heathendom, has become, once for all, disciplined and habituated to look upon the senses as tempters which lead down into the mire; to which the pleasurable is the forbidden and sexual attraction a disgrace. (2:209)

Shakespeare becomes the victim of the same bigoted puritanism that Brandes had been exposed to in the confined atmosphere of late nineteenth-century Copenhagen. Scornful of Gervinus who had characterized *Troilus and Cressida* as "a good-naturedly humorous play" and "a purely literary satire," Brandes is convinced that Shakespeare was lashing out at his own times when he wrote this play. The venom of Thersites runs in his veins for reasons we shall never fully know, but a source of the contempt and bitterness that permeate everything Shakespeare writes during these years may be traced in Ulysses's remarks to Achilles ("Time hath, my lord, a wallet at his back . . ." (3.3.139 ff), which seem out of character and at the same time strangely personal:

> How plainly is one of the sources betrayed here of the black waters of bitterness which bubble up in *Troilus and Cressida*, a bitterness which spares neither man nor woman, war nor love, hero nor lover, and which springs in part from woman's guile, in part from the undoubted stupidity of the English public. (2:222–23)

In his endeavor to give a psychobiographical interpretation of this difficult and in many ways enigmatic play Brandes makes many shrewd observations, but in the process he hardly does it full justice as drama. Especially he does not seem to question the view that Thersites speaks for the author.

It is an important compositional principle in Brandes's presentation to demonstrate thematic links between the plays in their alleged chronological order as this supports the thesis of the imprint of the artist's personality in his works. This is very striking in the transition from *Troilus and Cressida* to *Coriolanus.* As *Troilus and Cressida* was linked to its predecessor *Antony and Cleopatra* in the attitude to the female protagonists, so *Coriolanus* is linked to *Troilus and Cressida:*

> Shakespeare's aversion to the mob was based upon his contempt for their discrimination, but it had its deepest roots in the purely physical repugnance of his artist nerves to their plebeian atmosphere. It was obvious in *Troilus and Cressida* that the irritation with public stupidity was at its height. (2:228)

Brandes cites earlier examples of Shakespeare's aversion to the obnoxious smells of the mob. Nowhere is his aristocratic contempt for the mob, rooted in physical aversion to their stinking bodies, clearer than in the changes he made to the story of Coriolanus that he found in Plutarch. His denigration of the mob goes hand in hand with his glorification of Coriolanus: "Some few on this earth are men, the rest are spawn, as Menenius calls them; and so Shakespeare sympathises with Coriolanus and honours him" (2:246). He admits that the nature of the material required that the pride of Coriolanus should occasionally be expressed with repellant arrogance. "But we feel, through all the intentional artistic exaggeration of the hero's self-esteem, how there arose in Shakespeare's own soul, from the depth of his stormy contempt for humanity, a pride immeasurably pure and steadfast" (2:248). He is aware that the majority of critics both in the English-speaking world and in Germany will disagree with this reading of the play. They see the Roman people as good and amiable in the main, and Coriolanus as a man ruined by pride that degenerates into unbearable arrogance. They also tend to insist that Shakespeare was impartial in political matters, partly to fit him into the liberal ideas of a different age. Not so Brandes: "We have no interest, however, in refashioning Shakespeare. It is enough for us if our perception is fine and keen enough to recognise him in his works, and we must actually put on blinders not to see on which side Shakespeare's sympathies lie here" (2:239).

Brandes insists again and again that Shakespeare's scorn for the multitude grew out of his sense of lacking esteem for his profession, and that his chief consolation was the friendship and appreciation he had occasionally found in a few noble and noble-minded gentlemen. The arrogance that Shakespeare built into his Coriolanus and that he, in Brandes's view, approves and shares is clearly a view that Brandes will not only register with his fine and keen perception, but that he also, implicitly and explicitly, responds to with sympathy and maybe even identifies with. In spite of his claim that he has no interest in "refashioning Shakespeare," it is hard not to find the voice and the mind of "Branspeare" in the interpretation of these plays.

The all embracing gloom and disdain in Shakespeare's mind had not, however, found their ultimate expression in these two plays. *Troilus and Cressida* overflows with contempt for the feminine sex, for love and military glory. Coriolanus overflows with scorn for the masses:

> But the passionate disdain possessing Shakespeare's soul is destined to a stronger and wilder outburst in the work he next takes in hand. The outbreak in *Timon* is against no one sex, no one caste, no one nation or fraction of humanity; it is the result of an overwhelming contempt, which excepts nothing and no one, but embraces the whole human race. (2:253)

Timon of Athens is a key text for the argument Brandes presents, and as such gets an attention that is out of proportion with its merits. It is also a text that presents problems for his argument because of the poor state of the text, the unevenness of the writing and especially the difficulty of establishing Shakespeare's share in it. Brandes dwells on this problem of attribution, but finds that in spite of these difficulties Shakespeare's leading idea and dominant purpose are never for a moment obscured:

> Like *Coriolanus*, this play was undoubtedly written in a frame of mind which prompted Shakespeare less to abandon himself to the waves of the imagination than to dwell upon the worthlessness of mankind, and the scornful branding of the contemptible. (2:260)

The misanthropy that had been building up in Shakespeare's mind for almost a decade reaches its climax in the play of Timon. In the last paragraph of Brandes's chapter on this play he sums up the mental development in Shakespeare it has been his ambition to trace, in words that echo the concluding paragraph in "Book First" where Brandes outlined the melancholy, pessimism, and misanthropy in the future course of Shakespeare's life and works:

> All that he has lived through in these last years, all that he has suffered from the baseness of other men, is concentrated in this colossal figure

> of the desperate man-hater, whose wild rhetoric is like a dark essence of blood and gall drawn off to relieve suffering. (2:270)

This is the turning point in Brandes's version of the story of Shakespeare's life. The dark cloud had burst and the skies were slowly clearing. He enters upon a period of convalescence. It is not necessary for an assessment of Brandes's method and achievement, his contribution to the Shakespearean criticism of his day, to look into the second half of "Book Third." But it is of some interest and relevance for the assessment of Brandes's place in the history of Shakespearean criticism to compare his approach and his conclusions with those of Edward Dowden, who was working along the same lines at the same time.

Dowden's book, originally published in 1875, has been reprinted many times and is well-known to this day. In the preface he explains that his book attempts "to connect the study of Shakspere's works with an inquiry after the personality of the writer, and to observe, as far as is possible, in its several stages the growth of his intellect and character from youth to full maturity." Unlike Brandes's survey his is not, however, strictly chronological. Its four hundred thirty pages are divided into eight chapters, most of which deal with groups of plays that belong together, for example, "The English Historical Plays" (ch. 4) and "The Roman Plays" (ch. 6), although there are also chapters on "Shakspere and the Elizabethan Age" (ch. 1) or "The Humour of Shakspere" (ch. 7). In this division *Coriolanus* is not surprisingly dealt with in the chapter on Roman plays, and *Troilus and Cressida* is hardly mentioned at all in the first edition (but was dealt with in the preface to the third edition). So the place left for *Timon of Athens* in Dowden's survey is in chapter 8: "Shakspere's Last Plays," where it is somewhat incongruously grouped with *Cymbeline, The Winter's Tale*, and *The Tempest*.

Dowden is a much more cautious critic than Brandes. As regards *Troilus* he is not prepared to commit himself on the issue of dating and finds that the interpretation of the play is as difficult as the ascertainment of the facts of its history. This "comedy of disillusion" may be the outcome of "a mood of contemptuous depreciation of life" in the years when he also wrote *Measure for Measure*. But whatever its date, Dowden finds in it a striking resemblance in its spirit and structure to *Timon of Athens*. Writing of *Coriolanus* he touches on Shakespeare's political views, although he insists that the tragedy of Coriolanus is personal rather than political. His guarded and balanced view that "in the play of Coriolanus, the intolerant haughtiness and injustice of the patrician is brutal and stupid, not less, but rather more, than the plebeian inconstancy and turbulence,"[16] would seem to make him one of the English critics Brandes refers to when writing about Coriolanus. In spite of his title Dowden is nowhere as daring in reconstructing the mind of the playwright on the evidence of the texts as Brandes is.

According to Dowden, in *Timon of Athens* Shakespeare's mood of indignation with the world attains its highest, its ideal expression, while in *The Tempest* we find the ideal expression of the temper of mind which succeeded his mood of indignation—the pathetic yet august serenity of Shakespeare's final period. Contrary to Brandes, however, Dowden finds evidence in the play of Shakespeare's sanity: "He could now so fully and fearlessly enter into Timon's mood, because he was now past all danger of Timon's malady" (p. 382). The Athenian misanthrope was a type Shakespeare *had* known, in his own breast, but he uses the play to "utter that wrath against mankind to which he had assuredly been tempted, but to which he never wholly yielded." Dowden makes a distinction between the accustomed, but mythical picture of a bright, gentle and genial Shakespeare and the man "actually discoverable behind the plays":

> It is impossible to conceive that Shakspere should have traversed life, and felt its insufficiences, and injuries, and griefs, without incurring Timon's temptation—the temptation to fierce and barren resentment."[17]

In creating a character such as Timon, Shakespeare, however, achieved a "dramatic remoteness from his own personality." The "proof" of the personal element, remote or otherwise, in his Timon or his Hamlet, Dowden finds in the principle of contrasting such characters with "foils" like Alcibiades or Fortinbras. The protagonists are obviously much more interesting to their creator:

> Can we doubt that the Hamlets and Timons of Shakspere's plays represent the side of the dramatist's own character, in which lay his peculiar strength; and also his special danger and weakness.[18]

At this point speculations about painful experiences which may have induced Shakespeare to create his bitter and world-weary heroes lead Dowden to a cautious use of the Sonnets:

> If the Sonnets of Shakspere, written many years before the close of Shakspere's career as a dramatist, be autobiographical, we may perhaps discover the sorrow which first roused his heart and imagination to their long inquisition of evil and grief, and which, sinking down into

> his great soul, and remaining there until all bitterness had passed away, bore fruit in the most mature of Shakspere's writings, distinguished as these are by serene pathetic strength and stern yet tender beauty.[19]

Dowden refuses, however, to involve himself in the conflicting theories of autobiographical "facts" behind the sonnets. He reads them for their spirit, which tells us something about Shakespeare's spirit: measureless personal devotion, sensitivity, and forgiveness; and indeed a taste for the blameful pleasures of the world, far from the proud virginity of Milton's poetry, but never hard, selfish, or cold-blooded. The emphasis is on the recovery, the ability to move on, grow and use past experiences with artistic detachment.

Interestingly, both Dowden and Brandes resort to a musical metaphor to describe Shakespeare's state of mind at the time when he wrote *Timon of Athens*. But Dowden sees this phase in the poet's life as one where he is coming to terms with past disappointments and moving toward a final serenity, and says that "the music of his life is a little lowered throughout; the pegs are set down." But for Brandes Shakespeare's art and Shakespeare's mind are "out of tune—out of tune!"

The difference in the conclusions Dowden and Brandes reach on the basis of studying the same material is of course striking and disturbing, and does indeed undermine the credibility of the undertaking. Brandes in particular, being the more daring and subjective reader, lends himself to criticism of circular reasoning. Again and again he repeats the formula that it is not difficult "to follow the mental processes from which this work evolved.[20] Sometimes he bases his argument on the scant biographical evidence. As he linked the death of Shakespeare's father to the writing of *Hamlet*, so he attributes the portrait of Volumnia to the death of Shakespeare's mother in 1608. The death of a mother is often the saddest a man can sustain, says Brandes. Of Shakespeare's mother we know little, "but judging from the affinity which generally exists between famous sons and their mothers, we may suppose that she was no ordinary woman" (2:227), and thus in the midst of all that was low and base in *Coriolanus* he created the sublime mother figure of Volumnia. More often Brandes speculates in very general terms on the personal experiences that shaped Shakespeare's mind and thus his plays. A striking example of this approach is the concluding lines of the chapter on *Timon of Athens* quoted above. The personal causes of this pervasive discord in Shakespeare's mind are shrouded in darkness, and the evidence for it stems almost exclusively from a reading of the plays in question. The comment on *Timon* stands as a postulate that can hardly even be said to be borne out by the lengthy discussion of the play. Much of the text is a somewhat tendentious summary of this play, but although this summary does suggest weaknesses in the character of the protagonist, Brandes explicitly claims that he at all times possesses the poet's sympathy and compassion. At no point does Brandes really question the playwright's relation to his character. Even so the analysis fails to convince the present-day reader, brought up on different critical principles than that Timon and the play about him have grown out of a soul steeped in despondency and misanthropy.

Not only the present-day reader may have reservations about Georg Brandes's undertaking; many of the contemporary reviewers voiced similar reservations. Even Dowden—who might be supposed to be favorably disposed toward the project—though describing Brandes's work as "a book of great value," warns his readers that they need to be on their guard against "Dr Brandes' transferences from the realm of conjecture and the region of public history into Shakespeare's private life."[21]

The publication of *William Shakespeare* in English was widely noted. Besides *The Daily Telegraph, The London Times* carried a largely appreciative review of "on the whole an admirable piece of work," though quoting Brandes's programmatic statement (cf. note 5 above) the reviewer adds that "from these words it will be seen that the author lays himself open to the criticisms which are sure to be levelled against the man who constructs a life out of materials of which many are inferential."[22] *The Academy* voices similar reservations about "an admirable and exhaustive survey of its subject," finding that "occasionally Herr Brandes seems to us to overstep the limits of permissible conjecture."[23] Several reviewers note the fact that the book was written for non-English readers in the first place, for example, in *The Saturday Review*, where it is said that "Throughout the Continent of Europe it has been received with enthusiasm, as the most mature expression of biographical criticism up to date. It is now subjected to the severest ordeal, it is submitted to the tribunal of English taste and knowledge." The reviewer's own verdict is that the book "is certainly the best existing general view of the life and labours of Shakespeare."[24]

On the other side of the Atlantic the reception was also mixed. The *New York Times* reviewer is full of admiration for Brandes's marvellous research and scholarship as well as his criticism:

> . . . all is done with a scholarship so superb, and in a fashion at once so masterly and sympathetic that the work is lifted to the level of greatness itself, far beyond Taine's dazzling, but half-comprehending criticism.

He finds, though, that a major defect of the book is "its continually recurring note of almost virulent animosity against the Puritan spirit."[25] Writing in *The Dial,* Melville B. Anderson was much less impressed. Although he admits that the book is skillfully written and contains "some interpretations that are brilliant and even illuminating," he finds that it "has the distinction of being the greatest literary disappointment of the period." It is an unsound book by a heavy-handed critic" as signally lacking in critical tact as we have seen him to be lacking in sanity of judgment and openness of mind."[26] To balance this scathing criticism, let Edmund Gosse have the last word, to be found in a survey article on "Shakespeare in 1898" that appeared in *The North American Review* (162:1898). As I have noted above, Gosse had known Brandes since his youth and begins his section on Brandes with some general remarks about his career. He goes on to remind his readers that the book was not originally intended for English students, which gives it a certain advantage. It takes a foreign critic to lift Shakespeare out of and above the contemporary literary milieu. "In its cunning mixtures of biography and criticism [it is] the best popular or general portrait of Shakespeare yet given to a Continental audience, certainly, and perhaps even to an English one." He concludes, though, with a certain reservation: "In his first volume he appears to me rarely to go amiss; in the second, I confess, I find his interpretation of the plays occasionally fantastic." This view was shared by Sidney Lee, who in his *A Life of William Shakespeare* refers to Brandes's book as "a somewhat fanciful study."

In spite of some adverse or mixed criticism there is no doubt that the publication of *William Shakespeare* in English was a success which added an Anglo-Saxon dimension to Georg Brandes's international reputation. This appears from the generous comments on his book in Augustus Ralli's *History of Shakespearian Criticism.* Writing in 1932 Ralli concludes that "though less than the greatest as a whole" Brandes has some first-rate remarks.[27]

By then Brandes's book had seen a great number of reprints, both in England and in the United States.[28] He had also been asked to provide introductions for a series comprising all of Shakespeare's works in separate volumes, published in 1904, as well as an edition known as "The Garrick Shakespeare" in 12 volumes (1905), volume 12 being *The Life and Work of William Shakespeare*, by Georg

Brandes, in which the contents of *William Shakespeare, A Critical Study* were redistributed and recycled.

The international circulation and reputation of Brandes's *William Shakespeare* outside the English-speaking world is beyond the scope of this article. In Denmark there was not unanimous and unmingled praise for the book. In any case it could hardly add to the eminent, if highly controversial, position Brandes held in Danish society. And whatever the verdict of his own age as well as posterity may be, there is no doubt that his book had a significant influence at the time on the interest in and knowledge of Shakespeare in his home country, which had only recently acquired a complete translation into Danish of the works of Shakespeare by the poet Edvard Lembcke; where Valdemar Østerberg was busy translating many of the plays on a philologically sounder basis; and where Otto Jespersen was making invaluable contributions to the general knowledge of English. Its lasting appeal, to this day, is more uncertain. Its scholarly importance is negligible, but Brandes was an inspired reader and an inspiring writer, so not only on his own premises, but also in a modern perspective does his reading of individual plays show remarkable psychological insight and critical acuity, well worth seeking out to this day.

Notes

1. The two-volume edition in English is a complete translation of the original. The two volumes contain the three "Books" of the original. Volume 1 was translated by William Archer; volume 2 partly by him and partly by various other translators.

2. Paul Rubow, *Georg Brandes' Briller* (København: Levin & Munksgaard, 1932), an augmented version of Paul Rubow, *Georg Brandes og den kritiske Tradition i det nittende Århundrede* (København: 1931). Neither is available in translation.

3. Rubow has dealt with this in an article from 1915, "Georg Brandes Forhold til Taine and Sainte-Beuve," reprinted in Paul Rubow, *Litterære Studier* (København: Levin & Munksgaard, 1928).

4. Georg Brandes, *William Shakespeare: A Critical Study,* 2 vols. London: William Heinemann (1:2).

5. Ibid., 2: 413.

6. To the Swedish poet Gustav Fröding. Quoted from Jørgen Knudsen, *Georg Brandes: Symbolet og Manden, 1883-1895,* 2 vols. (København: Gyldendal, 1994) 2:619, my translation.

7. Jørgen Knudsen is in the process of writing a comprehensive biography of Georg Brandes. Part Three: *Georg Brandes, Symbolet og Manden,* discusses Brandes and Shakespeare, 2:606–32.

8. Georg Brandes, *William Shakespeare: A Critical Study* (1898 edition), 1:50.
9. Ibid., end of ch. 11, 2:9.
10. Ibid., 2: 26–28.
11. Ibid., 1:154.
12. Georg Brandes, *Levned*, 3 vols. (København: Gyldendal, 1905–8) 3:380, my translation.
13. Brandes, *William Shakespeare,* 1:313.
14. Ibid., 1:160.
15. My translation of a passage in vol. 2, ch. 7 in Georg Brandes, *William Shakespeare, (*København: Gyldendal, 1912).
16. Edward Dowden, *Shakspere, A Critical Study of His Mind and Art* (London: Routledge & Kegan Paul, 1875), ch. 6, section 3; p. 326 in the 24th impression (1957), from which all my quotations are taken.
17. Ibid., 384.
18. Ibid., 393.
19. Ibid., 394.
20. Thus, for instance, about *Coriolanus*, 2:243.
21. Edward Dowden, "Dr. Brandes on Shakespeare," *The Bookman* (April 1898): 12–13.
22. *The Times,* 17 February 1898.
23. "A New Study of Shakespeare," *The Academy* (March 26, 1898): 339–40.
24. "Dr. Brandes on Shakespeare," *The Saturday Review*, (February 26, 1898): 298–99. The review in *The Spectator,* 7 May 1898, under the title "A Danish Study of Shakespeare" supposes that Brandes has written the book primarily for his countrymen.
25. "Shakespeare. Georg Brandes's Exhaustive Critical Study and Biography of the Poet." *The New York Times Saturday Review of Books and Art* (March 19, 1898):186.
26. Melville B. Anderson, "A Countryman of Hamlet upon Shakespeare," *The Dial* (June 1, 1898): 347–50.
27. Augustus Ralli, *A History of Shakespearian Criticism*, 2 vols. (London: Oxford University Press, 1932) 2: 139–56.
28. Information about English language editions of Georg Brandes's works can be found in "Georg Brandes—bio-bibliographical survey" compiled by Per Dahl and John Mott, printed in *The Activist Critic, A symposium on the political ideas, literary methods and international reception of Georg Brandes*, ed. Hans Hertel and Sven Møller Kristensen in *Orbis Litterarum*, supplement no. 5 (Copenhagen: Munksgaard, 1980).

"Heavy-headed revel east and west": Hamlet and Christian IV of Denmark

MICHAEL SRIGLEY

ALTHOUGH IT HAS OF COURSE ALWAYS BEEN RECOGNIZED THAT SHAKE-speare refashioned the ancient Amleth of Saxo Grammaticus into a contemporary Renaissance prince, the full implications of this modernization have not been fully grasped. Hamlet is made to attend the Lutheran university of Wittenberg, founded only in 1502 and after 1517 the natural choice for young wellborn Danes like Rosencrantz and Guildenstern to pursue their studies. There Hamlet is attended by Horatio as the customary preceptor of the period of young noblemen and members of royalty attending university or touring Europe. He is interested in the plays written and acted at the university as were his contemporaries at Oxford and Cambridge, and gives a warm welcome to old friends when a troupe of actors arrives at Elsinore. The same updating of old material is found in the presentation of Denmark as a country under military threat, building up its fleet, casting bronze cannons and buying up weapons abroad. As will be shown, this matches the military preparations of the Danes under Christian IV in the years before and after 1603. What interest, it might be asked, would an English audience have in such allusions to contemporary Denmark or to such matters as Danish drinking habits? As I shall suggest, interest in Denmark and things Danish reached a high point in England during the first decade of the reign of Christian IV, and culminated in his long-heralded visit to England in 1606 to meet once more his brother-in-law, James I, and his own sister, Queen Anne.[1]

In 1603, when the so-called pirated edition of *Hamlet* (Q1) appeared, the political and cultural ties between England and Denmark were at their most intimate. In the same year James VI of Scotland had become James I of England and entered England with his Danish queen. As we shall see, an embassy traveled from England to Denmark in 1603. A Danish embassy came to England in the same year and in the ambassador's suite was a certain Rosenkrantz. In 1606 after some delay Christian IV paid a state visit to his brother-in-law, James and his sister Anne, and again as we shall see, on several occasions this was celebrated by the two kings in bouts of heavy drinking. By the time of Christian's visit, a second edition of *Hamlet* (Q2) had been "Newly imprinted and enlarged to almost as much againe as it was, according to the true and perfect Coppie," as the title page has it. That a new and more accurate copy of the play should be printed to replace the inaccurate version of Q1 is understandable. More puzzling is the claim that the play is almost twice the length of an earlier version. Could this be an indication not so much that Shakespeare restored the play to its original full length, but that for some reason he took the opportunity to almost double its length? Given the special ties that existed between England and Denmark during the opening years of James I's reign, I would like to explore the possibility that the second quarto of 1604–5 was revised and extended with an eye to the expected visit of Christian IV to England which after some delay finally took place in the summer of 1606.

Among the differences between the Q2 *Hamlet* of 1604–5 and both Q1 and the Folio edition of 1623 there is one in particular which may have a bearing on Christian IV's visit a little more than a year later.[2] In Q1 Hamlet's conversation with Horatio about the heavy drinking of the Danes is ten lines long, while in Q2 this is extended to thirty-one lines. In F1 the exchange between them is reduced to the length it had in Q1, with only a few minor differences. Dover Wilson in his note to lines 17–38 in his Cambridge edition suggests that the additional lines were cut from F1 "possibly because it was considered politically dangerous after 1603 with a Danish Queen (Anne, the consort of James I) on the throne."[3] But this would not explain why the longer version was printed in early 1605 by which time Anne had already settled in England and could, had she wished, have objected to them as a slur on her own countrymen. She might in fact have regarded Hamlet's speech, if she had read or heard it, as a justified yet discreet criticism of her countrymen as heavy drinkers. Its discretion has been noted by others. Hamlet's extended discussion of the drinking habits of the Danes can be read not so much as an attack on them for their toping as a sort of defense of them. This is the thrust, I believe, of Hamlet's argument in the early part of his speech:

> This heavy-headed revel east and west
> Makes us traduced and taxed of other nations.
> They clepe us drunkards, and with swinish phrase

Soil our addition, and indeed it takes
From our achievement, though performed at height,
The pith and marrow of our attribute.

(1.4.17–22)

Hamlet is saying that the reputation of the Danes for drunkenness detracts from the real achievements of the Danes, even the most outstanding of them. He goes on to vary the argument by providing what might be called a genetic explanation: their tendency to excessive drinking is one example of "some vicious mole of nature in them, / As in their birth, wherein they are not guilty (Since nature cannot choose his origin)" or "the stamp of one defect" in an individual, which

Being nature's livery, or fortunes star,
His virtues else be they as pure as grace,
As infinite as man may undergo,
Shall in the general censure take corruption
From that particular fault.

(31–36)

This is more an apology rather than an accusation. Hamlet is maintaining that the natives of any particular country are born with a specific weakness of character. In the case of the Danes, this is a weakness for drink. This, however, should not derogate from their otherwise high achievements or blind us to the virtues they possess, for in judging others there is a tendency to allow one fault or weakness to outweigh their good qualities.[4]

The reputation of the Danes and their king for excessive drinking was well known in England before Christian IV's visit of 1606. Ever since James as King of Scotland had crossed to Norway and Denmark in 1589–90 to claim Christian's sister, Anne, as his bride, political and cultural contacts between Britain and Denmark had steadily increased, and there were many Englishmen and Scots visiting Denmark who on their return could report on the carousing of the Danes. For example, the celebrated lutenist, John Dowland, appointed personal lutenist to Christian IV, had ample opportunity to observe as well as indulge in the "heavy-headed revels" during his period of service from 1598 to mid-1603 when he returned to England to publish his *Lachrimae or Seaven Teares*, with a dedication to Christian's favorite sister, Queen Anne.[5] During his time in Denmark, Dowland, despite being highly paid for his services, eventually ran into financial difficulties, and Diana Poulton suggests a possible reason for this. She writes:

> Dowland would have encountered heavy drinking . . . at the Danish Court. . . . It would be tempting to suggest that perhaps he too fell into the habit of excessive drinking.[6]

As she points out, life at Elizabeth's court was different from that of Christian's:

> Her abstemiousness in eating and drinking were matter for comment, and even those of her circle who drank heavily, in her presence found it politic to remain sober. In Denmark things were very different. When Shakespeare makes Hamlet speak the following lines he is merely describing conditions that were known to exist at Christian's Court.[7]

After citing from the speech of Hamlet's we have been considering, Poulton says of Christian IV: "In short, His High and Mighty Majesty was frequently dead drunk."

There is much evidence for the truth of this assertion. In what follows I shall first quote or summarize the evidence given in the volume in the series *Danmarks Historia* entitled *Christian IV.s Tidsalder 1596–1660* by Svend Ellehøj, where he discusses "the King's liking of strong drink and women,"[8] as well as other Danish sources, and then I shall go on to give an account of Danish toping drawn from various English accounts and finally describe Christian's reveling while visiting James I and his own sister Anne in 1606.

According to Ellehøj, Christian revealed his weakness for drink soon after his accession in 1596. He writes:

> It could happen that while entertaining visitors from abroad or consulting with his advisers Christian IV could be drunk three days running, but in his countrymen's eyes this was no shame, and admiringly they noted that the king's enormous physical strength enabled him to get up at dawn to go hunting despite the fact that he had had to be carried to bed in his chair after the previous evening's bout of drinking. Christian IV remained a heavy drinker down to old age. [It was related in 1643] that the King after completing his offical business in the morning, spent practically every afternoon drinking. . . . Eske Brok kept a diary recording meetings with the King in 1598, marking various entries with a cross to indicate that they had a 'god rus' [a good binge; Hamlet's "rouse"] together. The cross was heavily scored on those occasions when there was no drinking because of the presence of, say, the Archbishop.[9]

The code probably originated with the King himself, for it is known that "in his diary he marked with a cross the dates when he had been carried to bed, and added a second, or even a third if he had been excessively drunk or practically paralyzed."[10] Sivert Grubbe, one of Christian's principal secretaries, described in his diary a "god rus" (Hamlet's "rouse" again) he had had with the King. After drinking heavily long into the night, the King asked if there were any young girls available in Grubbe's inn. He said there were, and that he also had an English drink called *Rose de Sole* obtained from a visiting English ship. They drank bumpers from a bowl passed round the table. It tasted like brandy, the King said, but was, he explained, wine that had been distilled by the sun. It was so strong that the drinkers finally could not stand upright.[11] What happened about the girls is not recorded, but as will be seen from accounts of his visit to England in 1606, womanizing was another of Christian's royal weaknesses.

Where the Danish King led, his courtiers followed. "The courtiers drank from eight to twelve quarts of beer per day, and Queen Sophia [Christian's mother] two gallons of Rhenish wine."[12] In *Hamlet*, the Danish king "drains his draughts of Rhenish Rhine down" (1.4.10) and the Clown remembers how Yorick once "poured a flagon of Rhenish on my head" (5.1.169). Shakespeare, it seems, accurately associated Rhenish wine with Denmark.[13] Among the Ordinances issued by Christian IV to limit the spread of the plague is the following extraordinary recommendation: "There must be plenty of beer for the children, lest thirst drive them to drink water."

We gain further insight into the heavy drinking of the Danes and their king from an account of an English embassy to Denmark in 1603. There are reasons for believing that Shakespeare had either read this account or heard of what happened from someone on this diplomatic mission. The account was made public in the 1605 edition of Stowe's *Annales* (1434–37) and was written by William Segar, Garter King at Arms, who had officiated at the preliminary conferring of the Order of the Garter on Christian in the Castle at Elsinore.

Leading the embassy was the Earl of Rutland. He and his entourage sailed from Gravesend on June 28, 1603, and landed at Elsinore on July 7.[14] Two days later they set out for Copenhagen in coaches and wagons to meet the Danish king. On the way, they were met by one of his ministers, Henrik Ramel, who delivered an oration in Latin, announcing among other things that "in all the townes and villages where they passed, Wine and Beere, with other victuall," would be "plentifully and freely offered unto all men."[15] This was their first indication of Danish hospitality where drink was concerned. More were to follow. Arrived in Copenhagen, they were received by Christian IV, long orations were delivered, and afterward the Danish king "discoursed a while in the Italian tongue with the embassadour."[16] The large company then proceeded to the church where the baptism of the king's son was to take place, led by "the Kings Trumpets formost sounding" and by "the kettle drums," the latter a novelty to the English when Christian visited England in 1606.[17] The drum-march and fanfares may be recalled in the amplified stage direction of F1:

> Rosincrance, Guildenstone, and other Lords attendant, with his Guard carrying Torches. Danish March. Sound a Flourish.

After the christening, the ambassador and his followers were entertained at a feast. Segar's disapproving account of it is couched in terms that Shakespeare seems to echo in *Hamlet*:

> To be briefe, it were superfluous to tell you of all superfluities that were used, and it would make a man sick to heare of their drunken healths; use hath brought it into a fashion, a fashiõ made it a habit, which ill beseemes our natiõ to imitate.[18]

As Dover Wilson noted, "these last words come very close to Hamlet's" comments on Danish drinking habits at 1.4.13–19. They also echo Hamlet's words to his mother on the power of "habit" or "use" to either corrupt or improve human nature, since "use almost can change the stamp of nature" (3.4.161–70).

Another feature of Segar's account seems also to have lodged in Shakespeare's memory to reappear in Marcellus's speech describing the warlike preparations in Denmark. He asks if anyone can tell him

> Why this same strict and most observant watch
> So nightly toils the subject of this land,
> And why such daily cast of brazen cannon,
> And foreign mart for implements of war;
> Why such impress of shipwrights, whose sore task
> Does not divide the Sunday from the week;
> What might be toward, that this sweaty haste
> Doth make night joint-labourer with the day:
> Who is't can inform me?
>
> (1.1.71–79)

Horatio explains that it is in response to a threat of invasion by young Fortinbras of Norway. I suggest that Horatio is referring to the Denmark of Christian IV's time and not to the remote world of

Amleth of the chronicles. By 1603, Norway had long been absorbed into the Danish realm and was therefore no threat to Christian IV who was king of both Denmark and Norway. The threat rather came from Charles IX of Sweden. The dominion established by Denmark over the Baltic Sea had become a threat to Sweden and in the early years of the seventeenth century, Charles IX was preparing to go to war with Denmark. Christian IV responded with an extensive program of shipbuilding, armaments and fortifications. Some of its results were seen by the Earl of Rutland on his visit to Denmark and were recorded by Segar.

On July 11th the English guests were

> entertained with the sight of . . . the Arsenall or storehouse of the kings municians, which truely when it shall performed, will be one of the most excellent provisions in Christendom. There was but one side of it built, the other lay in their foundations, the Fabrication is of three lofts, in the nethernmost is Artillery upon cariages, so neate and cleane kept, that the brasse is as bright as gould, and the Iron as black as Jet, the Bullets are built in piles according to their bore, & all provisions so readie & necessary, as it not to expresse with words, what it is in forme, so is the middle house of Armours, Pike, & shot, Ensignes, Drums, & all martiall instruments else the upper loft with Powder, Cordage, and other necessaries is plentifully stored.[19]

The following day was "spent in seeing the king of Denmarks ships, and other complements."[20] Christian IV took special pride in his navy and had built up a fleet of warships, including the massive *Tre Kronor* or *Admiral* of fifteen hundred tons which was to attract huge crowds when he arrived at Gravesend in 1606 to visit James I and his sister. The English visitors also witnessed "the daily cast of brazen cannon" on their return to Elsinore. They were taken by Christian to see "certaine Water-milles (of his owne device) for the forging, hammering, and boaring of his Ordinance, both great and small: in which workes a dozen men did (with much ease) the offices of three or foure score."[21] Obviously, the visitors were impressed by the extensive military preparations that had been undertaken by Christian IV. The huge Arsenal had been started in 1598 and was ready in 1604. The Cannon Hall was reputed to be "the longest vaulted room in Europe."[22] The Warehouse had been started in 1602 and was ready in 1606. Over the entrance to the Arsenal, Christian had had the following words inscribed: "I fredens tid at haeve tankt på krigen, fortryder ingen; på tvungen krig er en raetfaerdig sag"—"To have thought of war in times of peace will offend no-one; in an enforced war it is a just thing." In addition to building the Arsenal and other warehouses, Christian had also been engaged in strengthening the fortifications of Copenhagen and building bastions along the coast facing Sweden as a frontier defense against an expected attack from the Swedes. Marcellus's question about the warlike preparations of the Danes and Horatio's explanation of all this military "post-haste and romage in the land" (1.1.107) have no parallel in the remote world of Amleth. They do, however, exactly match the actual military measures being taken by Christian IV in about 1603 to prepare for the war with Sweden which broke out in 1609. It can be added that, perhaps not unexpectedly, Christian, having completed his military preparations, subsequently turned to building a huge brewery in Copenhagen between 1610 and 1618.

The scale of these warlike preparations during the opening years of Christian IV's reign to meet the growing threat from Sweden is, I believe, reflected in Marcellus's blatantly anachronistic speech quoted above. The casting of bronze cannons, the import of weapons, and the

> impress of shipwrights, whose sore task
> Does not divide the Sunday from the week,

or night from day, which he reports, tallies closely with the hectic defensive measures being taken in Denmark during the early years of the seventeenth century.

On July 13, the King and the Earl of Rutland with their retinues left Copenhagen and returned to Elsinore to carry out the ceremony of investing Christian IV with the Order of the Garter. This was performed by William Segar, Norroy King of Arms, in the Great Hall of the Castle there. He describes the Great Hall in the following passage:

> it is hanged with Tapistary of fresh coloured silke without gold, wherein all the Danish kings are exprest in antique habits, according to their severall times, with their armes and inscriptions, conteining all their conquests and victories.[23]

We learn from Skovgaard that the tapestries, which were used to cover the walls of the Great Hall on important occasions, were designed by Frederik II's court painter, Hans Knieper of Antwerp, and woven at Elsinore in 1581–86.[24]

Segar's description of the Great Hall in Kronborg Castle at Elsinore may have given the hint to Shakespeare when he wrote the scene when Hamlet compels his mother to look

upon this picture, and on this,
The counterfeit presentment of two brothers.

(3.4.53–54)

Dover Wilson plausibly suggests that these are full-length portraits, rather than miniatures, and resemble those described in the German version of *Hamlet*, *Der bestrafte Brudermord*, as hanging in a "gallery," just as they did at Elsinore.[25] During the ceremony of investiture,

> the Castell discharged fiftie canon, and the king of Englands ship lying before the Castell, reported as many.[26]

When the investiture was over, the Earl of Rutland invited the Danish King

> aboard the English ship, and had a banket prepared for him upon the upper decks, which were hung with an Awning of cloath of Tissue, every health reported sixe, eight, or ten shot of great Ordinance, so that during the kings abode, the ship discharged 160. shot.[27]

Did not the booming reports of the great ordnance at Elsinore also reverberate in Shakespeare's mind when he came to write these lines in *Hamlet?*

No jocund health that Denmark drinks today,
But the great cannon to the clouds shall tell,
And the king's rouse the heaven shall bruit again,
Re-speaking earthly thunder.

(1.2.125–28)

A final dinner is given to the jaded English guests by the Lord Chamberlain, Henrik Ramel, at his own house near the Castle. Segar's comment again suggests that there was excessive tippling even on this occasion and that the principal English guest, the Earl of Rutland, had had enough:

> The cheare was great, and my lord being weary of those Bachinall entertainments, took there his leave of the kings maiesty, entending that night to lye aboard, for his more speedy despatch homewards: the king by no perswasion could alter his determination.[28]

The weary Earl had no doubt heard some Dane boast like Hamlet: "We'll teach you to drink deep ere you depart" (1.2.175) and been half deafened by the beating of the kettledrums, the braying of loud trumpets and the thunderous boom of the cannon. On Tuesday, July 19, after ten days of feasting, the *Golden Lion* set sail for England: "our ship saluting the castell, was resaluted by the same: and the king standing upon a counter scarpe that lay into the sea, gave fire to a Canon with his owne hand for our last farewell."[29] Had the King looked down from his vantage point on the escarpment down at the water below he would have seen what Horatio so vividly evoked in order to warn Hamlet against following the Ghost:

> What if it tempt you toward the flood, my lord,
> Or to the dreadful summit of the cliff
> That beetles o'er his base into the sea,
> And there assume some other horrible form,
> Which might deprive your sovereignty of reason,
> And draw you into madness?
>
> (1.4.69–74).

Segar's caustic remarks on the inebriation of the Danes during his visit to Christian IV and his reference to "those Bachinall entertainments" that the Earl of Rutland finally found so exhausting could have been read in England sometime after March 1605 when they appeared as a last minute addition to Stowe's *Annales.* Private reports would also have been made by an additional member of Rutland's suite on the return of the embassy to England, one who was well versed in the drinking habits of the Danes.

The extra passenger aboard the *Golden Lion* when it left Elsinore was in all probablility the celebrated lutenist, John Dowland. As mentioned earlier, Dowland sailed back to England some time in the middle of 1603 to publish his *Lachrimae or Seaven Teares* with a dedication to Christian's sister, Queen Anne. The court accounts show that on July 15, 1603 there was advanced

> to Johannes Dowland, lutenist, as his salary for three months to be reckoned from the 18th of May last until the 18th of August next in this present year.[30]

Poulton notes that Dowland left Denmark at some unknown date after May 18, and that "how he made the journey is not known."[31] It seems likely, however, that since Dowland received his advance salary on July 15 he would have boarded the *Golden Lion* at Elsinore when it set off for England just three days later on July 19, no doubt as weary of the endless "rouses" as Rutland was. It has also been suggested that Inigo Jones, after returning from Italy, had sailed on the outward journey from England with the Earl of Rutland to visit Christian IV, and then returned with Christian's brother, Ulrik, when he sailed to Scotland in 1604 to visit his sister Anne at Holyrood House.[32] Both Dowland and Inigo Jones would have had much to report concerning the drinking habits of the Danes.

Before leaving Denmark for England, as it were, I would like to mention briefly the tradition that Shakespeare also spent some time in Denmark. It is known that an English troupe was employed at the Danish court at Elsinore in 1586, probably on the recommendation of the Earl of Leicester, and that it included three "comedians"—William Kemp, George Bryan and Thomas Pope—all of whom, along with Shakespeare, joined the Chamberlain's Men in 1594. It has been suggested that it was from them that Shakespeare received information about Elsinore and that he alludes to their visit to Elsinore in 1586 in the arrival of the players in *Hamlet* at Elsinore .[33] It has even been suggested that Shakespeare was with this troupe in Elsinore in 1586.[34] It is not impossible, in my view, that in 1586 when he was twenty-two years old, during the so-called "lost years," Shakespeare did in fact travel with the Earl of Leicester's Men to Denmark.

The visits of Englishmen to Denmark were reciprocated by the visits of Danes to England. Where *Hamlet* is concerned, mention must be made of the stay in England of two Danes with familiar names: Frederik Rosenkrantz and his friend, Knud Gyldenstierne. As Frederik Rosenkrantz (1571–1602) has been taken as the original of the Rosencrantz in *Hamlet*, a few words about him are in place. He was sent by his father, Holger Rosenkrantz, to study at the two main Lutheran centers of learning, Rostock University in 1586–89 and Wittenberg University in 1589–91. After completing his studies, Rosenkrantz went on a tour of Europe that took him to Italy, Sicily and Malta and in 1592 he visited England in the company of his friend and fellow student, Knud Gyldenstierne. According to a biographical account of Frederik Rosenkrantz, there can be little doubt that "his stay in England with Knud Gyldenstierne was the occasion for introducing these two Danish noblemen into *Hamlet*."[35] Another Rosenkrantz visited England in connection with James's coronation in London in 1603. This was young Holger Axelsen Rosenkrantz (1586–1647), a member of the same powerful noble family in Denmark. He came in the retinue of the Danish Chancellor, Christian Friis, and attended the coronation. No doubt the opportunity was taken by the Danish Chancellor to discuss the forthcoming state visit of Christian IV to England. Brief mention can also be made of yet another Danish diplomatic mission to England that took place in the autumn of 1605 by which time the second quarto of *Hamlet* had been published. It was headed by Henrik Ramel, described in a contemporary English document now as Christian's "Principal Secretary and Counsellor of Estate," the same who provided the Earl of Rutland and his company with heady "Bachinall entertainments" at his house in Elsinore two years earlier. On behalf of the Danish king, Ramel was "solemnly installed in the order of Knighthood of Garter" at Windsor on September 8. It was probably on this occasion that final discussions took place concerning the forthcoming visit of Christian IV. In the long list of Danish noblemen and functionaries who received presents from James in 1606, yet another member of the Guildenstierne family, "Magnus Gildenstierne," is recorded as having been given "one chain of gold."[36] Hamlet as Renaissance prince rather than Amleth also studied at Wittenberg and, in his fictive life, would therefore have known Frederick Rosenkrantz and Knud Gyldenstierne both in Denmark and at Wittenberg which they attended in 1586–89. As we learn from the meeting between Hamlet and his fellow students in the Q1 version of the play of 1603, he was then their boon companion,

> *Ham.* What, Gilderstone, and Rossencraft,
> Welcome kinde Schoole-fellowes to *Elsanoure*.
>
> *Gil.* We thanke youre Grace, and would be very glad
> You were as when we were at *Wittenberg*.[37]

Wittenberg University was founded in 1502, and after 1517 became a major center of the Lutheran Reformation. As Dover Wilson remarks, the reference to Wittenberg indicates that Hamlet "was of Protestant upbringing" and would have been "swayed by Protestant prepossessions," especially where the nature of the Ghost was concerned.[38]

In view of the close dynastic, political and cultural ties between Britain and Denmark that reached a climax with the accession of James I to the English throne and the visit of Christian IV in 1606, a play like *Hamlet* set in Denmark and with the old Danish Amleth reborn as a Renaissance prince who had studied at Wittenberg would seem to invite a search for topical allusions. Just as Hamlet is presented in the play as a Renaissance prince, so Christian was regarded as the first Renaissance prince to reign in Denmark. Both had received the humanist education of the period, both took a keen interest in the theater,[39] and both visited the country of the mad English. Hamlet and Christian IV were also alike in another respect. Although Hamlet is presented early in the play as a young man still at university, we learn from Yorick later in the play that he is thirty years old.[40] This has puzzled generations of critics. Dover Wilson comments that Yorick's information

> fixes the age of Ham[let] in so pointed a fashion that as most agree Sh[akespeare] clearly attached importance to it; and yet this age does not at all tally with the impression of youth of the play.[41]

He suggests that this discrepancy was probably "due to revision," that is, the revision involved in expanding an earlier *Hamlet* into the Q2 version of the play.[42] But the question remains of why Shakespeare should have given his princely university student the impossible age of thirty. Since no plausible explanation for this has been found, I would like to make the following very tentative suggestion.

Making the big assumption that Shakespeare was asked, perhaps late in 1604, to prepare a version of *Hamlet* suitable for acting before Christian IV on his forthcoming visit to England, he found it appropriate to make Hamlet about ten years older. This could have been out of consideration for Burbage who in 1606 was about forty years old and perhaps objected to playing the part of a Danish teenager. But Shakespeare may have had another reason. As mentioned above, Hamlet and Christian IV were not unlike in certain respects. They differ, however, in age. In the first four acts of the second quarto Hamlet is presented as a university student of perhaps eighteen to twenty years, whereas Christian when he arrived in England in 1606 was some ten years older than Hamlet the university student. Born in April, 1577, Christian was in fact twenty-nine years old or in his thirtieth year when he arrived in England. In order to strengthen the general similarities of the two Danish princes, Shakespeare decided, I suggest, to make Hamlet thirty years old.

As mentioned earlier, Christian was notoriously a heavy drinker. At the same time it appears that he did not allow his drinking to interfere with his duties as a king. He was an early riser, loved riding and hunting, and was a hardworking and efficient manager of his country's affairs. At receptions and with friends he relaxed and, as we know, often drank deeply. Aware perhaps of the reputation of his countrymen for heavy drinking, Christian took special measures on his visit to England to keep the lower ranks at least of his large retinue as sober as possible. In his account of *The Entertainment of the King of Denmark, 1606*, Henry Robarts mentions this ban on heavy drinking:

> For the government of his followers of all sorts, according to his Kingly pleasure, he ordained a Marshal, who had Under-Marshals many, with great charge from his Majestie, that if any man of his company should be drunke, or otherwise to abuse himselfe in any maner towards Englishman, or his own followers, to be punished sharply; such is the Royall care of his Excellencie, which is duely executed.[43]

The punishment given to offenders is described by Henry Robarts in his second tract, *England's Farewell to the King of Denmark, 1606*:

> such as they found druncke were brought to a house appoynted for their prison, where their thumbes were nayled togeather and nayled by it to a post; where they remayned till some suit was made for their deliverie, and hartie repentance for their faults; the due execution whereof kept them in such awe, that you should seldome after the first weeke see any of them out of order.[44]

Such draconian measures, of course, were not applied to the noblemen or high officials in Christian's suite, and, as will be seen, led by Christian himself, they too drank heavily and riotously while in England in the relative privacy of palaces and country houses.

If the Hamlet of the second quarto was intended to bear a vague resemblance to Christian IV, Hamlet's condemnation of the heavy drinking of his compatriots would have to be tempered by an understanding of this weakness based on his own personal experience. He is therefore made to speak as a Dane himself who has followed the "custom" of wassailing. When Horatio asks whether it is a custom of the country to drink as rowdily as Claudius and his courtiers are doing, Hamlet replies:

> Ay marry is't,
> But to my mind, though I am native here,
> And to the manner born, it is a custom
> More honoured in the breach than the observance.
> (1.3.13–16).

Hamlet speaks as a Dane used to the custom of drinking on such occasions. "We'll teach you to drink deep ere you depart" (1.2.175), he says ironically to Horatio on his arrival at Elsinore. Born to the custom, he accepts it. What he condemns is excessive, "swinish" drinking. He is not a teetotaler calling on the Danes to give up drink, but rather a fellow drinker urging them to observe moderation in their drinking habits. He well knew the power of a "dram of eale," if the final word means "ill" or "evil" to corrupt the "noble substance" of a human being "to his own scandal" (1.4.37–39).[45]

Christian IV would not, I believe, have been offended at finding himself mirrored in Hamlet, even if the final words of Hamlet's speech to Horatio describing the corrupting effect of drink come close to describing the effect on his limbs of the several drams of *Rose de Sole* he took with friends in a Danish tavern. He may have noted that Hamlet as the heir apparent has been having a liason with one of the court ladies, the daughter of the Lord Chamberlain. Hamlet, as Christian well knew, could not marry her, for, as Laertes warns Ophelia, "his will is not his own" (1.3.17). Polonius repeats the warning, pointing out to her that if she is not careful she may tender him "a fool" (1.3.109), which Dover Wilson, following Dowden, suggests means "a baby."[46] Christian, as the father of a brood of illegitimate children, would have recognized the situation, had he seen the play, for he too had an eye for a pretty woman.

Christian finally arrived in England on 16 July 1606, aboard his fifteen hundred ton flagship, the *Trekronor* and during his stay there for about a month, he was royally and extravagantly entertained by his brother-in-law, James I.[47] This involved a lot of sightseeing and much feasting. There were visits to the City of London, Greenwich Palace, Hampton Court, Windsor Castle and to Theobalds, the imposing country residence of Robert Cecil, Earl of Salisbury. There were many banquets, many speeches, and diverse entertainments.[48] Among the latter were three plays performed by Shakespeare's company, the King's Men.[49] From the court records we learn that "John Hemynges, one of his Maiesties players" received payment "for three playes before his Maiestie and the Kinge of Denmarke." Two of these performances took place at Greenwich in July and August of 1606 and the third was at Hampton Court on August 7. Unfortunately the titles of the plays are not given, and we cannot be sure that *Hamlet* was one of them. But even if it was, how much of it would Christian have been able to follow? We saw earlier that although Christian IV knew Latin, German, French, Italian, and Spanish, he does not seem to have mastered English. But there is evidence that Christian was provided with some help in following at least one of the English plays he attended. This is found in a long Latin poem published in 1607 by Edmund Bolton, under the title *Tricorones sive Soles Gemini in Britannia: Carmen de Christiani IV. Regis adventu in eandem*, ("The Triple Crowns and Twin Suns in Britain: A Song on the Arrival of King Christian IV in this Country").[50] There is one passage in it which gives a fascinating glimpse of a play being performed before Christian at Greenwich toward the end of his visit:

> Hisce acupictores auleae, his pingat ISAAC
> Historiis tabulas: En personata subintrat
> Fabula & ANGLIACè scire attentissimus heros
> Iam nimium vellet, vendente interprete vappas,
> Sal comicus reges, & totam perfricat aulam;
> Dij, queis sunt hominum res, & commercia curae,
> Qui reges agere, & vulgus, sua quemque videtis,
> Quam læta haec facies?[51]

The poet calls on court-weavers to record these scenes in tapestries and on a certain "Isaac"[52] to paint them in pictures. He continues: "Lo, an enacted play [masked actor] enters stealthily and immediately the eager hero [Christian IV] has a great desire to understand [the drama] in English, even as the interpreter 'sells [him] flat wine' [makes a poor job of translating the actor's words]; comic wit strikes both at the kings and the whole court; ye gods, who see the preoccupations and cares of affairs of human beings that kings and commoners act out, how joyful this sight is."

Written in the margin opposite "ANGLIACè" are the words "Comœdia vernacula ANGLORUM lingua"—"a comedy in the vernacular tongue of the English." The fact that the performance was in English explains why the Danish king immediately wished he could understand what was being said. It is of special interest that an interpreter was on hand to help Christian, but apparently he did not succeed too well in his task.[53] This play is almost certainly one of the two plays recorded as having been performed at Greenwich before "his Maiestie [King James] and the Kinge of Denmarke" in July and August. We learn from Bolton's *Tricorones* that it was a comedy. In what other ways could Christian have been helped to follow a play in English such as this, or for that matter *Hamlet*, if he saw it?

There are a number of possibilities. As we have seen, an interpreter was available for Christian during the performance of the comedy at Greenwich. He could also have been given a summary of the play's action and this would at least have enabled him to follow the plot. In the case of *Hamlet*, it is also possible that he was familiar with the tale as found in Saxo Grammaticus or in Belleforest. The dumb show preceding Hamlet's play for the King and Queen would at least have enabled Christian to follow this play within a play, and in using it in this way, Shakespeare may also have fol-

Orditur? ducitur ad finem? macte vir armis,
Consilioque magis, charùm caput, ipse PHILIPPVS *Comes MONTEGOMERICVS.*
Lux HERBERTORVM, nec nunc a fratre secundus
Natu maiori, rege indulgente IACOBO,
Cedere non dedignetur, non florida turma
Magnatum ANGLORVM: Neque vos RAMSAEVS, & HAIVS *Vicecomes HADINTONIAE, & Baro HAIS.*
NORDOBRITANNORVM par florentissimum abestis.
Hisce acupictores aulæa, his pingat ISAAC
Historijs tabulas: En personata subintrat
Fabula & ANGLIACÈ scire attentissimus heros *Comœdiæ vernacula ANGLORVM lingua.*
Iam nimiùm vellet, vendente interprete vappas,
Sal comicus reges, & totam perfricat aulam;
Dij, queis sunt hominum res, & commercia curæ,
Qui reges agere, & vulgus, sua quemque videtis,
Quam læta hæc facies? succedit musica laruis, *Musice;*
Et iàm cùm serum pleno micat agmine cœlum,
Ipsaque nox nutat, somnoque immersa quiescit,
Et iocus, & lusus circumuolitantque, vigentque,
Nectitur hora horæ, ac in lucem vertitur vmbra;
Exclamatque aliquis (nec fortè EPICVREVS ille) *Somnus incusatur.*
Cur nisi cum requie superesse dedere beatis
Numina? cur somnos? Nimirùm est summa voluptas
Alternare vices, & non his vsque carere.
Manè canes adsunt, tremulæ discurrere damæ, *Venatio.*

Page 27 of Edmund Bolton, *Tricorones sive Soles Gemini in Britannia* (London, 1607).

lowed the custom of English traveling companies on the Continent of giving dumb shows depicting the main action of plays in English so that their audiences there could follow it. In his *An Itinery* (London, 1617), Fynes Moryson gives a description of an English troupe led by Robert Browne performing in English at Frankfurt am Main in 1592 before an audience that had no English:

> So as I remember that when some of our cast dispised players came out of England into Germany, and played at Franckford in the tyme of the Mart, hauing neither a Complete number of Actours, nor any good Apparell, nor any ornament of the Stage, yet the Germans, not understanding a worde they sayde, both men and wemen, flocked wonderfully to see theire gesture and Action, rather than heare them, speaking English which they understoode not, and pronouncing peeces and Patches of English playes, which my selfe and some English men there present could not heare without great wearysomenesse.[54]

The vivid "gesture and action" of the actors constituted a form of dumb show, but it appears that real dumb shows preceding the spoken play were also staged by traveling English companies for the benefit of non-English audiences.

As Dahlberg has argued in her work on strolling players in seventeenth-century Sweden, Germany and elsewhere, the preliminary dumb show was called the "Englische Praesentation," and continued to be used even by German acting groups in line of descent from the English troupes on tour in northern Europe from the 1580s onward.[55] It is therefore possible that in a production of *Hamlet* before the Danish king an "English presentation" or dumb show was enacted at the very beginning of the play so as to enable the king to follow the main plot. Such a preliminary dumb show would have resembled the dumb show which precedes the play within the play in *Hamlet* and which Ophelia finds so hard to understand.

An interesting note by Joseph Hunter in his *New Illustrations of the Life, Studies and Writings of Shakespeare* (1845, ch. 2, 249)[56] casts further light on the use of the dumb show by Danes. Hunter makes the comment that to represent

> the story of a play in dumb-show when the play itself is going to be performed appears a most extraordinary mode of procedure, and nothing like it has been traced in the usages of the English theatre, or, I believe, in the theatres of the more polished nations of Europe. . . . Ophelia's questions, 'What means this, my lord?' and 'Will he tell us what this show means?' prove that shows such as these made no part of the common dramatic entertainments of England. . . . No one has hitherto hit

> upon the true origin of the show in *Hamlet*. It seem that such strange and unsuitable anticipations were *according to the common practice of the Danish theatre*.

He then cites a seventeenth-century unpublished diary written by Abraham de la Pryme, relating how, in 1688, six thousand Danes landed at Hull and were quartered at Hatfield near Doncaster, "near to which the writer of the diary lived":

> Many of [the Danes] while they stayed here acted a play in their language, and they got a vast deal of money thereby. The design of it was Herod's Tyranny, the Birth of Christ, and the Coming of the Wise Men. They built a stage in our large court-house, and acted the same thereon. I observed that *all the postures were shown first*, namely, the king on his throne, his servants standing about him; and then, the scenes being drawn, *another posture came*, the murderous soldiers murdering the infants, and so on; and *when they had run through all so*, they then began to act both together. All which time they had plenty of all sorts of music of themselves, for [one] soldier played on one sort, and one another. I heard some of them say that some of these players belonged to the King of Denmark's play-house, that was set on fire and burnt when most of the nobles were beholding a play several years ago.

Such a practice could of course have originated with the English troupe of players, containing three of Shakespeare's own subsequent colleagues—William Kemp, George Bryan and Thomas Pope—which visited Elsinore in 1586. As we saw, it has been suggested that the play scene in *Hamlet* alludes to this same English troupe.[57]

Bolton's Latin account of Christian's visit to England does not, of course, mention his heavy drinking or the womanizing in which Christian indulged during his visit. Nor is there any mention of these habits, naturally, in the official account of his monthlong visit.[58] In private accounts we obtain a truer picture. The most graphic description of Christian and James in sodden, festive mood is found in the oft-quoted letter written by the witty Sir John Harington to Secretary Barlow concerning the Entertainment given by Robert Cecil, Earl of Salisbury, at his imposing country house, Theobalds. A few extracts will convey something of the "heavy-headed revel" that took place:

> The sports began each day in such a manner, and suche sorte, as well might have persuaded me of Mahomet's Paradise. We had women, and indeed wine too, of such plenty, that would have astonished each sober beholder . . . I think the Dane hath strangely wrought in our good En-

glish Nobles, for those whom I could never get to taste good liquor now follow the fashion, and wallow in brutish delights. The Ladies abandon their sobriety, and are seen to roll about in intoxication. In good sooth, the Parliament did kindly to provide his Majestie so seasonably with money; for there hath ben no lack of good livinge, shewes, sights, and banquettinges, from morn to eve.[59]

The ironic reference to the money provided by Parliament is to the annual subsidy, a substantial part of which the King and his Court squandered in about a month, giving rise to much criticism.[60] Harington goes on to describe a great feast and an after-dinner spectacle put on at Theobalds, in which the arrival of the Queen of Sheba at the Temple of Solomon was enacted. The Lady playing the part of Sheba was in her cups. Approaching the Danish king she tripped on a step and poured the contents of a casket over him:

Cloths and napkins were at hand, to make all clean. His Majestie then got up, and would dance with the Queen of Sheba; but he fell down, and humbled himself before her, and was carried to an inner chamber and laid on a bed of state; which was not a little defiled with the presents of the Queen which had been bestowed on his garments; such as wine, cream, jelly, beverage, cakes, spices and other good matters.[61]

The Presenters of the Entertainment who followed likewise "fell down; wine did so occupy their upper chambers."[62] Three court ladies next appeared in the roles of Hope, Faith and Charity. Hope was too drunk to speak and withdrew; Faith "left the Court in a staggering condition"; Charity failed to speak most of her part, and soon "returned to Hope and Faith, who were both sick and spewing in the lower hall." The other performers of the masque were in the same inebriated state. Harington sums up the evening as follows:

I have much marvelled at these strange Pageantries, and they do bring to my remembrance what passed of this sort in our Queen's days . . . but I did never see such lack of good order, discretion, and sobriety as I have now done.[63]

As Gifford, detecting the connection between Christian's visit and Shakespeare's *Hamlet,* later wrote:

This visit was a political misfortune. The arrival of his Danish Majesty was the signal for

heavy-headed Revel East and West.

The Danes brought with them their habitual propensity to drinking, and

James and his Courtiers complimented the strangers by partaking of their debaucheries.[64]

Harington pointedly referred to the entertainments at Theobalds as recalling a "Mahometan Paradise" with both wine and women available in abundance. Given Christian's predilections, it is likely that the Danish king indulged in both wine and women on this occasion as well as on a return visit to England in 1614. John Nichols provides some evidence of this:

> On both these occasions the two Monarchs were guilty of great intemperence; the Dane being addicted to drunkeness, to which James had not the least objection. To this Christian added several indelicate traits of manners to the Ladies about the Court, and particularly in his indecent behaviour to the wife of the High Admiral, the Countess of Nottingham, who resented it in a very spirited manner to the Danish Ambassador, in a letter which is preserved in Dr. Harris's Life of King James.[65]

Did, then, Christian IV witness a performance of Shakespeare's *Hamlet* during his visit to London in the late summer of 1606 as one of the three plays acted for James I and his guest by the King's Men that year? Though I have been unable to find conclusive evidence that Christian did see *Hamlet*, I find it difficult to believe that a play by England's leading playwright and a leading member of James's own company, and dealing with a Danish prince would not have been acted before Christian IV. As mentioned earlier, he was famed for his patronage of the theater in Denmark, and is known to have played roles in plays and spectacles performed at his own court. Had he seen *Hamlet*, the King of Denmark would have watched a play in which the mirror was held up to "the heavy-headed revels" habitually pursued by Christian and his Danish courtiers and would have heard Hamlet's long speech on the damage this had done to the reputation of the Danes by overshadowing their undoubted virtues. He would have heard those names so familiar to him, Rosencrantz and Guildenstern, ceremoniously (and slightly comically) repeated on a stage in England, and if a translator was present, he would have been able to follow Marcello's account of his own warlike preparations against Sweden—the casting of cannons, the buying of weapons, and the extensive shipbuilding, as it had been witnessed three years previously by the Earl of Rutland and his attendants. He may even have recognized in Hamlet's dalliance with Ophelia something of his own philandering at his own court in Denmark. Given the close ties that existed between Denmark and England following the marriage of Christian's favorite sister, Anne, to

James, as well as the long expected visit of Christian to his brother-in-law and his sister in England, it is plausible to think that Shakespeare would have been invited to rewrite and lengthen *Hamlet* especially for this visit. As we have seen, the King's Men, performed three plays before James I and Christian IV in 1606. It is not far-fetched to suggest that one of them could have been the revised *Hamlet* of 1604–5. If Hamlet's speech to the players had been translated for him, he might perhaps have found a special significance in Hamlet's remarks on

> the purpose of playing, whose end both at the first, and now, was and is, to hold as 'twere the mirror up to nature, to show virtue her own feature, scorn her own image, and the very age and body of the time his form and pressure (3.2.20–24).

Shakespeare is asserting the right of the playwright to reflect his own times, and hold up the mirror even to two toping monarchs. As he wrote, there was heavy-headed revel in both "east and west."

Notes

1. Christian succeeded his father, Frederik II, in 1588 and was crowned in 1596 when he came of age. James met Christian in 1590 in Denmark in connection with his marriage to Anne of Denmark in the Great Hall of Elsinore. James spent several months in Denmark, and took the opportunity of visiting Tycho Brahe's celebrated observatory, Uraniborg, on the island of Hven, where he had long discussions with the astronomer. See Joakim A. Skovgaard, *A King's Architecture: Christian IV and his Buildings* (London: Hugh Evelyn, 1973), 27.

2. Of the seven extant copies of Q2, three are dated 1604 and four 1605, suggesting that the quarto was printed both before and after the new year which then began on March 26.

3. See John Dover Wilson, *Hamlet* (Cambridge: Cambridge University Press, 1964), n. to 1.4.17–38. Unless otherwise stated, all quotations are from this edition of *Hamlet*.

4. Dover Wilson also read Hamlet's speech as an exoneration: "The habit [of excessive drinking] spoken of, therefore, is one that makes pleasing manners appear excessive, or that allows men to place a sinister interpretation on what is nothing but personal charm" (n. to 1.4.29–30). As suggested, I think that more than pleasing manners and personal charm are corrupted by a single fault. Its corrupting effect involves the denigration of real achievements and the highest virtues.

5. See Diana Poulton, *John Dowland* (London: Faber and Faber, 1982 edition) 60–62.

6. Ibid., 54.

7. Ibid., 52–53.

8. Svend Ellehøj, *Christian 4:s Tidsalder 1596-1660*, vol. 7 in *Danmarks Historie* (Copenhagen: Europarådets udestellning, 1964), 26. All translations here and from other Danish sources are my own.

9. Ibid., 23, 34.
10. See Skovgaard, *A King's Architecture*, 35.
11. Ellehøj, 36.
12. Skovgaard, 35, n. 5.
13. As Dover Wilson points out in his edition of *Hamlet*, n. to 1.4.8–9, Shakespeare may have recalled Marlowe's "He took his rouse with stoups of Rhenish wine" in *Dr. Faustus* (4.1.19).
14. The following account is based on John Stow, *Annales* (London, 1605),1433–37, which contains the account by William Segar of "The Earle of Rutland, his Ambassage into Denmarke."
15. Stow, 1434.
16. It is known that the King understood Latin, spoke German, French and Italian well, and had a smattering of Spanish but apparently no English. See Ellehøj, 24.
17. See John Nichols, *The Progresses, Processions, and Magnificent Festivities of King James the First* (London, 1828) 2: 65.
18. Stow, 1436.
19. Ibid.
20. Ibid.
21. Ibid.
22. Skovgaard, 37.
23. Stow, 1436.
24. Skovgaard, 19.
25. Dover Wilson, Cambridge edition of *Hamlet*, n. to 3.4.53. According to Charles Christensen, *Frederik IIs Renaescanceslot og dets senere Skaebne* (Copenhagen: Gads, 1950), 100, there were originally 111 portraits of Danish kings on display in the Great Hall at Elsinore. Perhaps Amleth's father would have been among them.
26. Stow, 1436.
27. Stow, 1436. The verb "reported" as used by Segar has the rare obsolete meaning in English of "to send back, re-echo," surviving in modern English in the "report" of a gun; the same notion of returning sound is conveyed by Shakespeare's choice of the word "re-speaking." See *OED,* "report" 9.b., *verb* with a quotation from Francis Bacon of sound echoing from a cave. Segar's words are cited under 9.c. as carrying the rare and obsolete sense of "To fire a gun; to be the cause or occasion of firing," but the sense of 9.b. seems entirely adequate.
28. Stow, 1437.
29. Stow, 1437. The "counter scarpe" on which Christian stood may be part of the outworks added in 1585 to Kronberg by Frederik II, including "the massive 'Ridder Postej' that extended from the castle wall to the water's edge so as to command shipping in the Sound." See Skovgaard, 18. See also Charles Christensen, 187, for the tradition that the Ghost appeared in one of the bastions overlooking the Sound.
30. Cited in Poulton, 61.
31. Poulton, 60.
32. This was suggested by James Lees-Milne in his *The Age of Inigo Jones* (London: B. T. Batsford, 1953). The chief evidence for such a visit comes from John Webb, Jones's apprentice and assistant. He claims in his *Stone-Heng. A Roman Work and Temple* (London, 1663) that it was Christian IV who "first engrossed *Him* to himself, sending for him out of *Italy*, where, especially at *Venice,* he had many *years* resided." Claims that Jones designed such buildings as Christian's

new palace of Rosenberg have been disputed. See Skovgaard, 122, for a discussion of these claims.

33. See Gunilla Dahlberg, *Komediantteatern i 1600-talets Stockholm* (Stockholm: Kommittén för Stockholmsforskning, 1992), 32–33 and n. 5 for bibliography.

34. See Dahlberg, 33, n. 5, for the works arguing for and against the idea that Shakespeare visited Elsinore.

35. Dover Wilson (Cambridge edition of *Hamlet*, additional notes, 293–94) cites a letter to the *Times Literary Supplement* (28 January 1926), where the writer refers to "one Frederik Rosenkrantz . . . a member of a Danish diplomatic mission sent to Queen Bess. . . . In 1593 he had married a Guildenstern and was accompanied by his wife's brother, a Guildenstern. These two men were both graduates of Wittenberg University and described as dashing and accomplished men of the world." Victor E. Thoren in his *The Lord of Uraniborg: A Biography of Tycho Brahe* (Cambridge: Cambridge University Press, 1990), 429, n. 53, suggests that this was probably the son of Knud Henriksen Gyldenstierne whose wife was a second cousin of Tycho Brahe. The *Dansk Biografisk Leksikon* (Copenhagen, 1941) 20, 90, states that Frederik Rosenkrantz was unmarried but was related to the Guildensterns through his mother Karen Gyldenstierne. It also suggests that he is the model for the Rosencrantz of *Hamlet*.

36. Nichols, *Progresses* 1: 604.

37. *Hamlet*, ed. G. B. Harrison (Edinburgh: Edinburgh University Press, 1966) 32.

38. See Dover Wilson edition of *Hamlet*, n. to 1.2.113 and *Introduction*, li.

39. Christian took roles in plays and court masques and encouraged the performance of plays at court. In 1594 his brother-in-law, the Hertig of Braunschweig sent a company of players under the leadership of the Englishman, Thomas Sackville to him. See *Christian IV og Europa*, Steffen Heiberg, ed. (Copenhagen: Foundation for Christian IV Year, 1988) 143–44.

40. See Dover Wilson, Cambridge edition of *Hamlet*, 5.1.143–57.

41. See n. to 5.1.143–57 in Dover Wilson edition of *Hamlet*.

42. See the New Variorum edition of *Hamlet* (1963), vol. 1, n. to 5.1.153, for a survey of critical opinion on Hamlet's age. In his edition of the Arden *Hamlet*, Harold Jenkins has a longer note to 5.1.139–57 on the "apparent allusion" to Hamlet's age where he dismisses the Burbage hypothesis and argues that the number "thirty" is an inexact "round number."

43. See Nichols, 2: 57.

44. Ibid., 2: 85.

45. A dram as a measure of strong drink is not recorded in *OED* until about 1700, though there are earlier examples of its use in connection with cordials, and yet Shakespeare's use of the word "dram" in the alcoholic context of the whole speech seems to anticipate its later usage, alongside its normal meaning in Shakespeare's day of "small in quantity."

46. See Dover Wilson's Cambridge edition of *Hamlet*, n. to 1.3.109.

47. A letter of 18 July 1606, printed by John Nichols in his *The Progresses of King James* 2: 53, announces that "After many reports and long expecting, the King of Denmark is come hither." An extract from Stow's *Annales* in Nichols, *The Progresses* 2: 85, also related that "King James, upon long tarrying of the King of Denmark, rested very doubtful of his comming by reason the Sommer was so far spent."

48. To celebrate Christian's visit, almost a hundred scholars and students at Oxford contributed to a collection of Latin congratulatory poems entitled *Charites*

Oxonienses, sive Laetitia Musarum in auspicatissimo adventu . . . Christiani IIII. The manuscript presentation copy (Gaml. kgl. Saml. (Royal Library, Old Royal Collection) 879, fol.) is preserved in the Royal Library of Copenhagen. See Ethel Seaton, *Literary Relations of England and Scandinavia in the Seventeenth Century* (Oxford: Clarendon Press, 1935), 268 and n. 4.

49. Ethel Seaton has drawn attention to a Danish manuscript entitled "En kort og rigtig Relationskriffuelse om den Konglige Engelska Reise" (Kong. Bibl. Ny kong. Saml. (Royal Library, New Royal Collection), 995 ff. 12v., 15v.), mentioning the performance of a comedy before Christian IV on August 1, 1606. This may be the play described by Bolton. I have not been able to consult this manuscript. See Seaton, *Literary Relations between England and Scandinavia*, 67 and n. 4.

50. Edmund Bolton (1575–1633?), antiquary and poet, attended Trinity Hall, Cambridge and then entered the Inner Temple. As a Catholic recusant, he earned a precarious living as a writer, and is remembered as the proposer to James I of a royal academy or college, possibly on Baconian lines. James supported the project but died before it could be carried out.

51. Edmund Bolton, *Tricorones sive Soles Gemini in Britannia: Carmen de Christiani IV. Regis adventu in eandem* (Augustae Trinobantum [London], 1607), 27, lines 627–34. To the best of my knowledge, the reference in Bolton's poem to this performance of a play at Greenwich, mentioned at line 611, has not been previously noted. I am grateful for the learned assistance of Professor Hans Helander of the Classics Department, Uppsala University, for making this translation more accurate than it might well have been.

52. It is possible that the Isaac of the poem is the Dutch painter Pieter Isaacsz (1569–1665), born at Elsinore, who was appointed artistic adviser to Christian IV in 1607. Perhaps he accompanied the Danish king to England in 1606. More plausibly, Bolton's Isaac might well be Isaac Oliver, the celebrated miniaturist but also painter, active in England at this time. He was appointed "painter for the Art of Limning" in 1605 to Queen Anne, Christian IV's sister. In an anecdote of the period he is referred to as "Isaack the French Painter in Blackfriers." See Roy Strong, *The English Renaissance Miniature* (London: Thames and Hudson, 1983) 117–18.

53. That Christian's English was minimal or nonexistent is shown by the fact that on his arrival at Theobalds on 24 July 1606, he was first greeted by verses in English and then in Latin translation. The Latin he would have understood, but not the English. The verses were composed for the occasion by Ben Jonson. See Nichols, *Progresses* 2: 70–71.

54. Cited by Gunilla Dahlberg, *Komediantteatern i 1600-Talets Stockholm*, 365.

55. Dahlberg, 367, 407.

56. This is cited in the New Variorum edition of *Hamlet* I, n. to 3.2.127.

57. See Dahlberg, 32–33 and notes 3, 4, and 5.

58. See Nichols, *Progresses* 2: 54–69.

59. As Ethel Seaton pertinently remarks, "Sir John had evidently reached a Hamlet-like depth of depression" after witnessing the drunken spree at Court. See Seaton, *Literary Relations of England and Scandinavia*, 68.

60. Nichols, 2: 72. James I is said to have spent nearly the whole of the subsidy of £453,000 granted by Parliament during the visit of Christian IV and of the Prince de Vaudemont that immediately followed. See Nichols, 2: 69, n. 1.

61. Nichols, 2: 72.

62. Ibid., 73.

63. Ibid.

64. Ibid., 70, n. 1.

65. Ibid., 69, n. 1.

The Stockholm 1944 Anti-Nazi *Merchant of Venice:* The Uncertainty of Response

GUNNAR SORELIUS

IN THE LONG HISTORY OF THEATRICAL PRODUCTION AND CRITICISM OF *THE* Merchant of Venice the figure of Shylock, whether he has been seen as a representative of his race or not, has on the whole been treated either as a comic figure or as a tragic figure more sinned against than sinning. Interpretations of Shylock as an outright villain seem to be unusual. In Shakespeare's own time, however, although there is no direct evidence for this, it seems to be taken for granted that Shylock was looked upon as a comic figure who because of his greed, revengefulness, lack of pity and his hatred of Christians is rightly humiliated, severely punished and literally laughed out of court. In this respect *The Merchant,* as far as Shylock is concerned, is a very classical drama, more reminiscent of Jonsonian comedy than of the new genre of romantic drama that is largely Shakespeare's creation. In the first part of the eighteenth century an adaptation by George Granville, *The Jew of Venice,* which became the form in which the play was performed for a long time, "lightened" the character of Shylock.[1] It is interesting for our purposes to see that Granville's Shylock is not forced to convert to Christianity, as he is in the original. Charles Macklin, whose interpretation of the play was first seen in 1741, used a version for his view of the play that restored it to something closer to the original than the George Granville adaptation. He played Shylock as a "terrifying" villain who was both fierce and relentless, and may thus be an exception to the rule that he has not usually been looked upon as an altogether unsympathetic character. Edmund Kean's interpretation in the early years of the next century made Shylock into an intense and tragic character at the same time as he was deeply intellectual and deeply human. William Charles Macready created a dignified and stately Shylock but one who was "consumed with malice."[2] Edmund Kean's son Arthur Kean subsequently acted Shylock with his wife Ellen Tree as Portia, but in their productions elaborate scenery seems to have been more important than character interpretation. Henry Irving appears to have managed to make Shylock both a typical representative of his race and of suffering humanity in general. He also revived an older tradition of speaking with an oriental rather than a middle European accent. Halio points out that Irving's interpretation has been influential to our own day and mentions Laurence Olivier's Shylock as an example.[3]

After World II, Halio says, "directors found the Holocaust impossible to ignore."[4] The production we are going to look at indicates that the impact on the interpretation of Shylock of the tragic fate of Jews in the war years started before the end of the war. Conversely, in Nazi Germany *The Merchant of Venice* from 1933 onward was used quite extensively in the campaign against Jews, perhaps most often to ridicule them in the tradition of the comic Shylock.[5] There were also more neutral interpretations. Max Reinhardt, perhaps the most famous and influential theater director of the time, who was himself Jewish, produced a number of highly acclaimed productions of *The Merchant,* but these seem to have been nonpolitical, and are said to have had "a general atmosphere of laughter."[6] However, when he produced *The Merchant* at the nineteenth Biennal in Venice in 1934, the fact that Reinhardt, who had by now become "a particular *bête noire* of the Nazis,"[7] was even invited to Fascist Italy seems in itself to have been considered a political gesture.[8]

It is part of the complicated picture that there were also directly pro-Jewish productions in Nazi Germany during the war, so much so, that an "official" *Merchant of Venice* was put on in Vienna in 1943 directed by Lothar Müthel and with Werner Krauss as Shylock to "counteract the falsification of the Shylock character" which was said "to have been allowed to proliferate in recent years."[9] Werner Krauss was a well-known film star, famous for the title role in the expressionistic film *Dr. Calivari's Cabinet* and for his part in the Nazi anti-Jewish propaganda film *Jud Süss* produced in 1940. In Sweden *Jud Süss* was banned by the Censor the following year.[10] An interesting feature of Müthel's *Merchant* is that here Jessica was presented as the result of an adulterous union between Shylock's wife and a gentile, an attempt to tone down the scandal of the interracial marriage between Jessica and Lorenzo, although, as has been pointed out, according to Nazi doctrine she would still have been Jewish.[11]

The Merchant of Venice that was performed at the Royal Dramatic Theater in Stockholm, the national theater of Sweden, on 5 January 1944, about seventeen months before Germany capitulated in May 1945, would probably have qualified as an example of the kind of interpretation of Shylock that the Vienna production was intended to remedy. It is not possible to see from the minutes of the Theatre's Board of Directors when the decision to produce *The Merchant* was made. Decisions regarding repertoire seem to have been the responsibility of the director, but having in mind the long periods of rehearsal that the Theater is famous for, the decision should have been made early in the previous autumn.

The reactions of the audience, to the extent they can be ascertained fifty-five years after the event, from the written reports in newspapers and magazines, in reviews, in reports of interviews with those directly involved in the production, in the translation used, in the *Regiebuch* of the director, and in other sources, are highly ambiguous and range from enthusiastic endorsement of the anti-Nazi message that the production was understood by some to contain, to bitter regret that an anti-Semitic play such as *The Merchant* was put on at all. One way of explaining this discrepancy would be to say that these reactions simply reflect basic uncertainties in Shakespeare's text, but it is obviously also useful, from a historical as well as an aesthetic perspective, to try to see the production in the context of the historical and cultural background against which Shakespeare's drama was staged.

This background involves such trivial considerations as the fact that the 1943 season had been a failure for The Royal Dramatic Theater. Its new director, Pauline Brunius, needed a success to boost the prestige as well as the finances of her theater. And Shakespeare being, as Max Reinhardt is known to have expressed it, "the greatest and the quite incomparable piece of luck that has befallen the theatre,"[12] and who also (in the words of Dame Judi Dench) is, and presumably was, known in the trade as "the gentleman who pays his bill," may have been seen as an obvious choice. In addition the theater had over the years put on a number of very successful productions of *The Merchant* as well as other Shakespeare plays. One reviewer of the new production pointed out that *The Merchant of Venice* had in fact become the best-loved Shakespeare play in the Swedish theater.

Most importantly, there was a clear political intention in the choice of the play. For Alf Sjöberg, the director, it was an "indirect but poignant political gesture." He "wanted to interpret Shylock as a timeless and sympathetic representative of the Jewish race."[13] This wish was also shared by the theater's young new star, Holger Löwenadler, who had been cast for the role of Shylock.[14] The current persecution of the Jews, the knowledge of which was becoming more widespread, although its full nature was perhaps not yet fully grasped,[15] made Shakespeare's drama topical. It is also obvious that the theater now felt, in 1943, that it had to live up to demands to react against German war crimes that were increasingly being made on the national theater by the liberal and social democratic press. It was argued that the Royal Dramatic Theater as the foremost theater in the country ought to be the custodian of democratic and humanitarian ideas and ideals that other theaters had already embraced. It is also probable that it was felt that German pressure on Swedish public opinion to observe at least a neutral attitude toward the war between Germany and the allies could now be taken less seriously than before.[16] The Swedish government had in fact, presumably on instructions from the German Embassy in Stockholm, stopped the Norwegian dramatist Axel Kielland's patriotic drama *Om ett folk vill leva (If a people wants to live),* performed at the Nya Teatern in Stockholm the previous year, after only two performances. This was pointed out by a critic in connection with his review of the new *Merchant.* He also regretted that another freedom drama, the Danish Kaj Munk's *Niels Ebbesen* was not performed at the National Theater but had to be performed at a smaller theater, The Svenska Dramatikers Studio. It is interesting to note that this production was directed by the young Ingmar Bergman, further evidence that his early Nazi sympathies had by now radically changed.[17]

After the first night of Sjöberg's *Merchant of Venice* many reviewers recognized it as a brave decision to put on the play at all and to try to use it to criticize the German persecution of the Jews, but some also looked upon it as a somewhat foolhardy choice. It was evidently known that *The Merchant* had been used in exactly the opposite way as anti-Semitic propaganda in Nazi Germany.

Sjöberg's earlier Shakespeare productions included *Henry IV* in 1935, *As You Like It* in 1939 and *Much Ado about Nothing* in 1940. The last had had a record run of fifty-four performances. All these had used revised versions of the classical nineteenth-century Swedish translation by Carl August Hagberg, but for the new *Merchant* a new translation was commissioned. The task was entrusted to the well-known poet and member of the Swedish Academy, Hjalmar Gullberg, and to the equally well-known essayist, journalist, and champion of democratic values, Ivar Harrie, who had already translated the banned *Niels Ebbesen* the previous year. It is not known what instructions they were given, if any, but it seems obvious that they were chosen because of their anti-Nazi preferences. One reviewer ironically said that they had been told to remove the most anti-Semitic features of the play in order to adapt it to the interpretation that was going to be presented.

My own examination shows that in addition to the general modernization of language and syntax of the new translation, as it can be studied in the director's own *Regiebuch* in the archives of the theater, there were above all a number of cuts in the text. Most of these seem to have been made simply to shorten the time of performance. One significant alteration omits Portia's dismissal of the prince of Morocco before she has even set eyes on him in the concluding lines of act 1, scene 2: "I had rather he should shrive me than wive me" (lines 127–28). This may have been done to clear Portia of the racial prejudice she shows here and later when she bids the Prince of Morocco farewell after he has chosen the wrong casket: "A gentle riddance. Draw the curtain go, / Let all of his complexion choose so!" (This, however, was kept, perhaps because the corresponding lines in Hagberg's translation are less offensive, simply hoping "that all like him choose so.") It has been argued that the lines about Morocco's "complexion of a devil" were left out because Sjöberg wanted to draw a parallel between the Prince of Morocco and Shylock as two aliens of similar stature.[18] Sjöberg, who often analyzes Shakespeare's characters in terms of social class, comments in his direction notes that Morocco should be respected because of his high rank.[19]

If this change was intended to make it possible to draw a more sympathetic picture of Shylock, there are in fact other alterations which seem to paint a darker picture of him and seem to be more prejudiced against him, as when Shylock's reaction to Jessica's desertion that she "will probably suffer for this some time in the future" is changed to the more graphic wish that her "blood may one day be struck with my curse," which corresponds to the original English "She is damn'd for it" (3.1.29). Another example of this apparent blackening of Shylock is when Solanio says that he has never seen a person "so greedy for human blood," whereas in Hagberg's translation he says quite simply that he has never seen "a man so keen on another man's destruction," corresponding to Shakespeare's "so keen and greedy to confound a man" (3.2.275). A more practical alteration occurs at the end of act 3 where the order of the last two scenes is reversed so that the first half of the production can end with Portia and Nerissa leaving Belmont just before the intermission, obviously in order to accommodate the journey between Belmont and Venice more easily in the time scheme of the performance, and perhaps to facilitate the change of the quite elaborate scenery that was used.

The most significant alteration made in the whole drama may be the omission of the stipulation suggested by Antonio and confirmed by the Doge that Shylock, like Barabas in Marlowe's *Jew of Malta,* must convert to Christianity:

> Two things provided more, that for his favour
> He presently become a Christian.
>
> (4.1.382–83)

as well as the consequential harsh comment by Gratiano:

> In christ'ning shalt thou have two godfathers.
> Had I been judge, thou shouldst have ten more—
> To bring thee to the gallows, not the font.
>
> (4.1.394–96)

This omission is in fact something that Sjöberg's *Merchant* had in common with Granville's adaptation, but whereas the forced conversion was left out there to make the play more palatable to an audience that expected the play to be consistently happy, as French Classical aesthetics and taste required, in the case of the 1944 version this alteration bases the motivation of Shylock's guilt not on his religion but directly on his race, as was indeed the case in Nazi Germany. As was the case there Shylock could not be saved simply by changing his religion, as it is implied could be done in Shakespeare's drama, and perhaps in Shakespeare's time and generally in the early history of the persecution of Jews.[20] In Shakespeare Jessica is saved from any prejudice against her race simply by marrying the Christian Lorenzo, and, it is taken for granted, thereby becoming Christian. In Shakespeare it seems to me that Shylock is ridiculed for at least two reasons but neither of these necessarily have to do with race. One is his religion, but more important is his greed and vengefulness and unwillingness to change. Given a psychology which allowed for reformation and sudden change of character, Shylock could have exercised his free will and forgiven his enemies, which is really all that is asked of him. Race in the modern sense was of course not a category that Shakespeare's time recognized but an invention of the eighteenth century.[21] This change is perhaps not sufficiently noticed by modern commentators. Thus Pierre Lasry's television film *Shylock* has no mention of this.[22]

Sjöberg's conception of his production and the ways in which his direction changed during rehearsals has been described in some detail by Sverker Ek. The director had initially intended to use the yellow star that Jews were forced to wear in Nazi Germany. This was supposed to glow in the night scene in which Shylock contemplates Antonio's request for a loan (1.3), both as a symbol of religious trust and the alienation of the Jew. It would of course have been a strong sign of the topical nature of the production. Bassanio in his turn wears a white carnival mask to hide his identity, embarrassed as he is to have to approach the Jew.[23] In the end only the mask was kept. It seems that the yellow star was felt to be too provocative even at this relatively late stage of the war. A similar, topical reference could be seen in Bill Alexander's 1987 production with Antony Sher as Shylock, in which swastikas appeared as graffiti on the walls of Shylock's house.[24]

Sjöberg saw Shylock as a person with a fundamental urge to seek contact with Christians. According to Ek, pro-Jewish propaganda during the war often argued that Jews were nonaggressive by nature. Sjöberg makes Shylock try to take hold of Antonio's coat, a sign of his need for human contact. When he is rejected and Antonio tears himself loose from Shylock's grip, Shylock overreacts in his demand for a pound of flesh, which according to the director's comment in the *Regiebuch* was an old Venetian fine stipulated in the laws of Venice from time immemorial.[25] When Sjöberg produced *The Merchant* again in the same theater eighteen years later in 1962 he did in fact answer an observation made by a reviewer that *The Merchant* had been considered by the Third Reich and Goebbels as one of their "idealogically most valuable" dramas. An interesting part of this rejoinder again repeats the idea that Shylock's thwarted wish for human contact, "his longing for tenderness," in relation to Christian Venice is the key to his character.[26] In Sjöberg's production Shylock speaks his famous words "Hath not a Jew . . ." (3.1) directly to the two aristocrats Salarino and Solanio (Sjöberg makes much of the fact that there is a wide social gap between the Venetian upper crust and Shylock as a Jew) with a plea for equality and understanding. When the two noblemen look at each other, signaling that they have had enough of the Jew's ranting, put on their masks and leave the scene, Shylock "whines like a beaten dog." It is not until this late stage that his vindictiveness and hatred manifests itself, born as it were out of the contempt he is treated with by Venetian society. "Israel rises" is Sjöberg's comment in the margin of his *Regiebuch*.[27]

The pro-Jewish and anti-Nazi message was also conveyed through the way in which Sjöberg controlled the reactions of the audience, as when the trial scene was witnessed by a shouting crowd of rowdies that contemporary audiences, if they were so inclined, could easily associate with the Hitlerjugend of the time.[28] Their presence and behavior was obviously designed to create sympathy for the Jew and of course to draw a parallel between Nazi Germany and the drama. From the point of view of the style of direction it seems clear that Sjöberg had learned from Max Reinhardt both attention to detail as well as the ambition to create a theater in which every part contributed to the way in which the director tried to be in complete command of the theatrical experience, a style which is clearly visible also in his pupil Ingmar Bergman's theatrical work. Bergman has often expressed his admiration for Sjöberg, especially for his Shakespeare productions. Sjöberg, whose interest in the theater had been awakened at an early age,[29] may even have seen Reinhardt's *Merchant* when this was put on in Stockholm in 1920.[30] Sjöberg was then seventeen years old.

The reactions to the production varied radically from complete acceptance of the anti-Nazi message to bitter criticism that such an anti-Semitic drama had been put on at a time when active support was needed for the Jewish race. It is indeed puzzling how the same theatrical experience could be interpreted so differently by different people. By a curious accident the first night of the drama coincided with the news of the murder of Kaj Munk by the Germans on the previous day. At least one reviewer commented on this coincidence and regretted that the performance had not included a minute of silence to honor the dead hero, but added that it was obvious from the communal response of the audience that the message of the production, which according to the reviewer was intended to be an active support for Europe's Jews, had been understood and accepted.[31] Löwenadler had managed to create a Shylock that in its admirably unassuming way included all of the guilt of the pogroms and all of the boiling fury of the year 1943. The reviewer seems to be thinking here of the disgust that the news of the persecution and extermination of the Jews in Nazi Germany had given birth to the previous year in Sweden. The standing ovation that Löwenadler received when leaving the stage after the court scene was a tribute not just to the art of the actor but a tribute to a cruelly injured people. Thus, the reviewer says, "the audience remembered the night when tidings of the death of Kaj Munk reached the Northern peoples."

This was at the same time the most sympathetic and most enthusiastic review that the production received. It was also the best example of a review that wholeheartedly grasped and embraced the anti-Nazi message that the director had wanted to convey. Others were on the whole more cautious in their interpretation. In this they may have taken their cue from one of the translators, Ivar Harrie, who, somewhat strangely given the ambition to speak up for the persecuted Jews of Europe, offers a curiously noncommittal picture of Shylock in his introductory note in the program. Harrie recognizes that Shylock has influenced the image of the typical Jew ever since Shakespeare's time and can be recognized in modern anti-Semitism, but that for a hundred years or more he has also been looked upon as a tragic figure, whose fate is that because of the way he has been treated, he can no longer respond to the humanity that Portia represents. One reviewer refers to this program note, evidently reading it in the spirit in which it was conceived, and finds it natural that the Theater whose "young actors" had just put on Schiller's libertarian drama *Don Carlos* wanted to recruit Shakespeare for the side of the angels and press *The Merchant* for anything that could be used to fight Nazism.[32] Another reviewer voices the view that it could be argued that it had been unwise to put on this particular Shakespeare play at this particular time, but to abstain from performing *The Merchant* would be to give him over to the Germans. He praises particularly the fact that the new interpretation more clearly than had been done before manages to demonstrate that Shylock has become what he is because of the society in which he finds himself. He is persecuted not because he is evil but he is evil because he is persecuted. The reviewer refers particularly to the scene that had been added in Sjöberg's production in which a party of carnivaling revelers jeer cruelly at Shylock when he has just realized that his daughter has deserted him.[33]

Other reviewers, who realized that the production they had seen had an honorable aim, nevertheless feared that it would encourage hatred of the Jews. Several writers regretted that the play had been put on at a time, "when the Jewish race was being cruelly eradicated by the Hitler-Himmlish soldiery."[34] It was also said that the choice of play was especially odious at a time when the government had decided that all Danish Jews were to be given refuge in Sweden.[35] The reviewer also notices that Löwenadler's Merchant was "sympathetic only in part" and makes the comment that "of the two great citizens of the [cultural] world, Wagner and Shakespeare, it has been possible to try to show that the latter had no anti-Semitic intent in *The Merchant,* but that no claim of this nature has ever been made concerning Wagner's attitude towards Shylock's people." Other reviewers thought that Löwenadler's Shylock was in fact not very different from other interpretations, or even the anti-Semitic Jew of Nazi propaganda. His Shylock was no doubt someone that Shakespeare and his contemporaries would have approved of, and "presumably also Julius Streicher."[36] Streicher was of course the editor of the anti-Semitic magazine *Der Stürmer,* who was to be sentenced to death in the Nuremberg trial and executed in 1946.

It is not clear who influenced the interpretation of Shylock most, the director or the actor. As we have seen, Löwenadler and the director agreed on making *The Merchant* an anti-Nazi manifestation. In his political interpretation Sjöberg seems to have been influenced by the *Lear* he had seen performed by the Jewish theater in Moscow in 1935. He has himself written in his notebook that this made an immense impression on him. This theater visit was made in the company of Gordon Craig,[37] who commented on the same occasion, "I don't think I have understood Shakespeare properly until tonight." Craig is of course famous for the importance he attached to the interpretation and vision of the director. In this respect Sjöberg seems to have followed in the footsteps of Craig, whom he called the first great pioneer of the modern theater.

The 1944 production imitated the Moscow *Lear* also in the way it mixed the political with the poetical, although some reviewers noticed that the romantic and comic parts often dwarfed the tragic

The court scene in Alf Sjöberg's *The Merchant of Venice.* Photograph by Almgren & Preinitz. Courtesy of the Royal Dramatic Theatre, Stockholm.

strain of the play. A great deal of the success of Sjöberg's *Merchant* was no doubt due to the highly artistic rendering of the romantic plot and to the elaborate decor. In his stage design he followed Craig in part. The court scene, for example, was modernistically simple. But he also carefully recreated the Italian Renaissance atmosphere of particularly the comic part of the drama. In the Belmont scenes with the three caskets, for example, the scenery was inspired by Tiepolo's mural painting of "The Banquet of Antony and Cleopatra" in Pallazo Labia in Venice.[38] His *Regiebuch* also shows how much attention Sjöberg attached to the incidental music that had been specially written by one of the foremost Swedish composers of the day, Dag Wirén, and to the choreography. One is reminded that Bergman did something similar in his *Winter's Tale* a few years ago.

What seems in retrospect the most important modification in the traditional way of presenting Shylock as a man speaking either with an oriental or a Middle European accent was that Löwenadler used his own normal Swedish voice, thus bringing the character much closer to his audience and avoiding the ridicule or contempt associated with a thick foreign accent in any language. The only other example of this seems to be Patrick Stewart in the 1987 production at The Other Place in Stratford-upon-Avon. Although Löwenadler did not speak with a Jewish accent, very heavy makeup was used to make Shylock look almost like a caricature of a Jew. *Söndags-Nisse-Strix,* a comic periodical, which regretted that *The Merchant* had been presented at all, a sentiment which, as we have seen, was shared by a number of other voices, asked humorously if the board of governors of the Royal Dramatic Theater owned shares in a daily called *Dagsposten,* which sympathized with the Nazis and received financial support from Nazi Germany. It even hinted somewhat illogically that Löwenadler was Jewish himself: "Does Mr Löwenadler appear bearing an Arian certificate, and if so, has he faked it?"[39]

Sjöberg's *Merchant* was an enormous success and was seen by almost sixty thousand people during fifty-six consistently sold-out performances setting a new record for the Theater. According to a notice in a newspaper people fought for tickets. The King, the Queen, and the Crown Prince saw the play, as did on a later occasion the King's brother the painter-prince Eugene, as was reported in the press. There was also a radio version.

As to the anti-Nazi message of the production, it is obvious that the original strong wish on the part of the director and the actor performing Shylock to make *The Merchant* into a significant pro-

Holger Löwenadler as Shylock in Alf Sjöberg's *The Merchant of Venice.* Photograph by Kerstin Bernhard. Courtesy of the Royal Dramatic Theatre, Stockholm.

Jewish manifestation and an equally strong criticism of Nazi Germany was toned down in the actual performance, as the leaving out of the yellow stars indicates. It created strong although conflicting reactions in the audience, especially as to whether a play like *The Merchant* by its very nature encouraged anti-Semitic feelings. A drama's meaning is of course not constructed entirely by its creator, a mild form of a cliché in modern critical thinking which would argue that the author plays no role whatsoever in this respect; but neither is it entirely constructed by the director, even if Sjöberg may have thought so, inspired as he was by Craig, who had become a personal friend from their time together in Moscow. Nor is it created by the actors who in this case seem to have done their best to make the play an unequivocal anti-Nazi manifestation. This was of course especially true of the interpreter of Shylock. The evidence of the reports of the reviewers as well as the evidence of the discussion occasioned by the performance indicates that the meaning of a play like *The Merchant of Venice* is very volatile. Spectators can to some extent be controlled by the director. Programs and reviews may also influence their response, but in the last analysis their own experiences and prejudices decide what a play means. "Nothing," after all, as Portia says, "is good (I see) without respect" (5.1.99).

Notes

1. My summary of the critical and stage history of *The Merchant* is largely derived from Jay Halio's Oxford edition (Oxford: Clarendon Press, 1993).
2. Halio. 66.
3. Ibid., 69.
4. Ibid., 73.
5. John Gross, *Shylock: Four Hundred Years in the Life of a Legend* (London: Chatto & Windus, 1992), 294–97; Halio, 81.
6. J. L. Styan, *Max Reinhardt* (Cambridge: Cambridge University Press, 1982).
7. Gross, 297.
8. Rudolf Wendbladh, "'Köpmannen' på hemmaplan, *Stockholms-Tidningen,* 31 January 1944.
9. Georg Svensson in *Bonniers Litterära Magasin*, February 1944.
10. Bo Heurling, ed., *Bra Böckers film och TV lexikon* (Bra Böcker: Höganäs, 1985), 1: 224–25.
11. Gross, 295.
12. Quoted by Styan, 51.
13. Sverker R. Ek, *Spelplatsens magi: Alf Sjöbergs regikonst* (Värnamo: Gidlunds, 1988), 158.
14. Lars Öhngren, *Att vara skådespelare* (Stockholm: Natur och Kultur, 1963), 127–28.
15. Ek notices that the news of the death camps was at first taken to be Soviet propaganda (160).
16. See Willmar Sauter, *Theater als Widerstand. Wirkung und Wirkungsweise eines politischen Theaters. Faschismus und Judendarstellung auf der schwedischen Bühne, 1936-1941, diss. 1973.* See also Per Lysander, "Dramaten bugade djupt för de tyska herrarna," *Dagens Nyheter*, 13 April 1997. On German attempts to influence public opinion during the war and before, see Åke Thulstrup, *Med lock och pock: tyska försök att påverka svensk opinion, 1933-45* (Stockholm: Bonniers, 1992).

17. Nils Beyer "Hösten 1943 i rampljuset," *Tiden*, No. 1 (1944): 38–42. *Niels Ebbesen,* which was banned by the Germans in Denmark and which seems to have been stopped when a production was planned at the Royal Dramatic Theater, is set in the Middle Ages and tells the story of the pacifist country squire Niels Ebbesen who reluctantly revolts against the tyrannical invader of Denmark, the German Count Gerhard of Holstein, and kills him with his own hands. The allegory of the drama is obvious. Count Gerhard is Hitler who says: ". . . And what is then my task? I will tell you. It is to found a kingdom based on mercy, justice and peace. I am the merciful one because I destroy those that are not fit to live. I am the just one because I give victory to the strong. I am the peace because peace is only possible where there is only one ruler whom all obey mutely and blindly" (81). The drama ends in jubilation. Niels Ebbesen is addressed by the representative of the people of Denmark: "You have slain our enemy. But far more you have given us back our faith. So lead us then. Lead us now and through the centuries. Whenever Denmark sinks, lift us up again." Niels Ebbesen promises the Danish people never to give up until "we have chased all those who want our destruction back over the border, or under the ground, whichever they themselves prefer, for we must be free if we want to live" (98–99). One can hardly think of a more powerful protest against the German occupation. In Sweden it was no doubt also noticed that at one point Count Gerhard threatens to invade Sweden (85–86). The quotations, in my translation, are from the Swedish translation, by Ivar Harrie (Stockholm: Bonniers, 1942). On Ingmar Bergman and Nazism, see my published lecture, in Swedish, "Ingmar Bergmans Shakespeare," *Kultur och samhälle i språkets spegel,* ed. Gunilla Gren-Eklund (Uppsala, 1999), 153–71.

18. Ek, 170.

19. *Regiebuch:* "Here speaks the stranger, of a different race, but sufficiently respected because of his high rank."

20. On anti-Semitism generally becoming defined in terms of race rather than religion in the nineteenth century, see Gross, 291–92.

21. In spite of Shylock's talk of his "nation" (3.1.53).

22. National Film Board of Canada, 1999.

23. Ek, 161.

24. Halio, 77.

25. Ek, 162.

26. *Dagens Nyheter*, 11 December 1962. The reviewer was the well-known writer and critic Ebbe Linde.

27. Ek, 162.

28. Ibid., 162.

29. Ibid., 30.

30. Styan, 61, 146.

31. Arthur Nordén in *Norrköpings Tidningar*, 10 January 1944.

32. "C. B-n." in *Nya Dagligt Allehanda*, 6 January 1944.

33. Nils Beyer in *Socialdemokraten*, 7 January 1944.

34. Anonymous review in *Aftontidningen*, 16 January 1944.

35. "Th:son" in *Sydsvenska Dagbladet*, 6 February 1944.

36. Svensson, 149.

37. Ek, 125.

38. Ibid., 168–69.

39. No. 4, 1944.

Notes on Contributors

KEITH BROWN is a professor at the Institute of British and American Studies of Oslo University, Norway. He has published and edited work on a variety of literary topics both in English and Norwegian. His study *Shakespeare: Mannen, Tiden, Verket* appeared in 1998.

NIELS B. HANSEN is associate professor of English at the University of Copenhagen, Denmark.

ROGER D. SELL is J. O. E. Donner Professor of English Language and Literature at Åbo Akademi University, Finland. His most recent books are *Literature and Communication: The Foundation of Mediating Criticism* (2000), and *Mediating Criticism: Literary Education Humanized* (2001).

ALF SJÖBERG (1903–80) was chief director at the Royal Dramatic Theater, Stockholm, for many years and an internationally renowned film director.

GUNNAR SJÖGREN (1897–1979) was the author of a number of books and articles in Swedish on Shakespeare and his time and Shakespeare and Scandinavia.

KRISTIAN SMIDT is Professor Emeritus of English literature at the University of Oslo and has published a number of books on Shakespeare in English and Norwegian, and some on modern authors (Joyce, T. S. Eliot).

GUNNAR SORELIUS is Professor Emeritus at the University of Uppsala, Sweden. He has published books and articles on theater history, Shakespeare, and Shakespeare and Sweden.

MICHAEL SRIGLEY is a senior lecturer in the English Department, University of Uppsala, Sweden. He has published two full-length studies on Shakespeare and one on Alexander Pope.

AUGUST STRINDBERG (1849–1912) is Sweden's foremost dramatist.

CLAS ZILLIACUS teaches comparative literature at Åbo Akademi University, Finland. His translation of *Hamlet* into Swedish (1983), earned him a Finnish Ministry of Culture Award.

Index